W9-CEW-013

Catholic Identity
School Edition

Sadlier

WE·BELIEVE ™

We Are God's People

WITH PROJECT DISCIPLE

Pray
Learn
Celebrate
Share
Choose
Live

Grade Six

S Sadlier

This advanced publication copy has been printed prior to final publication and pending ecclesiastical approval.

Acknowledgments

Excerpts from the English translation of The Roman Missal, © 2010, International Committee on English in the Liturgy, Inc. All rights reserved.

Excerpts from the English translation of the *Catechism of the Catholic Church* for the United States of America, copyright © 1994, United States Catholic Conference, Inc.—Libreria Editrice Vaticana. English translation of the *Catechism of the Catholic Church: Modifications from the Editio Typica* copyright © 1997, United States Catholic Conference, Inc.—Libreria Editrice Vaticana. Used with permission.

Scripture excerpts are taken from the *New American Bible with Revised New Testament and Psalms* Copyright © 1991, 1986, 1970 Confraternity of Christian Doctrine, Inc., Washington, D.C. Used with permission. All rights reserved. No part of the *New American Bible* may be reproduced by any means without permission in writing from the copyright owner.

Excerpts from the English translation of *Lectionary for Mass* © 1969, 1981, International Committee on English in the Liturgy, Inc. (ICEL); excerpts from the English translation of *Rite of Holy Week* © 1972, ICEL; excerpts from the English translation of *Rite of Penance* © 1974, ICEL; excerpts from the English translation of *The Liturgy of the Hours* © 1974, ICEL; excerpts from the English translation of *A Book of Prayers* © 1982, ICEL; excerpts from the English translation of *Order of Christian Funerals* © 1985, ICEL; excerpts from the English translation of *Rite of Confirmation* (2nd Edition) © 1975, ICEL; excerpts from the English translation of *Book of Blessings* © 1988, ICEL All rights reserved.

Excerpts from *Catholic Household Blessings and Prayers (Revised Edition)* © 2007, 1988, United States Conference of Catholic Bishops, Inc. (USCCB), Washington, D.C. Used with permission. All rights reserved.

English translation of the Glory to the Father, Lord's Prayer, Apostles' Creed, Nicene Creed, *Te Deum Laudamus*, and the *Sanctus* by the International Consultation on English Texts (ICET).

Excerpts from the General Audience of Pope Francis, May 22, 2013, and from his *Evangelii Gaudium, Apostolic Exhortation on the Proclamation of the Gospel in Today's World*, November 24, 2013, copyright © Vatican Publishing House, Libreria Editrice Vaticana.

Excerpt from *Dei Verbum, Dogmatic Constitution on Divine Revelation*, Pope Paul VI, November 18, 1965.

Excerpt from United States Conference of Catholic Bishops, *The New Evangelization: Disciples on Mission in the World* copyright © United States Conference of Catholic Bishops, Washington, D.C. All rights reserved.

Excerpt from Pope John Paul II, *Redemptoris Missio, On the Permanent Validity of the Church's Missionary Mandate*, December 7, 1990, © Vatican Publishing House, Libreria Editrice Vaticana.

Excerpt from the General Audience of Pope John Paul II, January 13, 1988, copyright © Vatican Publishing House, Libreria Editrice Vaticana.

"We Believe, We Believe in God," © 1979, North American Liturgy Resources (NALR), 5536 NE Hassalo, Portland, OR 97213. All rights reserved. Used with permission. "God, Creator, God Most High," © 1998, Janet Vogt. Published by OCP Publications, 5536 NE Hassalo, Portland OR 97213.

All rights reserved. Used with permission. "I Know You Are God," © 1995, Janet Vogt. Published by OCP Publications, 5536 NE Hassalo, Portland OR 97213. All rights reserved. Used with permission. "And It Was Good," © 1990, North American Liturgy Resources (NALR), 5536 NE Hassalo, Portland, OR 97213. All rights reserved. Used with permission. "Water of Life (Aqua de Vida)," © 1994, Jaime Cortez. Published by OCP Publications, 5536 NE Hassalo, Portland OR 97213. All rights reserved. Used with permission. "Be Not Afraid," © 1975, 1978, Robert J. Dufford, SJ and New Dawn Music, 5536 NE Hassalo, Portland, OR 97213. All rights reserved. "City of God," © 1981, Daniel L. Schutte and New Dawn Music, 5536 NE Hassalo, Portland, OR 97213. All rights reserved. Used with permission. "Wherever You Go," Weston Priory, Gregory Norbet, OSB. Copyright © 1972, from the recording "Wherever You Go," The Benedictine Foundation of the State of Vermont Inc., Weston Priory, Weston, Vermont, U.S.A. Used with permission. "Psalm 122: Qué Alegría/I Rejoiced," Music and verse text © 1997, Jaime Cortez. Published by OCP Publications, 5536 NE Hassalo, Portland, OR 97213. All rights reserved. Used with permission. English refrain © 1969, 1981, ICEL. Spanish refrain © 1982, Sobicain. All rights reserved. Used with permission. The English translation of Psalm 122 response from Lectionary for Mass © 1969, 1981, 1997, International Committee on English in the Liturgy, Inc. All rights reserved. "Prepare the Way," © 1997, Paul Inwood. Published by OCP Publications, 5536 NE Hassalo, Portland, OR 97213. All rights reserved. Used with permission. "Psalm 98: All the Ends of the Earth," Music © 1999, 2000, Barbara Bridge. Published by OCP Publications, 5536 NE Hassalo, Portland, OR 97213. All rights reserved. Used with permission. Refrain © 1969, ICEL. Verse © 1970, CCD. All rights reserved. The English translation of Psalm 98 response from Lectionary for Mass © 1969, 1981, 1997, International Committee on English in the Liturgy, Inc. All rights reserved. "Though the Mountains May Fall," © 1975, Daniel L. Schutte and New Dawn Music, 5536 NE Hassalo, Portland, OR 97213. All rights reserved. Used with permission. "Christ, Be Our Light," © 1993, Bernadette Farrell. Published by OCP Publications, 5536 NE Hassalo, Portland, OR 97213. All rights reserved. Used with permission. "Luke 1: Magnificat/Benedictus," © 1992, 2000, Paule Freeburg, DC and Christopher Walker. Published by OCP Publications, 5536 NE Hassalo, Portland, OR 97213. All rights reserved. Used with permission. "My God, My God," © 1988, 1989, 1990, Christopher Walker. Published by OCP Publications, 5536 NE Hassalo, Portland, OR 97213. All rights reserved. Used with permission. "Resucitó/He Is Risen," Music © 1973, Ediciones Musical Pax. Sole U.S. Agent: OCP Publications. English text © 1988, OCP Publications, 5536 NE Hassalo, Portland, OR 97213. All rights reserved. Used with permission. "Pescador de Hombres/Lord, You Have Come," Spanish text and music © 1979, Cesáreo Gabaráin. English translation by Robert C. Trupia, © 1987 by OCP Publications, 5536 NE Hassalo, Portland, OR 97213. All rights reserved. Used with permission. "Jesus Is Risen," Music © 1992, Barbara Bridge. Text © 1992, Barbara Bridge and Owen Alstott. Published by OCP Publications, 5536 NE Hassalo, Portland, OR 97213. All rights reserved. Used with permission. "Spirit of God, Come to Us," © 1989, Sr. Veronica McGrath and Carey Landry. Administered by OCP Publications, 5536 NE Hassalo, Portland, OR 97213. All rights reserved. Used with permission. "God Has Chosen Me," © 1990, Bernadette Farrell. Published by OCP Publications, 5536 NE Hassalo, Portland, OR 97213. All rights reserved. Used with permission. "Who Am I?" Music and text © 1999, Christopher Walker and Paule Freeburg, DC. Published by OCP Publications, 5536 NE Hassalo, Portland, OR 97213. All rights reserved. Used with permission. "Envía Tu Espíritu," © 1988, Bob Hurd. Published by OCP Publications, 5536 NE Hassalo, Portland, OR 97213. All rights reserved. Used with permission.

William H. Sadlier, Inc.
25 Broadway
New York, NY 10004-1010

ISBN: 978-0-8215-3056-6
10 11 12 13 14 SHNW 26 25 24 23 22

The Subcommittee on the Catechism, United States Conference of Catholic Bishops, has found the doctrinal content of this series, copyright 2015, to be in conformity with the *Catechism of the Catholic Church*.

The Sadlier *We Believe* Program was drawn from the wisdom of the community. It was developed by nationally recognized experts in catechesis, curriculum, and child development. These teachers of the faith and practitioners helped us to frame every lesson to be age-appropriate and appealing. In addition, a team including respected catechetical, liturgical, pastoral, and theological experts shared their insights and inspired the development of the program.

Contributors to the inspiration and development are:

Dr. Gerard F. Baumbach
Professor Emeritus, Institute for Church Life
Director Emeritus of the Echo Program
University of Notre Dame

Carole M. Eipers, D.Min.
Vice President, Executive Director
  of Catechetics
William H. Sadlier, Inc.

Theological Consultants

His Eminence Donald Cardinal Wuerl, M.A., S.T.D.
Archbishop of Washington

Most Reverend Edward K. Braxton, Ph.D., S.T.D.
Official Theological Consultant
Bishop of Belleville

Reverend Joseph A. Komonchak, Ph.D.
Professor Emeritus of Theology and Religious Studies
The Catholic University of America

Most Reverend Richard J. Malone, Th.D.
Bishop of Buffalo

Reverend Monsignor John E. Pollard, S.T.L.
Pastor, Queen of All Saints Basilica
Chicago, IL

Scriptural Consultant

Reverend Donald Senior, CP, Ph.D., S.T.D.
Member, Pontifical Biblical Commission
President Emeritus of Catholic Theological Union
Chicago, IL

Catechetical and Liturgical Consultants

Patricia Andrews
Director of Religious Education
Our Lady of Lourdes Church,
Slidell, LA

Reverend Monsignor John F. Barry, P.A.
Pastor, American Martyrs Parish
Manhattan Beach, CA

Reverend Monsignor John M. Unger
Deputy Superintendent for Catechesis
  and Evangelization
Archdiocese of St. Louis

Thomas S. Quinlan
Director, Religious Education Office
Diocese of Joliet

Curriculum and Child Development Consultants

Brother Robert R. Bimonte, FSC
President, NCEA

Sr. Carol Cimino, SSJ, Ed.D.
Superintendent, Catholic Schools
Diocese of Buffalo

Gini Shimabukuro, Ed.D.
Professor Emeritus
Catholic Educational Leadership Program
School of Education
University of San Francisco

Catholic Social Teaching Consultants

John Carr
Director
Initiative on Catholic Social Thought and Public Life
Georgetown University

Joan Rosenhauer
Executive Vice President, U.S. Operations
Catholic Relief Services
Baltimore, MD

Inculturation Consultants

Allan Figueroa Deck, S.J., Ph.D., S.T.D.
Rector of Jesuit Community
Charles Casassa Chair of Catholic Social Values
Professor
Loyola Marymount University

Kirk P. Gaddy, Ed.D.
Middle School Team Leader/Religion Teacher
St. Francis International School
Silver Spring, MD

Reverend Nguyễn Việt Hưng
Vietnamese Catechetical Committee

Dulce M. Jiménez-Abreu
Director of Bilingual Programs
William H. Sadlier, Inc.

Mariology Consultant

Sister M. Jean Frisk, ISSM, S.T.L.
International Marian Research Institute
Dayton, OH

Media/Technology Consultants

Sister Judith Dieterle, SSL
Past President, National Association of
    Catechetical Media Professionals

Robert Methven
Vice President, Digital Publisher
William H. Sadlier, Inc.

Robert T. Carson
Media Design Director
William H. Sadlier, Inc.

Writing/Development Team

Rosemary K. Calicchio
Executive Vice President, Publisher

Blake Bergen
Director of Publications

Joanne McDonald
Editorial Director

Regina Kelly
Supervising Editor

William M. Ippolito
Director of Corporate Planning

Martin Smith
Planning and Analysis
    Project Director

Dignory Reina
Editor

Peggy O'Neill
Digital Content Manager

Contributing Writers
Christian Garcia
Kathy Hendricks
Shannon Jones
Theresa MacDonald
Gloria Shahin

Suzan Laroquette
Director of Catechetical
    Consultant Services

Judith A. Devine
National Sales Consultant

Victor Valenzuela
National Religion Consultant

Publishing Operations Team

Carole Uettwiller
Vice President of Planning and
    Technology

Vince Gallo
Senior Creative Director

Francesca O'Malley
Art/Design Director

Cheryl Golding
Production Director

Monica Reece
Senior Production Manager

Jovito Pagkalinawan
Electronic Prepress Director

Design/Image Staff
Kevin Butler, Nancy Figueiredo,
Stephen Flanagan, Lorraine Forte,
Debrah Kaiser, Cesar Llacuna,
Bob Schatz, Karen Tully

Production Staff
Monica Bernier, Robin D'Amato,
Rachel Jacobs, Carol Lin,
Vincent McDonough,
Yolanda Miley, Laura Rotondi,
Allison Stearns

We are grateful to our loyal *We Believe* users whose insights and suggestions have inspired *We Believe: Catholic Identity Edition*—the premier faith formation tool built on the six tasks of catechesis.

Contents

SEASONAL CHAPTERS

WE✦BELIEVE

The *We Believe* program will help us to

learn

celebrate

share

and

live our Catholic faith.

Throughout the year we will hear about many saints and holy people.

Saint Agnes

Saint Alphonsus Liguori

Saint Angela de Merici

Saint Bonaventure

Saint Catherine of Siena

Saint Catherine Laboure

Saint Cecilia

Saint Elizabeth of Portugal

Saint Genevieve of Paris

Saint Ignatius of Loyola

Saint Joan of Arc

Saint John

Saint Jerome

Saint Lawrence

Saint Martin of Tours

Mary, Mother of God

Saint Mary Magdalene

Saint Maximilian Kolbe

Saint Paul

Venerable Pierre Toussaint

Saint Stephen

Saint Thomas Aquinas

Paint

Together, let us grow as a community of faith.

Welcome!

✝ We Gather in Prayer

Leader: Welcome, everyone, to Grade 6 *We Believe*.
As we begin each chapter, we gather in prayer.
We pray to God together. Sometimes, we will
read from Scripture; other times we will say the
prayers of the Church or sing a song of thanks
and praise to God.

Today, let us sing the *We Believe* song!

♫ We Believe, We Believe in God

Refrain:

We believe in God;
We believe, we believe in Jesus;
We believe in the Spirit who gives us life.
We believe, we believe in God.

We believe in the Holy Spirit,
Who renews the face of the earth.
We believe we are part of a living Church,
And forever we will live with God.

(Refrain)

Each day we learn more about God.

In each chapter, we find four main faith statements. They start the day's lesson. They focus us on what we will be learning about in the lesson.

WE GATHER

✝ *Thank you, God, for all our classmates.*

Then we

think about
talk about
act out
draw about
write about

Life

at school
at home
in our parish
in our world
in our neighborhood

Talk about your life right now. What groups, teams, or clubs do you belong to?

Why do you like being a part of these groups?

What does belonging to these groups tell other people about you?

When we see **We Gather** we begin by taking a moment to pray.

When we see **We Believe** we learn more about our Catholic faith.

WE BELIEVE

We learn about:

• the Blessed Trinity—God the Father, God the Son, and God the Holy Spirit

• Jesus, the Son of God, who became one of us

• the Church and its history and teachings

• the Mass and the sacraments

• our call to be a disciple of Jesus.

UNIT 1 Forming the Covenant
"I praise you, so wonderfully you made me;
   wonderful are your works!"   (Psalm 139:14)

UNIT 2 Building the Covenant Nation
"Sing to the LORD, for he is gloriously
   triumphant."   (Exodus 15:21)

UNIT 3 Redefining the Covenant People
"Rise up in splendor! Your light has come,
   the glory of the Lord shines upon you."   (Isaiah 60:1)

UNIT 4 The Covenant Fulfilled in Jesus
"And a voice came from the heavens, saying, 'This is my
   beloved Son, with whom I am well pleased.'"(Matthew 3:17)

> A major theme in your *We Believe* textbook this year is learning more about God's love for his people, and his action in their lives throughout history. Your book is divided into four units.

Watch for these special signs:

Whenever we see ✝ we make the Sign of the Cross. We pray and begin our day's lesson.

📖 is an open Bible. When we see it with a blue Scripture reference, what follows is a paraphrase of the Bible. When we see a black reference like this (John 13:34), that passage is directly from the Bible.

When we see 🏃 we do an activity.
We might:

• talk together

• write a story

• draw a picture

• act out a story or situation

• imagine ourselves doing something

• sing a song together, or make up one

• work together on a special project.

There are all kinds of activities! We might see 🏃 in any part of our day's lesson. Be on the lookout!

Can you guess what 🎵 means? That's right, it means it is time to sing, or listen to music. We sing songs we know, make up our own, and sing along with those in our *We Believe* music program.

When we see **Key Words** we review the meanings of important faith words we have learned in the day's lesson.

As Catholics...

Here we discover something special about our faith. We reflect on what we have discovered and try to make it a part of our life. Don't forget to read it!

13

WE RESPOND

We can respond by:

- thinking about ways our faith affects the things we say and do

- sharing our thoughts and feelings

- praying to God.

Then in our home, neighborhood, school, parish, and world, we say and do the things that show love for God and others.

When we see **We Respond** we reflect and act on what we have learned about God and our Catholic faith.

Draw yourself doing something that shows you are a disciple of Jesus Christ.

We are so happy you are with us!

We sharpen our disciple skills with each chapter's Project Disciple pages!

Show What you Know
We "show what we know" about each chapter's content. A disciple is always learning more about his or her faith.

Celebrate!
As disciples, we worship God.

↳ **DISCIPLE CHALLENGE**
We take our disciple skills one step further.

Grade 6 Chapter 9

PROJECT DISCIPLE

Pray Learn Celebrate Share Choose Live

Show What you Know

Design a "desktop wallpaper" summarizing the Israelites' journey through the wilderness. Include Key Words and captions in your design.

What's the Word?

"[Jesus] took Peter, John, and James and went up to the mountain to pray. While [Jesus] was praying his face changed in appearance and his clothing became dazzling white. And behold, two men were conversing with him, Moses and Elijah, who appeared in glory and spoke of his exodus that he was going to accomplish in Jerusalem." (Luke 9:28–31)

• Underline the phrase that describes the Transfiguration of Jesus.
  (This description tells of the Transfiguration of Jesus.)
• what Moses and Elijah were speaking about.
  Jesus' exodus was his suffering, Death, Resurrection, and Ascension.)

webelieveweb.com

116

Celebrate!

Catholics inherited some customs of worship from the Jewish People. One custom is the use of music and songs. Moses' sister Miriam played a tambourine with joy when the people gained their freedom. The Jewish People often praised God with pipes and cymbals, trumpets and horns, lyres and harps. As Catholics, we celebrate with these instruments and many others. Organs, pianos, drums, and guitars—all can help us to "Sing to the Lord a new song" (Psalm 149:1).

↳ **DISCIPLE CHALLENGE** Create a playlist of songs to praise God.

Fast Facts

Moses is mentioned in the New Testament, more than any other Old Testament person. References to him are found in the Gospels of Matthew, Mark, Luke, and John; in the Acts of the Apostles; these Epistles: Romans, 1 Corinthians, 2 Corinthians, 2 Timothy, Hebrews, and Jude; and in the Book of Revelation.

8:26 PM
PLAYLIST

Take Home

Share these verses from Psalm 119 with your family.

"Lord, teach me the way of your laws;
I shall observe them with care.
Give me insight to observe your teaching,
to keep it with all my heart.
Lead me in the path of your commands,
for that is my delight."
(Psalm 119:33–35)

117

What's the Word?
Here we read and respond to Scripture.

Fast Facts
Fast Facts help us to learn even more about our faith.

Take Home
We always get the chance to share our faith "at home."

There are **LOADS** of **ACTIVITIES** that make us better disciples! Just look at this additional list.

Question Corner—take a quiz

Make It Happen!—living out what we have learned

What Would You Do?—making the right choices

Reality Check—here we can express our ideas and choices

Picture This—a great way for us to see and show our disciple skills

Pray Today—talking and listening to God

Saint Stories—finding great role models

More to Explore—activities to develop our comprehension and Internet skills

Now, Pass It On!—invites us to witness to our faith

And every chapter ends with a Chapter Test!

15

You are on a journey to continue to grow as a disciple of Jesus Christ. You can strengthen your Catholic Identity through these new features:

Catholic Identity: Retreats

provide time for you to reflect on what it means to be a Catholic. There are four retreats in your book.

Bringing the Retreat Home helps you to share the theme and highlights of each retreat.
Why We Believe as a Catholic Family helps you and your family to uphold and explain your Catholic faith to others.

Catholic Identity: Q & A offers you a way to

review what the Church teaches. The more you know these truths the more you strengthen your Catholic Identity.

Catholic Identity: Home Companion

provides you and your family with a resource of prayers, practices, and other information to enrich your identity as a Catholic family.

Student and Family resources are available at: **religion.sadlierconnect.com**

16

✝ Celebrating Catholic Identity: CREED

Divine Revelation

Part 1   I Open My Heart

Ever since he created us, God has been continually inviting us into a closer relationship with him. God has revealed himself to us in Sacred Scripture. He also makes himself known to us through his creation, and through his presence and grace in our lives each day.

How has God made himself known to you? Maybe you see God in nature, in the love of your family, or in the loyalty of your good friends. Write about ways you know God through the people and events in your life.

_____

_____

_____

_____

_____

_____

_____

_____

Divine Revelation

Part 2 We Come Together for Prayer

Leader: "God has revealed himself to [us] by gradually communicating his own mystery in deeds and in words" (*CCC*, 69). When God makes himself known to us, he invites us to respond with faith.

Reader 1: "Faith is the realization of what is hoped for and evidence of things not seen." (Hebrews 11:1)

Leader: Let us pray. Lord God, hear our voice in prayer, and open our hearts to you as you make yourself known to us. Teach us to respond with faith. God, you made yourself known to our Old Testament ancestors in faith. Throughout their history, you called them back to yourself and offered them salvation. In words and deeds, you showed your great love for them. You made yourself fully known to them and to all your people when you sent your Son Jesus into the world.

Reader 2: "No one has ever seen God. The only Son, God, who is at the Father's side, has revealed him." (John 1:18)

All: Jesus, draw us closer to you, that through you we may know God's everlasting love.

Leader: What did Jesus say and do that helps you to understand God's love for all people? List two or three words that remind you what Jesus teaches you about God's love. (*All silently write responses.*)

_____

_____

_____

_____

_____

Jesus, thank you for teaching us that God . . . (*All share the words they listed.*)

Leader: Let us conclude by praying an Act of Faith.

All: (*Pray the Act of Faith found in the **Catholic Identity Home Companion** "Creed" section at the end of this book.*) Amen.

Divine Revelation

Part 3 I Cherish God's Word

"No one comes to the Father except through me. If you know me, then you will also know my father. From now on you do know him and have seen him." (John 14:6–7)

READ the quotation from Scripture. Read slowly. Pay close attention to what you are reading.

REFLECT on what you read. Think about:

- How well do I know Jesus? How strong is my relationship with him?

- How well do I know God the Father? How can I be more aware of his presence in my life?

- How can Jesus' words in Scripture help me understand who God is?

SHARE you thoughts and feelings with God in prayer. Let your thoughts and feelings come naturally. Speak to God as a friend.

CONTEMPLATE, or sit quietly and allow your attention to remain focused on God's Word in the Scripture passage from the Gospel of John above.

Jesus Teaching by the Seashore, by James J. Tissot (1836–1902)

Divine Revelation

Part 4   I Value My Catholic Faith

With your group, participate in the "Revelation Gallery Walk," exploring ways we can know God. After each station on the walk, jot down an important insight.

Station 1: Our Desire for God _____

_____

Station 2: Seeing God in Scripture and the Church's Liturgy _____

_____

Station 3: Seeing God in All Things _____

_____

Station 4: Jesus, the Fullness of God's Revelation _____

_____

Share one of your insights with the group. Write this insight on the banner below. You can decorate your banner if you wish.

Divine Revelation

Part 5 I Celebrate Catholic Identity

Work with your group to develop a plan for how you will respond to God's presence and his invitation to a closer relationship with him. Your plan should cover specific steps you will take in the coming week.

Weekly Planner

Choose one or more steps from your weekly plan, and discuss ways to put them into action.

 1

 2

3

 4

5

 6

 7

Divine Revelation

Part 6 I Honor My Catholic Identity

Leader: Lord God, open our hearts so that we may know you and see you in our lives each day. Guide us as we reflect on this day. (*Leader will lead the group in the following reflection, pausing after each part.*)

Leader: Let us be aware of God's presence. Be still and rest in God's presence. Be aware of God's presence with you now and in every moment of the day.

Leader: Let us reflect on your day with gratitude. Recall the gifts that God has given you this day. What have you received? Pause and give God thanks for all his gifts to you.

Leader: Let us ask for the help of the Holy Spirit. How have you responded to God's presence and love this day? How can you grow more loving in your response to him?

Ask the Holy Spirit to enlighten you so you may see God in all things.

Leader: Let us review your day. Reflect on the details of your day. Think about choices you made, words you said, feelings you had. What motivated your words and actions? When was God in your heart and mind? When were you not aware of his presence?

Leader: Let us look toward tomorrow. Imagine Jesus sitting at your side. Express sorrow for any wrongdoing. Tell him your hopes for tomorrow, and ask him to help and guide you. Let us pray.

All: God, our Father, I offer you today all that I think and do and say. I offer it with what was done on earth by Jesus Christ, your Son. Amen.

Bringing the Retreat Home

Divine Revelation

Retreat Recap

Review the pages of your child's *Celebrating Catholic Identity: Creed* retreat. Ask your child to tell you about the retreat. Talk about Divine Revelation:

- God makes himself known to us.
- God invites us to respond in faith.
- God is fully revealed in his Son, Jesus Christ.

Share a story of a time when someone in your family experienced God's presence in a special way.

The Word of God

This year, your child will learn that the Bible, also called *Sacred Scripture* or simply *Scripture*, is the written record of God's Revelation and his relationship with his people. Together read the section "Reading the Bible . . . in Five Easy Steps" in the *Catholic Identity Home Companion* at the end of your child's book. Look up the Scripture passage named in the five steps, and read it together. Write and discuss what you learn from the passage.

Take a Moment

God reveals who he is and invites us into a closer relationship with him. A busy family life may not always give us opportunities to recall those important family moments that have strengthened our relationship with God and one another. Keep a family journal in which to record and appreciate these moments.

Family Prayer

Pray these words together this evening at mealtime.

Lord, bless our family gathered here today. We thank you for your loving protection and guidance.

Your love brings us strength and comfort, and unites us as a family. May your peace dwell in our home.

For more resources, see the *Catholic Identity Home Companion* at the end of this book.

Catholic Identity Retreat

Why We Believe
As a Catholic Family

What if someone asks us:

- Why do Catholics believe that Divine Revelation is handed on through both Scripture and Tradition?

The following resources can help us to respond:

Out of love for us, God reveals who he is. Divine Revelation is God's making himself known to us. Revelation has been handed on through the Bible, or Scripture, and through Tradition. Maybe you have encountered others who view the Bible as the only source of Revelation. Or maybe you have heard Catholic teachings questioned for "not being in the Bible."

Scripture and Tradition go hand in hand. Tradition is the Revelation of the Good News of Jesus Christ as lived out in the Church, past and present. Tradition includes teachings and practices handed on orally from the time of Jesus and his Apostles. It includes the creeds, or statements, of Christian beliefs. It also includes the teachings and documents of the Church, the Church's worship, and other practices. An example of Tradition is the Nicene Creed we pray at Mass. Scripture and Tradition shape our faith in Jesus Christ and our life as his disciples.

What does Scripture say?

"When [Jesus] was raised from the dead, his disciples remembered that he had said this, and they came to believe the scripture and the word Jesus had spoken." (John 2:22)

"They devoted themselves to the teaching of the apostles and to the communal life, to the breaking of the bread and to the prayers." (Acts of the Apostles 2:42)

"All scripture is inspired by God and is useful for teaching, for refutation, for correction, and for training in righteousness, so that one who belongs to God may be competent, equipped for every good work." (2 Timothy 3:16–17)

The written message of Scripture and the spoken message of Tradition have been handed on by the Apostles to the whole Church. Scripture is God's Word, written by human authors under the inspiration of the Holy Spirit. Tradition consists of all that the Church has learned with the guidance of the Holy Spirit, including her teachings, documents, worship, prayer, and other practices. The Holy Spirit inspires both Scripture and Tradition. We need both to understand how to live as God's people.

What does the Church say?

Scripture and Tradition are "one sacred deposit of the word of God" (Dogmatic Constitution on Divine Revelation, 10).

"The Church, to whom the transmission and interpretation of Revelation is entrusted, 'does not derive her certainty about all revealed truths from the holy Scriptures alone. Both Scripture and Tradition must be accepted and honored with equal sentiments of devotion and reverence.'" (CCC, 82 with quote from Dei Verbum, 9)

"This living transmission, accomplished in the Holy Spirit, is called Tradition, since it is distinct from Sacred Scripture, though closely connected to it. Through Tradition, 'the Church, in her doctrine, life, and worship perpetuates and transmits to every generation all that she herself is, all that she believes.'" (CCC, 78 with quote from Dei Verbum, 8 § 1)

Notes:

Forming the Covenant

Seasonal Chapters

DEAR FAMILY

In Unit 1 your child will grow as a disciple of Jesus by:

- appreciating Scripture and Tradition as God's Revelation of himself

- praising God as the source of all life and living as the image of God

- recognizing the truths taught in the Genesis stories of creation and of Original Sin

- understanding God's promise to send a Savior and his covenant with Noah

- learning about the patriarchs, our ancestors in faith, and Abraham, the father of God's people.

What's the Word?

All of Sacred Scripture is the Word of God. We learn about God through Scripture in ways similar to the ways we learn about characters in books: what the person says, what the person does, how the person acts, what the person thinks, what others say about the person, how others react to the person. For each one of these ways, give an example of what we learn about God from the Bible.

Picture This

In each of the Units there is a timeline of our faith. Look at the timeline on pages 20–21. Go over it as a family and invite members to share what they remember of each of the Scripture events cited. If there is an event that no one recalls, read it in your Bible (or look for it in your child's book) and share it with your family. At the end of Unit 1, return to this timeline and have your child share one event they learned about.

Reality Check

"The relationships within the family bring an affinity of feelings, affections, and interests, arising above all from the members' respect for one another."
(*Catechism of the Catholic Church*, 2206)

Show That You Care

God created us in his image and likeness and so every person reflects God's goodness. As a family, name the ways each member of your family reflects God. Say a prayer of thanks for each member and the God-given gifts they have.

Question Corner

Chapter 5 introduces men and women who were important to God's people in the Old Testament: Abraham, Isaac, Jacob and Joseph, Sarah, Rebekah, Rachel, and Leah. Who are the men and women who have been important to your family through generations? Tell some of their stories to your children. Pray for all of your ancestors together.

Take Home

Be ready for this unit's Take Home:

Chapter 1: Discussing the readings for next Sunday's Mass

Chapter 2: Planning a family "movie night"

Chapter 3: Sharing ways to be a steward

Chapter 4: Recognizing the Good News

Chapter 5: Going where God leads

God's Revelation

✝ We Gather in Prayer

Leader: O living God,
Our journey of faith leads us on
the path to you.
Your magnificent deeds are
words of strength and hope for us.
Open our hearts to listen to your
living Word.

Reader 1: "You formed my inmost being;
you knit me in my mother's womb.
I praise you, so wonderfully you made me;
wonderful are your works!"

(Psalm 139:13–14)

All: Your Word is a light to my path, O Lord.

Reader 2: "I raise my eyes toward the mountains.
From where will my help come?
My help comes from the LORD,
the maker of heaven and earth."

(Psalm 121:1–2)

All: Your Word is a light to my path,
O Lord.

Leader: O God of creation, you made
all things good. Help us to see
the work of your hands in the
world and in our lives. May we
always praise you for your
wonderful deeds!

♫ God, Creator, God Most High

Refrain:
God, Creator, God Most High,
be our ever present light.
Be among us, here before us, God
within us.

You are light for the world.
You are light for the lost to see.
Out of darkness we come to the
light of your love,
for your Word is a lamp unto our feet
to guide us. (Refrain)

You restored night to day.
You commanded the dark to cease.
By your promise of love we shall
not walk in fear.
We shall walk in the light of hope
and peace to guide us. (Refrain)

Abby ♡

Story of creation

First humans

Sin changes humanity

The story of Cain and Abel

The story of the Tower of Babel

We can know God through his creation.

+12 / 12

WE GATHER

✝ *O God, help us to know you.*

What are the ways that you discover new ideas or gather new information?

The intenet or books

How do you use your senses—sight, hearing, taste, touch, and smell—to help you to gain information?

I can lision to people. I can
hear people.

How does your own experience help you to learn about yourself and the world?

It help me by give me a
push that somethins is good or bad

How does the experience of other people help you to learn things?

New word, new items, new style

WE BELIEVE

One very important factor in learning is thinking. When we think, we are using our natural ability to reason and to come to sound conclusions. These conclusions can even be tested logically and scientifically.

The ability to reason is a gift that all human beings have. And through reason humans have drawn many conclusions about God. For centuries, great thinkers have developed reasonable theories for God's existence. The simplest of these theories is based on the idea that a machine, such as a watch or a computer, does not make itself. It has a maker. The reasonable conclusion is that the same principle applies to the universe. The universe has a maker. We believe that the maker, or Creator, of the universe is God.

POSTCARD

20

God establishes covenant with Abraham

Abraham's faith is tested by God

Isaac becomes patriarch

Jacob tricks Esau

God renews covenant with Jacob

God changes Jacob's name to Israel

Joseph is sold into slavery

Joseph works for pharaoh

Joseph's brothers go to Egypt

Joseph and his brothers reconcile

The World Around Us In his writings Saint Paul reminds us that the human mind can find God "in what he has made" (Romans 1:20). For example, by looking at the vast expanses of space through a telescope we get to know something of God's power. By discovering more about the universe we get to know about God's knowledge and wisdom. By smelling a flower on a cool summer morning we can experience God's beauty.

By noticing the great variety of plant and animal life in the world we can come to understand God's generosity. By appreciating how tenderly a mother sheep cares for her newborn lamb we can see a glimpse of God's loving kindness. And by observing human life, the greatest and most astounding creation in the universe, we get another glimpse into who God is. Learning

about who we are, how we think and behave, and what we hope for helps us to think about what God must be like.

So by making use of all of our natural gifts, and those of other people, we get to know about our world, about ourselves, and about God. These are purely natural ways of coming to know God. They help us to believe in God and to understand that it is reasonable to believe in him. However, these natural means are all limited. We need something else to get to know God better. God has to tell us about himself.

WE RESPOND

Look at the photos on these pages. Which ones help you to know what God is like? Why?

Make a postcard of another scene that reminds you of God. In a caption on the card, explain why the scene makes you think of God. With your class decide on a special place to display all the cards.

God makes himself known through Divine Revelation.

WE GATHER

✝ *Loving God, teach us your ways.*

Think about a movie or television show about people who are friends. How do they trust one another? share with one another? know and care about one another?

WE BELIEVE

God wants us to have a close friendship with him. He loves us so much that he confided in us. He told us about himself. He revealed himself to us. *Reveal* means "to make known." **Divine Revelation** is God's making himself known to us.

God did not reveal himself by writing us a letter or sending an e-mail. God has made himself known to us through his mighty deeds and by his interactions with his people throughout time.

Although God spoke to individual men and women about himself and his plan for his people, his message was for the whole community. God made it clear that he wanted to have a loving relationship with all people. In revealing himself, God answered all sorts of questions that human beings ask but cannot answer on their own. Revelation made it possible for humans to know God more deeply and to respond to him in a way that was otherwise not possible.

However, God did not reveal himself all at once. God has made himself known gradually over a long period of time. God's Revelation of himself began with the creation of the first human beings and their descendants. It continued through the ancient Israelites and the Jewish People.

God's Revelation is full and complete in his only Son, Jesus Christ. By sending his Son, God tells us what we need to know about himself. In the Gospel of John we read, "No one has ever seen God. The only Son, God, who is at the Father's side, has revealed him" (John 1:18).

22

Jesus Christ is the only Son of God who became man. Jesus shows us God his Father's love. In learning about Jesus Christ, we learn about the Father. When we follow Jesus' example of living, we grow closer to the Father. Together with the Father, Jesus sends God the Holy Spirit to strengthen us. The Holy Spirit helps us respond to God's great love for us. God the Father, God the Son, and God the Holy Spirit are the Blessed Trinity. The **Blessed Trinity** is the Three Persons in One God.

The Holy Spirit guides the Church to understand God's Revelation and to apply it in our lives. As the Church, we try to live by God's laws. We live in hope of eternal life with God—where we will have a clearer understanding of God's plan. Only then will God be completely known by us. As Jesus said, "Now this is eternal life, that they should know you, the only true God, and the one whom you sent, Jesus Christ" (John 17:3).

Reread pages 22 and 23. Highlight or underline ways God revealed himself.

Key Words

Divine Revelation God's making himself known to us

Blessed Trinity the Three Persons in One God: God the Father, God the Son, and God the Holy Spirit

WE RESPOND

God speaks to all of us every day. How is God speaking to you today?

Almighty God, thank you for revealing yourself to us in your only Son, Jesus Christ. Praise and glory to you! Amen.

23

God's Revelation is handed down through the Bible and Tradition.

WE GATHER

✝ *Loving God, guide us in truth.*

How do you know about your relatives who lived before you? How can you pass on memories of your family to the next generation?

WE BELIEVE

God's Revelation of himself took place from the beginning of time. The events and the recollections that people had of God were passed on from generation to generation. And people's living experience of God helped to shape what would eventually be written down.

God's Revelation of himself has been handed on through the *Bible* and through *Tradition*.

The Bible The **Bible**, also called *Sacred Scripture* or simply *Scripture*, is the written record of God's Revelation and his relationship with his people. The Bible is a book of faith and is unlike any other book. It has a divine author, God, and many human authors, or biblical writers. These writers used their own words and expressions and chose the way to organize their writings. But as they worked, they were guided by God the Holy Spirit.

The special guidance that the Holy Spirit gave to the human writers of the Bible is called **Divine Inspiration.** This inspiration of God the Holy Spirit guaranteed that the human writers wrote without any error God's saving truth. For that reason God is the true author of the whole Bible.

Thus, the Bible is the *Word of God*. We treat the Bible with reverence because it is God's Word to us today. From the Bible we learn how to relate to God—Father, Son, and Holy Spirit.

Tradition Tradition is the Revelation of the Good News of Jesus Christ as lived out in the Church, past and present. Tradition includes teachings and practices handed on orally from the time of Jesus and his Apostles. It includes the creeds, or statements, of Christian beliefs. It also includes the teachings and documents of the Church, the Church's worship, and other practices. Tradition is the source of the Church's ongoing understanding of the meaning of Revelation and the ways to apply it to our lives.

The written message of Scripture and the spoken message of Tradition have been handed on by the Apostles to the whole Church. The bishops are the successors of the Apostles. With the pope as their head, they form the *Magisterium*, the living, teaching office of the Church. In Jesus' name and with the help of the Holy Spirit, the Magisterium interprets both Scripture and Tradition.

Through the centuries the Church has continued to share and build on the faith of the Apostles. The Church community in every generation believes and lives this faith and passes it on to future generations.

How are the Bible and Tradition the same? How are they different?

As Catholics...

The Church, primarily the bishops, has the task of interpreting and teaching Scripture. The bishops share this teaching responsibility with priests and laypeople. Many people help the bishops to interpret the meaning of Scripture. Some of these people are biblical scholars who find out the meanings of ancient words. They translate and study ancient scrolls. They visit places in the Middle East to find evidence of the Bible and how it was written.

Other scholars are archaeologists. They dig at sites in the Middle East to find artifacts—tablets, scrolls, jewelry, pots, and tools. They help us to understand how people lived in biblical times.

Who are some people who teach you about the Bible?

Key Words

Bible the written record of God's Revelation and his relationship with his people

Tradition the Revelation of the Good News of Jesus Christ as lived out in the Church, past and present

Divine Inspiration the special guidance that the Holy Spirit gave to the human writers of the Bible

WE RESPOND

Imagine that you have to teach this truth to your class: God's Revelation is passed on through the Bible and Tradition. Design a visual (poster, chart, screensaver, or other object) that might help the class to understand this truth.

The Bible is a collection of books.

✝ *Your Word, Lord, lights my way.*

🧍 What different kinds of things can you learn about the ocean from each of these types of books?

From a
Poetry Book

From a
Science Book

From an
Adventure Book

Religion
(Add your own)

WE BELIEVE

The word *bible* means "books." The Bible is not just one book but a small library of sacred, or holy, books. Through different literary forms, each book helps us to learn about God in a unique way. A *literary form* is a type of writing used to get a message across.

The Bible contains all kind of literary forms: ancient folktales, histories, novels, short stories, advice on living, codes of law, letters, prophecy, visions, poetry, hymns, and many other types of writing. Each book of the Bible is written in one or more of these literary forms.

There are seventy-three separate books in the Bible. And the Bible is divided into two parts called *Testaments*.

The *Old Testament* contains forty-six books originally written in Hebrew, Aramaic, or Greek. In the Old Testament we learn about God's relationship with the people of Israel.

In the tenth century before Christ (B.C.), the Israelite people first began to write down the stories that had been handed down by word of mouth for generations. But, it took almost a thousand years to assemble all the books of the Old Testament, since the writing of these stories continued until the first century B.C.

The books of the *New Testament*, however, were written more quickly. Only about sixty or seventy years passed between the Death of Jesus and the completion of the writing of the books of the New Testament.

The New Testament contains twenty-seven books originally written in Greek. The New Testament contains the story of Jesus, his mission, his first followers, and the beginning of the Church.

Together the Old and New Testaments make up the complete Bible.

WE RESPOND

When we refer to a citation from the Bible we refer to the name of the book, the chapter of the book, and verse(s) of the chapter. Thus, Genesis 1:1–2 refers to the Book of Genesis, chapter 1, verses 1 and 2.

🧍 Explain what the following citation means: Revelation 21:1–3.

Thank you, O God, for the gift of your Word in the Bible. Amen.

Books of the Bible

The Old Testament

Pentateuch ("Five Scrolls")

These books tell about the formation of the covenant and describe basic laws and beliefs of the Israelites.	Genesis	Exodus	Leviticus	Numbers	Deuteronomy

Historical Books

These books deal with the history of Israel.	Joshua	1 Samuel	1 Chronicles	Nehemiah	Esther
	Judges	2 Samuel	2 Chronicles	Tobit	1 Maccabees
	Ruth	1 Kings	Ezra	Judith	2 Maccabees
		2 Kings			

Wisdom Books

These books explain God's role in everyday life.	Job	Proverbs	Song of Songs	Wisdom	Sirach
	Psalms	Ecclesiastes			

Prophetic Books

These books contain writings of the great prophets who spoke God's Word to the people of Israel.	Isaiah	Ezekiel	Amos	Nahum	Haggai
	Jeremiah	Daniel	Obadiah	Habakkuk	Zechariah
	Lamentations	Hosea	Jonah	Zephaniah	Malachi
	Baruch	Joel	Micah		

The New Testament

Gospels

These books contain the message and key events in the life of Jesus Christ. Because of this, the Gospels hold a central place in the New Testament.	Matthew	Mark	Luke	John

Letters

These books contain letters written by Saint Paul and other leaders to individual Christians or to early Christian communities.	Romans	Colossians	Titus	2 Peter
	1 Corinthians	1 Thessalonians	Philemon	1 John
	2 Corinthians	2 Thessalonians	Hebrews	2 John
	Galatians	1 Timothy	James	3 John
	Ephesians	2 Timothy	1 Peter	Jude
	Philippians			

Other Writings

	Acts of the Apostles	Revelation

PROJECT

Pray
Learn
Celebrate
Share
Choose
Live

Show What *you* Know

Complete the crossword puzzle using the

Across

3. the Three Persons in One God: God the Father, God the Son, and God the Holy Spirit

Down

1. the Revelation of the Good News of Jesus Christ as lived out in the Church, past and present

2. The special guidance that the Holy Spirit gave to the human writers of the Bible is known as Divine _____.

3. the written record of God's Revelation and his relationship with his people

4. Divine _____ is God's making himself known to us.

Crossword answers:
- 1 Down: Tradition
- 2 Down: Inspiration
- 3 Across: Blessed Trinity
- 3 Down: Bible
- 4 Down: Revelation

Picture This

A *logo* is a uniquely designed symbol to represent a name, a company, etc. Design a logo to represent the Blessed Trinity.

Pray
Learn
Celebrate
Share
Choose
Live

Saint Stories

Saint Jerome was born in the fourth century. He studied in Rome and learned Greek and Latin. He became a monk, and went to live in the desert to fast, pray, and focus on God. Jerome studied the writings of the Old Testament and the Hebrew language. With his skill in Hebrew and Greek, Jerome translated the Bible into Latin. Many people were able to read and study Scripture because of Jerome's translation. Saint Jerome is one of the Church's great biblical scholars. We celebrate his feast day on September 30.

DISCIPLE CHALLENGE

- Underline the phrase that describes why Jerome went to live in the desert ✓
- What helped Jerome translate the Bible into Latin?

  His skill in Hebrew and Greek.

Fast Facts

The shortest book in the Bible is the Second Letter of John. It has only 13 verses. The Book of Psalms, with 150 psalms, is the longest book in the Bible.

Take Home

Visit *This Week's Liturgy* on www.webelieveweb.com for the Sunday Mass readings and holy day liturgies, as well as activities. Find this week's readings. Read and talk about them. Select an activity to do together.

Make it Happen

Look at the chart on page 27. Take the time to become more familiar with the books of the Bible.

Now, pass it on!

CHAPTER TEST

Write the letter that best defines each term.

1. _____ Divine Revelation

2. _____ Bible

3. _____ Tradition

4. _____ Divine Inspiration

   a. written record of God's Revelation and his relationship with his people

   b. a type of writing used to get a message across

   c. the special guidance that the Holy Spirit gave to the human writers of the Bible

   d. God's making himself known to us

   e. the Revelation of the Good News of Jesus Christ as lived out in the Church, past and present

Write True or False next to the following sentences.
Then change the false sentences to make them true.

5. _____ The Magisterium is the living, teaching office of the Church.

_____

6. _____ The Blessed Trinity is the Three Persons in One God.

_____

7. _____ We learn about God's relationship with the people of Israel in the New Testament.

_____

8. _____ Tradition is the written record of God's Revelation and his relationship with his people.

_____

Write a paragraph to answer this question.

9–10. How has God revealed himself to us?

_____

_____

_____

_____

Creation

✝ We Gather in Prayer

Leader: O God of creation,
You have given us wonderful gifts!
We praise and thank you for all
that you have created.

Reader: "All good giving and every
perfect gift is from above, coming
down from the Father of lights."
(James 1:17)

Leader: We thank you for our gift of life.

All: We praise you God.

Leader: We thank you for our sense
of smell, hearing, and touch.

All: We praise you God.

Leader: We thank you for our
families and friends.

All: We praise you God.

Leader: We thank you for our
abilities and talents.

All: We praise you God.

♫ I Know You Are God

In the morning's first sunlight, I know you
are God.
In the gentle and starry night, I know you
are God.
I see in your majesty all that you are to me,
in each and ev'rything, I know you are God.

In your loving forgiveness I know you
are God.
In your kindness, compassion I know you
are God.
My trust rests in you alone, source of all
peace and hope;
bless the Lord, O my soul, I know you
are God.

31

The Book of Genesis is about beginnings.

WE GATHER

✝ *God, we thank you for being with us always.*

Think about the beginning years of your life. Describe your earliest memories or something your family has told you about your early life. What have they told you about events in your family that took place before you were born?

WE BELIEVE

The history of God and his people covers thousands of years. It is recorded in the Bible. Each part, or period, of this story connects in a special way with the covenant. The **covenant** is an agreement between God and his people.

This chart divides this lengthy history into smaller periods. The chart lists historical periods that are presented in the Bible and indicates some books of the Bible that describe each period.

Historical Period	Books of the Bible
Prehistory	Genesis
The Patriarchs	Genesis
Israel in Egypt	Exodus
The Wilderness Experience	Exodus, Leviticus, Numbers, Deuteronomy
Settling the Land	Joshua, Judges, Ruth
The United Kingdom	1–2 Samuel, 1–2 Kings, 1–2 Chronicles, Psalms
The Divided Kingdom	2 Kings, 2 Chronicles, Amos, Hosea, Micah, Isaiah, Jeremiah, Nahum
The Babylonian Captivity	Lamentations, Ezekiel, Isaiah, Daniel, Esther
Return to the Homeland	Ezra, Nehemiah, Tobit, Judith, Jonah, Ecclesiastes
Israel Among the Nations	1–2 Maccabees, Daniel, Sirach
Jesus' Earthly Ministry	Matthew, Mark, Luke, John
The Early Church	Acts of the Apostles, Letters, Revelation

Genesis means beginning. The **Book of Genesis** is the first book in the Bible, and it is about beginnings. In the first eleven chapters of Genesis, we read about prehistory, the events from creation down to the time of Abraham. These chapters contain stories that describe the beginning of God's relationship with humanity. These stories are very old and are not necessarily about factual events. Instead the stories tell of religious truths about God and his actions and interactions with humanity.

The stories contain vivid descriptions and imagery, repeat details often, and have simple plots with not many characters. These features made it easy for people to understand the meaning of the stories, to remember them, and to pass the stories down through the ages.

The biblical writer used symbols to tell a realistic story and at the same time to give the deeper meaning of the story. The symbols used in the Bible express ideas and beliefs about God and his actions throughout history.

In the first eleven chapters of Genesis, the stories are sometimes separated from each other by genealogies, or family trees. The genealogies tell how people are related to one another and how they are part of God's family.

The Gates of Paradise, by Lorenzo Ghiberti (1378–1455), depict Old Testament scenes. Baptistery of the Duomo, Florence, Italy

covenant an agreement between God and his people

Book of Genesis the first book in the Bible

WE RESPOND

Think about all the "beginnings" that have taken place in your life. You might include the first time you rode a bicycle or the time when you first received Holy Communion.

Write a prayer asking God to continue to help you in all your "beginnings."

God thankyou for all
that you have done
for me help me in
all my beginnings
Amen.

God created the universe.

✝ *O God, how wonderful is your universe!*

Have you ever looked at the night sky filled with stars? What did you wonder about?

WE BELIEVE

Through the ages people have wondered about the universe: Where did it come from? How did it begin? Who created it? Why was it created? When did it start?

Scientists have focused on the problems of *how* and *when* the universe and all of life came into being. They have discovered many facts and have come up with some very interesting theories. The Church recognizes the importance of these studies. However, science cannot answer the questions of *who* created the universe, *why* it was created, and *where* it is going. These questions can only be answered in faith. So we look to Scripture and Tradition for the answers to these questions. And in the Book of Genesis we find two accounts of creation.

The First Creation Account In Genesis 1:1—2:4, we find a beautiful and imaginative story of the creation of the universe. In simple but poetic language, the biblical writer tells us that God freely created the universe over a six-day period. A *day* in this story does not mean twenty-four hours. In fact, *day* does not represent any definite period of time. Scholars think the biblical writer showed God creating the universe in six days because that was the normal workweek of the Israelites who lived at the time the story was written.

In the creation story God spoke and everything was created: light, sun, moon, stars, sky, water, earth, sea, fish, plants, animals, and humans. By God's word the universe came into being. And at each stage God saw that what he created was good. Then on the seventh day God rested.

Day 1

"God said, 'Let there be light,' and there was light." (Genesis 1:3)

Day 4

"God said: 'Let there be lights in the dome of the sky . . .' God made the two great lights, the greater one to govern the day, and the lesser one to govern the night; and he made the stars."
(Genesis 1:14, 16)

This creation account is not meant to be a scientific study of creation. It is not an exact recording of God's work within a certain time frame. However, it is the story that revealed to God's people the truths about creation: everything in existence is created by God, and everything that God created is good and depends on him.

First Story of Creation

"In the beginning, when God created the heavens and the earth, the earth was a formless wasteland, and darkness covered the abyss, while a mighty wind swept over the waters." (Genesis 1:1–2)

Day 2

"God said, 'Let there be a dome in the middle of the waters, to separate one body of water from the other.' And so it happened." (Genesis 1:6)

Day 3

"God said, 'Let the water under the sky be gathered into a single basin, so that the dry land may appear . . . ' Then God said, 'Let the earth bring forth vegetation: every kind of plant that bears seed and every kind of fruit tree on earth that bears fruit with its seed in it.' " (Genesis 1:9, 11)

Day 5

"God said, 'Let the water teem with an abundance of living creatures, and on the earth let birds fly beneath the dome of the sky.' " (Genesis 1:20)

Day 6

"God said, 'Let the earth bring forth all kinds of living creatures: cattle, creeping things, and wild animals of all kinds' . . . Then God said: 'Let us make man in our image, after our likeness' . . . male and female he created them.

God blessed them, saying: 'Be fertile and multiply; fill the earth and subdue it. Have dominion over the fish of the sea, the birds of the air, and all the living things that move on the earth.' . . . God looked at everything he had made, and he found it very good." (Genesis 1:24, 26, 27, 28, 31)

 In groups portray the events of creation in a dramatic representation.

WE RESPOND

What does creation tell us about God's love? his wisdom? his power? his goodness?

Heavenly Father, thank you for your wonderful gift of creation.
Amen.

Day 7

"Thus the heavens and the earth and all their array were completed. Since on the seventh day God was finished with the work he had been doing, he rested on the seventh day from all the work he had undertaken. So God blessed the seventh day and made it holy, because on it he rested from all the work he had done in creation.
Such is the story of the heavens and the earth at their creation." (Genesis 2:1–4)

God is the source of all life.

WE GATHER

✝ *God, there is nothing you cannot do.*

🧍 Choose one of your favorite characters from a book, television show, or movie. Then with a partner describe two positive qualities about that character. How does the character show these qualities?

WE BELIEVE

The first account of creation in Genesis 1:1—2:4 not only tells us about creation, it also tells us about God. To begin with, the account shows us that God is the one, true God. In other words, God is unique. There is no other God. This understanding of God is very different from the one held by other ancient peoples.

They believed that there were many gods and even thought of objects as gods. They often worshiped the sun or moon, other forces of nature like the weather, or ideas like fate or justice.

From the first account of creation we learn how the one true God was different from the many false gods or idols that were the focus of beliefs in ancient times. The first creation account makes it clear that the God we worship is a personal God, not an object or an idea. God is a living being, and is the source of all life. In fact, God is the greatest of all beings. God is the supreme being who creates all life and keeps it in existence.

Throughout history God has continued to reveal himself as the one who is the source of all creation. In the Bible we find many references to God as Creator.

Old Testament	New Testament
"Our help is in the name of the LORD, the maker of heaven and earth." (Psalm 124:8)	"The God who made the world and all that is in it, the Lord of heaven and earth, does not dwell in sanctuaries made by human hands, nor is he served by human hands because he needs anything. Rather it is he who gives to everyone life and breath and everything." (Acts of the Apostles 17:24–25)

The first account of creation helps us to know some of God's attributes, or qualities.

• God is eternal. This means that God always was and always will be. God is changeless and timeless.

Unlike the Israelites, other ancient peoples worshiped false gods that were born, usually in some fantastic way, and could die.

• God is all-powerful. This means that God can do anything. God is perfect.

Here again God differs from the false gods that other ancient peoples believed in. They believed that their gods made mistakes and sometimes failed. They often pictured these gods as guilty of terrible evils.

• God is all-knowing. This means that God knows everything—past, present, and future. Yet God's knowledge never keeps people from choosing and acting freely.

Unlike the Israelites, other people believed in false gods that did not know everything, could not do everything, and often tried to keep the people from making their own decisions.

• God is ever-present. This means that God is everywhere at all times.

False gods that other people believed in could not be present everywhere and always. They were often described as traveling from place to place, just like human beings.

The first creation account tells us so much that we need to know about God. However, human words and ideas can only explain so much. That is why God will remain a mystery to us in this life. We will only have full and complete knowledge of God in eternal life.

To help you remember the attributes of God, use words and images to complete this diagram.

sacrect

God is . . .

loved

thought of

Thank you God!

the greatest of all

God Stars

WE RESPOND

Which of God's attributes best describes your own experience of God? Why?

Human beings are created in God's image and likeness.

WE GATHER

✝ *Loving Father, you are always by our side.*

🧑 In a group brainstorm words that can be used to describe the term *human beings*. Then write a definition of the term.

imperfect, hardworking, living,

WE BELIEVE

The account of creation that begins the Book of Genesis indicates that God created not only the universe but all the living things in it. However, there is something strikingly different in the description of the creation of humans.

"God created man in his image;
in the divine image he created him;
male and female he created them."

(Genesis 1:27)

The biblical writer is telling us that only human beings are made in the image and likeness of God. We are like God because as human beings each one of us is a unique person who possesses a human dignity. **Human dignity** is the value and worth that comes from being made in God's image and likeness. Both males and females are created in God's image and likeness—different but equal. And God found that good. Girls and boys, women and men, all share the same human dignity, and are created to share in God's friendship.

Of all the creatures humans alone are created by God with **free will**, the freedom and ability to choose. God also gave each man and woman a **conscience**, the ability to know the difference between good and evil, right and wrong. We alone are able to think and love and form relationships. We alone can know and love our Creator. God calls us to be open to his love and to the love of others. He calls us to love as he loves and to live in his friendship.

Being made in the image and likeness of God carries with it serious responsibilities. We are called to respect and care for all that God has given us. And since our free will makes us responsible for our own thoughts and actions, we must make our choices carefully. We are called to choose what is good and right and to act in the image and likeness of our Creator.

WE RESPOND

 Fill out this pledge card.

I am made in God's image and likeness.

I accept the responsibility and will try to live out this responsibility by

always pickins good and going to church.

Thank you, God, for making me in your image and likeness. Amen.

Abby
(Name)

Key Words

human dignity the value and worth that comes from being made in God's image and likeness

free will the freedom and ability to choose

conscience the ability to know the difference between good and evil, right and wrong

PROJECT

Show What *you* Know

+10/10

Unscramble the Key Words to complete the sentences below.

Free will

EREF LILW	NUHAM GNYIIDT	KOBO ISESGNE FO
ECCNICSENO		VATNNEOC

1. The first book of the Bible, the _Book of Genesis_, contains two accounts of creation.

2. Of all creatures created by God, we alone were created with _free will_, the freedom and ability to choose, and with _conscience_, the ability to know the difference between good and evil, right and wrong.

3. The _covenant_ is an agreement between God and his people.

4. Each one of us is a unique person who possesses _human dignaity_, the value that comes from being made in God's image and likeness.

Celebrate!

On or around the feast day of Saint Francis of Assisi, many parishes hold a special ceremony. Parishioners take their animals, including pets and even work animals, to church. Some churches have a procession. Others simply have the animals gather for a blessing. Saint Francis of Assisi believed that humanity was connected to all of God's creation in a brotherhood. Saint Francis is the patron saint of animals and of ecology, which is the study of the relationship between living things and their environment.

↳ DISCIPLE CHALLENGE

• When is Saint Francis of Assisi's feast day?

Oct 4.

• Does your parish have a special ceremony or procession for the blessing of animals? If so, describe it.

No it dose. well not that I know of.

D1SC1PLE

Pray
Learn
Celebrate
Share
Choose
Live

More to Explore

womb

The Vatican Observatory is one of the world's oldest astronomical institutes. It was founded in 1582. The observatory has two research centers, one in Castel Gandolfo, Italy, and one in Tucson, Arizona. The Tucson center telescope is the first optical-infrared telescope to be used to study light at the farthest points of the universe. The center in Italy has a unique collection of meteorites that are used to study the history of the solar system. Studying science is a way to grow closer to God by appreciating the wonders of God's creation.

What are other ways to appreciate the wonders of God's creation?

Spread the Good News

Boing to school.

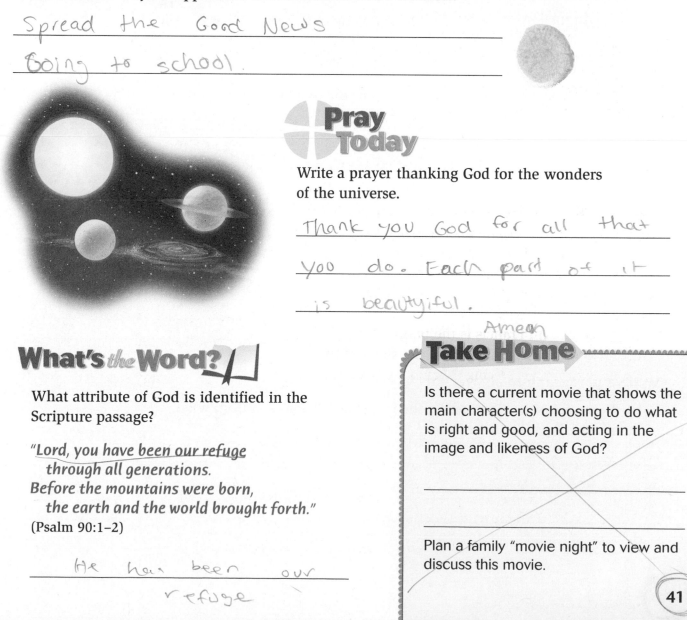

Pray Today

Write a prayer thanking God for the wonders of the universe.

Thank you God for all that you do. Each part of it is beautyiful.

Amean

What's the Word?

What attribute of God is identified in the Scripture passage?

"Lord, you have been our refuge through all generations.
Before the mountains were born,
the earth and the world brought forth."
(Psalm 90:1–2)

He has been our refuge

Take Home

Is there a current movie that shows the main character(s) choosing to do what is right and good, and acting in the image and likeness of God?

Plan a family "movie night" to view and discuss this movie.

41

see google classroom

CHAPTER TEST

Circle the letter of the correct answer.

1. The _____ is an agreement between God and his people.

    a. Bible   **b.** creation   **c.** covenant

2. Biblical writers used _____ to tell a realistic story and at the same time to give the deeper meaning of the story.

    a. attributes   **b.** symbols   **c.** scholars

3. _____ is the freedom and ability to choose.

    a. Genesis   **b.** Free will   **c.** Conscience

4. _____ is the source of all life.

    a. The Bible   **b.** The Book of Genesis   **c.** God

Short Answers

5. Why is Genesis an appropriate name for the first book of the Bible?

    _____

6. What is a truth that the first creation story reveals to us?

    _____

7. God has many attributes; list three.

    _____

8. What is human dignity?

    _____

Write a paragraph to answer this question.

9–10. Because we were created in the image and likeness of God, what responsibilities do we have?

    _____

    _____

    _____

    _____

People Turn from God

3

✝ **We Gather in Prayer**

Leader: Blessed be the God of creation who forms us like clay in the hands of a potter.

All: Blessed be God now and for ever.

Reader 1: "This word came to Jeremiah from the LORD: Rise up, be off to the potter's house; there I will give you my message.

Reader 2: I went down to the potter's house and there he was, working at the wheel. Whenever the object of clay which he was making turned out badly in his hand, he tried again, making of the clay another object of whatever sort he pleased.

Reader 3: Then the word of the Lord came to me: Can I not do to you, house of Israel, as this potter has done? says the LORD.

Reader 4: Indeed, like clay in the hand of the potter, so are you in my hand, house of Israel." (Jeremiah 18:1–6)

The Word of the Lord.

All: Thanks be to God.

43

God created human beings, body and soul.

WE BELIEVE

After the opening story of creation, the Book of Genesis provides a second story of creation. We can read it in Genesis 2:5–25. In this second account of creation, the biblical writer describes that God created humans *before* he created plants and other creatures. Thus, the two creation stories differ. Yet both accounts make the same point: God created humanity as the high point of creation, giving us great dignity and power.

Scripture makes this clear:

"What are humans that you are mindful of
 them,
 mere mortals that you care for them?
Yet you have made them little less than a
 god,
 crowned them with glory and honor.
You have given them rule over the works of
 your hands,
 put all things at their feet." (Psalm 8:5–7)

The Second Creation Account The biblical writer tells us that God created humans by taking a lump of clay from the earth and using it to form the body of the first man. This creation account is very old, yet it agrees with the idea from today's modern scientific study: Our human bodies are made out of the same elements as the rest of the universe.

In this story we read "the LORD God formed man out of the clay of the ground and blew into his nostrils the breath of life, and so man became a living being" (Genesis 2:7). This symbolizes that God gave humanity life. This breath of life from God refers to our **soul**, the invisible spiritual reality that makes each of us human. The soul is immortal; it will never die.

This story makes it clear that humans are a union of a visible, physical body and an invisible, spiritual soul. Every human being is unique, yet each of us is made body and soul. And one day we will die and our bodies will turn to dust. But our souls, the breath of God in us, will live forever. At the end of time, our body and soul will be reunited when Christ comes again at the Last Judgment.

44

soul the invisible spiritual reality that makes each of us human and that will never die

We also find in this second story of creation that God said, "It is not good for the man to be alone. I will make a suitable partner for him" (Genesis 2:18). So God created many wild animals and birds and then finally, while the man slept, God took one of his ribs and created the first woman. When the man woke up and saw this woman he said,

"This one, at last, is bone of my bones and flesh of my flesh" (Genesis 2:23).

God's creation of woman from the rib of man symbolizes that females and males share the same human dignity and are equal. This also reminds us that all humans are united to one another. We all have one true Father—God. It is God who has created us and has breathed life into us. We are all created to share in God's own life, and to help one another to know and love God.

WE RESPOND

We all have gifts and abilities. What are some of yours? How do you use your unique gifts and abilities to help others know and love God? How do they use their gifts to help you?

🎵 And It Was Good

Ev'rything was now in place, earth and sky and sea; then God blew a mighty breath making you and me.

And it was good, good, very, very good, and it was good, good, very, very good, and it was good, good, very, very good, it was very, very, very good.

45

God called us to be stewards of creation.

God told the first human beings, "Be fertile and multiply; fill the earth and subdue it. Have dominion over the fish of the sea, the birds of the air, and all the living things that move on the earth" (Genesis 1:28).

God told the first man and woman to bring new life into the world and thus create the human family. He asked them to be responsible for the earth and all the living things in it. Then God allowed humans to be partners with him and with one another in continuing his work of creation.

God put the first man and woman in the beautiful garden in Eden and shared his own friendship and life with them. They also had use of all the gifts of creation. The garden was a symbol that the biblical writer used to show the happiness that human beings had in the presence of God.

The biblical writer tells us about another symbolic event: God gave humans authority over all the animals by allowing them to name the animals. To the ancient Israelites, people had authority over those whom they named. So humans were called by God to be the caretakers of creation.

Of all of God's creatures, humans alone have the ability to care for creation and make it prosper. In fact, that is exactly what stewardship involves—authority and responsibility. A **steward** is a person who is given both the authority over what he or she cares for and the responsibility for seeing that it lives and grows. So from the very beginning, all humanity was called to be stewards of God's creation.

Stewards Today   Today people around the world are trying to carry out their responsibilities as God's stewards of creation. Many people work to protect our environment by recycling and using resources wisely. Some plant new trees to maintain the world's forests. Other people work to stop air and water pollution, and to protect our wildlife. Scientists and farmers find ways for us to safely grow enough food to feed all the people in the world. By caring for creation, we show respect for the creator.

steward a person who is given both the authority over what he or she cares for and the responsibility for seeing that it lives and grows

WE RESPOND

We are all called to take care of creation every day. What specific things can we do to:

use water wisely _turn off the water when bürshin te_

recycle _Throw the right stuff away._

take care of pets _Take them outside or for walks_

protect the environment _Not throw trash out of window_

other _Taking care of the earth_

Plan to do one of these things with your family next week.

Thank you, Lord, for making us the stewards of this beautiful world we live in.
Amen.

Evil entered the world through a human act.

WE GATHER

✝ *God, help us in our choices.*

What are some of the reasons that people make choices that lead them away from God and others?

WE BELIEVE

In Chapter 3 of the Book of Genesis, the biblical writer uses a story with many symbols and other storytelling devices to teach important truths about sin and suffering. As the story opens, the first man and woman were living in a beautiful garden in Eden. They had everything they needed for a happy life. They were God's friends, and because of this friendship they had happiness and harmony in their lives. In fact, they were at one with God, each other, and the rest of creation. They were living in the original state of innocence, holiness, and justice for which God had created them.

The first humans were free to do whatever they wanted except one thing: they could *not* eat the fruit of the tree of the knowledge of good and bad. God told the man that if he ate from it, he would die. This warning about the forbidden fruit symbolizes that friendship with God depends on complete trust in God and on following his will for us. It reminds us that, as created beings, we are limited and we must respect those limitations.

But we learn from the story that the first man and woman disobeyed God. A serpent spoke to the woman and said, "God knows well that the moment you eat of it [the fruit] your eyes will be opened and you will be like gods who know what is good and what is bad" (Genesis 3:5). She believed the serpent. So she picked some of the fruit and ate it. Then she offered some to the man, who also ate it.

This story is filled with symbols. The serpent represents the Devil, who tempted the woman to do evil. The fact that the woman believed the serpent reminds us of just how attractive evil can be. Eating the fruit symbolizes a choice. It shows that because of our free will, humans have the power to make choices that can lead to good or to evil.

As the story continues the first man and woman realized the seriousness of their actions. They became frightened of God and hid from him. But God knew what they had done, and, as the story closes, God sent them out of the garden. They no longer had any right to be there.

This story tells of a very real truth—the choice of the first humans to turn away from God and lose their close friendship with him. Of their own free will, they chose to turn from God. By their own actions, the first man and woman broke their friendship with God and let evil into the world. And this is when pain, sorrow, and death also entered into human life.

WE RESPOND

🏃 With a group discuss recent news stories that show people who are suffering in some way. How can they be comforted? Illustrate ways that you and your class can help people who are suffering in your own school and neighborhood.

Loving God, comfort us in our sufferings. Guide us, too, in helping others who are suffering and in need of comfort.

All people suffer from the effects of Original Sin.

WE GATHER

✝ *Lord, deliver us from evil.*

What might damage your relationship with a friend or a family member? Explain.

WE BELIEVE

The story of the first human beings, whom we call Adam and Eve, shows how close the relationship between God and human beings originally was. It also shows how that relationship was broken by human actions.

The first humans disobeyed God. Instead of respecting God's warning and trusting his words, they turned away from him. They selfishly did what *they* wanted, rather than what God commanded. In other words, they committed a sin. **Sin** is a thought, word, deed, or omission against God's law.

This sin of the first humans took away their original innocence, holiness, and justice. They lost the harmony they felt with God, with each other, and with the rest of creation.

The first humans had committed personal sin because they personally chose to turn from God and failed to love and obey him. Their personal sin was the first sin and is called **Original Sin**. Original Sin weakened human nature and brought ignorance, suffering, and death into the world. This wounded human nature was passed on to the rest of humanity. Thus, we all suffer from the effects of Original Sin, though it is not a sin for which we are personally responsible.

Key Words

sin a thought, word, deed, or omission against God's law

Original Sin the first sin that weakened human nature and brought ignorance, suffering, and death into the world; we all suffer from its effects

God's Mercy Even though the first human beings turned away from God, God did not turn away from them. He did not abandon humanity. Instead God promised to show them his mercy. He said;

"He will strike at your head,
     while you strike at his heel." (Genesis 3:15)

This is very symbolic language, telling us that God would send a descendant of the first man and woman to rescue humanity from evil one day. This was God's promise that sin and evil would one day be overcome.

So humanity was *not* completely lost. Human nature was wounded, but not totally destroyed. Humans were still a part of God's good creation, and God still loved all those he created. But because of Original Sin, human nature needed to be restored to its original relationship with God. And in his mercy, God would provide for this.

As Catholics...

Our Lord and Savior Jesus Christ, as true God and true man, is free from all sin, including Original Sin. He died and rose to free us from sin. Because Mary was to be the Mother of the Son of God, she was blessed by God in a special way. Mary was free from Original Sin from the moment she was conceived, and she did not commit sin during her entire life. We call this truth the Immaculate Conception.

Mary, under the title of the Immaculate Conception, is the patroness of the United States. The whole Church celebrates the Feast of the Immaculate Conception on December 8. In the United States this feast is a holy day of obligation.

How does your parish celebrate this feast?

WE RESPOND

Write a prayer asking God to keep us close to him.

God please be close to me during my toughest times and be close to me while i'm writing this prayer.
                    Amen.

PROJECT

Show What *you* Know

Write a summary of the second creation story.
Use the **Key Words** in your summary.

God mad a man out of clay and he named him Adam. Whit adams rib he created a women named Eve. They didn't have origail sim. He put them in the granden and told them not to the apple from the tree. Adam and eve were temted by the devil and ate the apple from the tree. That kaow sin became.

Celebrate!

Mary was free from Original Sin from the moment she was conceived. This truth is the Immaculate Conception.

As a parish, we gather together to celebrate the Immaculate Conception.

↳ **DISCIPLE CHALLENGE** When and how do we celebrate the Immaculate Conception?

December 8th, we go to eurch and celebrae her.

DISCIPLE

More *to* Explore

Dangers such as pollution and climate change threaten the environment. The National Catholic Rural Life Conference (NCRLC) helps families in rural farm areas with these and other problems. The conference reminds us of our call to the stewardship of all creation. The NCRLC is concerned about scientific advances in growing food. Members speak out to make sure that Catholic social teachings guide us in making decisions about our environment. The NCRLC calls on all people to respect life, uphold human dignity, and show respect for creation.

↳ DISCIPLE CHALLENGE

- Search the NCRLC Web site (www.ncrlc.com).
- Choose one of the programs or issues. Prepare to report on it to the class.
- Visit *Lives of the Saints* on www.webelieveweb.com to learn more about the NCRLC patron saints.

Question Corner

In the Book of Genesis, we learn God gave humanity "dominion over . . . all the living things that move on the earth" (Genesis 1: 28). *Dominion over* implies being a steward and having responsibility for living things. What are you responsible for?

_____

Make *it* Happen

Your local food bank needs volunteers and donations. Write one way you and your friends can help.

_____

_____

_____

Now, pass it on!

Take Home

Talk about the word *steward* with your family. Point out that all members of your family are stewards—each is given the authority over what he or she cares for and the responsibility for seeing that it lives and grows. Share some ways that each member of your family is a steward.

Write True or False for the following sentences.
Then change the false sentences to make them true.

1. _____ In the stories of creation in the Book of Genesis, we find out that God's greatest creation was humanity.

_____

2. _____ God calls each of us to be responsible for the earth and all the living things in it.

_____

3. _____ Friendship with God depends on complete trust in him and on following his will for us.

_____

4. _____ We are born with Original Sin and suffer from its effects because it is sin for which we are personally responsible.

_____

Write the letter that best defines each term.

5. _____ steward

6. _____ sin

7. _____ soul

8. _____ Original Sin

a. the first sin that weakened human nature and brought ignorance, suffering, and death into the world

b. a thought, word, deed, or omission against God's law

c. the invisible spiritual reality that makes each of us human and that will never die

d. person who is given both the authority over what he or she cares for and the responsibility for seeing that it lives and grows

e. the original state of innocence, holiness, and justice for which humans were created

Write a paragraph to answer this question.

9–10. How did God respond when Adam and Eve sinned?

_____

_____

_____

_____

✝ We Gather in Prayer

Leader: Sit quietly and think of a beautiful place. It might be a mountaintop, a park, a deep canyon, or the ocean's edge. Choose a place that makes you feel happy and peaceful.

Now imagine Jesus standing with you in your special place.

- What do you say to Jesus?
- What does he say to you?
- What do you want to ask Jesus?
- What do you want to thank him for?

Have a short conversation together, as friend with friend. Now let us pray together.

Leader: Jesus, Son of the living God,

All: have mercy on us.
(Response to all petitions.)

Leader: Jesus, splendor of the Father,
Jesus, king of glory,
Jesus, dawn of justice,
Jesus, Son of the Virgin Mary,
Jesus, worthy of our love,
Jesus, prince of peace,
Jesus, all-powerful,
Jesus, God of peace,
Jesus, our refuge,
Jesus, Good Shepherd,
Jesus, crown of all saints.

Leader: Christ hear us.

All: Christ hear us.

Leader: Lord Jesus, hear our prayer.

All: Lord Jesus, hear our prayer. Amen.

God promised to send a Savior.

WE GATHER

✝ *Glory be to the Father, and to the Son, and to the Holy Spirit.*

🧑 With your group brainstorm stories from books or television shows that are about broken friendships. What are the various outcomes of these stories?

They become friends again by saying sorry.

What caused these outcomes?

They relised that they were fighting about was stuiped

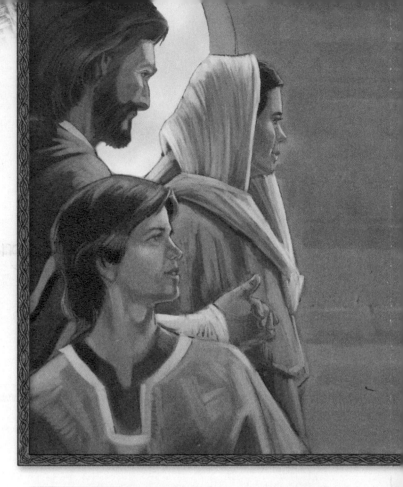

WE BELIEVE

We learn from the Old Testament that Original Sin separated human beings from God. Thus, even though they would try to do the things God asked, human beings would continue to sin. It would be very hard for them to have a close friendship with God again. Yet God would never stop loving people and forgiving them.

Humanity could not undo the effects of Original Sin. To fully restore the friendship with God that was broken by the first humans' disobedience, humanity needed God's help. They needed God to fulfill his promise to send a Savior. So God's people waited for the one who would bring humanity back to the perfect state of holiness in which God had created them. They believed that when the Savior came, he would completely restore their friendship with God.

Throughout the Old Testament the biblical writers reminded the people of God's promise. In his writings, the prophet Isaiah told of someone who would come to free humanity from sin and restore their friendship with God. Isaiah described this person as the *Suffering Servant.*

"Through his suffering, my servant shall
    justify many,
  and their guilt he shall bear."
(Isaiah 53:11)

This Suffering Servant referred to by Isaiah is God's own Son. For in the fullness of time God the Father sent his only Son to restore our relationship with him. Through Mary's obedience and acceptance of God's will, Jesus Christ, the Son of God became man. Jesus Christ, true God and true man, fulfilled all that God promised. Obedient to his Father, he died on the cross and rose from the dead to save all people from sin and to bring us the hope of new life. As Saint Paul wrote, "For just as in Adam all die, so too in Christ shall all be brought to life" (1 Corinthians 15:22).

As Catholics...

Because of Jesus Christ all people can once again share in God's life and friendship. We call this share in God's life and friendship *grace*, and we receive grace through the sacraments. A sacrament is an effective sign given to us by Jesus through which we share in God's life.

There are Seven Sacraments: Baptism, Confirmation, the Eucharist, Penance and Reconciliation, the Anointing of the Sick, Holy Orders, and Matrimony. Jesus instituted, or began, the sacraments so that his saving work would continue for all time. The sacraments truly bring about, or effect, what they represent. For example, in Baptism we not only celebrate new life, we actually receive new life in Christ. In Penance we not only celebrate that our God is forgiving, we actually receive God's forgiveness.

The sacraments are the most important celebrations in the Church. The sacraments join Catholics all over the world with Christ and with one another.

How are the sacraments an important part of your life and the life of your family?

The New Testament contains four separate books about Jesus. We call these the Gospels of Matthew, Mark, Luke, and John. The word *gospel* means "good news." The **Gospel** is the Good News about God at work in Jesus Christ.

In the Gospels we read of Jesus' work to bring hope to the poor and suffering, freedom to those who are persecuted, and healing to those who are sick. From the Gospels we learn that through his life, Death, and Resurrection, Jesus Christ makes it possible for all humanity to again share in God's life.

Key Word

Gospel the Good News about God at work in Jesus Christ

WE RESPOND

10-12

How does the way you live show that you share in God's life and friendship?

Father in Heaven, thank you for keeping your promise and sending your Son, Jesus Christ. Amen.

The first human family struggled because of Original Sin.

WE GATHER

✝ *Jesus, Savior, guide and protect all families.*

👤 What positive things can people do to handle the anger they might feel in certain situations?

1 telke a breck

WE BELIEVE

The story in the Book of Genesis continues by telling us about Adam and Eve's family. In the fourth chapter of Genesis we find out that Adam and Eve had two sons. The older son Cain was a farmer. His younger brother, Abel, was a shepherd.

By all appearances this family was loving and happy. Then something happened to set brother against brother. Both brothers made an offering of their goods to the Lord, but "the LORD looked with favor on Abel and his offering, but on Cain and his offering he did not" (Genesis 4:4–5).

The story does not explain why one offering was acceptable and the other was not. That was the biblical writer's way of indicating that we cannot always understand the ways of God and should not try to judge his ways. Yet Cain judged everything only from his own point of view. He felt that he had been treated unfairly, and he became very angry about it. Perhaps he was also envious of Abel's success.

The first human faimally struggled because of original sin.

In the story God saw what Cain was going through and offered him some advice. God told Cain that he could do the right thing and accept this situation. God assured Cain that he had the ability to overcome evil. But Cain could not rise above his anger. He took his resentment out on his innocent brother—Cain killed Abel. Murder, one of the worst effects of Original Sin, came into existence.

In the Genesis account, God asked Cain where Abel was. Cain replied, "I do not know. Am I my brother's keeper?" (Genesis 4:9). God was deeply offended and said to Cain, "What have you done! Listen: Your brother's blood cries out to me from the soil! Therefore you shall be banned from the soil that opened its mouth to receive your brother's blood from your hand" (Genesis 4:10–11).

Suddenly, Cain realized that he was being sent away and would lose God's protection. He feared that he himself would now be killed. Yet God came to Cain's aid. He put a mark on Cain. This showed that though he murdered Abel, Cain was protected by God. So even in this terrible circumstance God showed his great love for Cain.

The story of Cain and Abel can be understood on several levels. On one level it declares the sacredness of human life and prohibits murder of any kind. On another level it symbolizes the separation of human beings from one another. On a third level it is about accepting life as one finds it and respecting one another. And on a fourth level it is about the healing power of God's love.

Write a prayer for all families everywhere. Ask God to be with all families. Ask him to help families solve their problems in a loving and caring way.

God help the familys
in need. Help the ones
who have sined or torned
for you. Help them with
there needs.
Amena-

WE RESPOND

How can you show love for your family this week?

59

God made a covenant with Noah.

WE GATHER

✝ *Father, help us to be just in all our ways.*

Justice means respecting the rights of others and giving them what is rightfully theirs. Just comes from the word *justice*.

Who in your neighborhood or school would you describe as a just person? Why?

WE BELIEVE

As the Book of Genesis continues, we learn that God is greatly displeased with humankind. They were not being the faithful stewards of the world that they were created to be.

Genesis 6:7—9:17

So to Noah, who was a just man, God said, "I have decided to put an end to all mortals on earth; the earth is full of lawlessness because of them. So I will destroy them and all life on earth" (Genesis 6:13). Then God commanded Noah to build a great ark, a kind of ship. Noah was to fill it with two of every living thing, male and female, along with his wife and family.

When Noah had everything ready, God sent forty days and forty nights of continual rain. God allowed the seas to spill over onto the land and the floodwaters to slowly rise above the highest mountains. All life outside the ark was lost.

Eventually the floodwaters went down, and God allowed Noah, his family, and all the animals to leave the ark. In gratitude, Noah built an altar and offered God a sacrifice on it. God was pleased with this sacrifice and made

a covenant, or agreement, with Noah. In this covenant God promised that even if humanity failed him again, he would never send another flood to destroy life on earth. Through Noah God made an everlasting covenant with the whole of humanity. For that reason all people are called to friendship with God. All people are invited to enjoy God's love and forgiveness. The symbol of this promise was a rainbow. God told Noah, "This is the sign of the covenant I have established between me and all mortal creatures that are on earth" (Genesis 9:17).

The story of the flood, which is found in Chapters 6—9 of the Book of Genesis, revealed an important religious truth: God's forgiveness and love, and humanity's goodness, can overcome all evil. Yet, humanity lost its unity with the rest of creation because of its responsibility for the flood.

To symbolize God's justice and his love and forgiveness, the biblical writer used the powerful symbol of water in the story of the great flood. Water is always a very meaningful symbol. Water can be forceful and even threatening, yet it can be cleansing and calming.

A story of a great flood that almost destroys all life is very common among the ancient peoples of the world. The Genesis account of Noah and the flood is perhaps the most famous of these stories, but it is not original. It goes back to a much more ancient tale of a great flood. A version of this tale is preserved in the Epic of Gilgamesh, which was written sometime between 2000 and 1000 B.C.

Christian Symbolism: The Flood There is great meaning in the symbols found in the story of Noah. Some Christian writers think that the ark is a symbol of the Church: just as the ark saved Noah and all who were with him, so through the Church we are saved.

In the Church, the flood is a symbol of the waters of the Sacrament of Baptism. Through Baptism we are freed from Original Sin and all personal sins. Through Baptism God offers us his forgiveness and his love.

Just as Noah and his family were brought to a new life through the flood, in the waters of Baptism we are brought to a new life in Christ. Through the waters of Baptism, God begins a covenant relationship with each Christian. Just as the world was washed and made clean by the flood, we are washed and made clean in the baptismal water.

Design a stained-glass window that reminds you of God's friendship with all people.

WE RESPOND

🎵 Water of Life/Agua de Vida

Refrain:
> Water of life, holy reminder;
> touching, renewing the body of Christ.
> Water of life, holy reminder;
> touching, renewing the body of Christ.
>
> All generations, come forth and receive
> the blessing of this holy water;
> making us one with the God who forgives,
> the one who is faithful and just. (Refrain)

Refrain:
> Agua de vida, santo recuerdo;
> Une y renueva al cuerpo de Cristo.
> Agua de vida, santo recuerdo;
> Une y renueva al cuerpo de Cristo.
>
> Vengan, reciban el agua de paz,
> revivan su santo bautismo.
> Dejen atrás los rencores de ayer
> y vivan la nueva a lianza. (Refrain)

61

Tower of Babel, by Pieter the Elder Brueghel (1515–1569)

The unity of the human race was lost.

WE GATHER

✝ *Lord, help us to live as one world family.*

What are some of the causes of divisions in our world today? How can the world be more united?

WE BELIEVE

We now come to the very last event that the Book of Genesis records for the period called prehistory. In Genesis 11:1–9 we read the story of the Tower of Babel. This story symbolizes the separation among different groups of people. It symbolizes humanity's loss of unity and the development of different languages.

We read that at first "the whole world spoke the same language, using the same words" (Genesis 11:1). This symbolizes that all human beings were related. Because they were able to communicate, they could truly act as God's stewards of the earth. Part of God's plan for completing the work of creation involved humanity's spread across the face of the earth.

Yet, human beings feared this, since moving on would expose them to all sorts of dangers and weaken their ability to defend themselves. So they decided to resist God's plan: They would all settle in one place and build a great tower to live in. In the Book of Genesis this is referred to as the Tower of Babel.

The tower that they tried to build looked very much like an ancient structure called a *ziggurat*. A ziggurat is made of a series of smaller and smaller brick platforms, one on top of the other. On the top of the highest platform stood a temple. Long staircases led up to the various platforms and to the temple.

In the story the tower was a symbol of human resistance to God's will. The people who were building it did not trust God. They preferred to do things their way. God saw what human beings were doing and decided to stop them. He did this by confusing their language. As a result, humans could not understand one another and the unity of the human race was lost.

What do you think this expression means: "They don't speak the same language."

[handwritten] They don't think the same.

Misunderstandings Begin   Sometimes the only reason people disagree is because they do not understand one another. This misunderstanding can lead to suspicion, mistrust, and even open hostility. According to the biblical writer, this began to happen to the human race after Babel. Humanity began to lose its unity and break up into rival groups.

As the story closes, the process of populating the earth continued as God had planned. Now, however, humans spoke many different languages and had developed different ways of living and communicating. And throughout history the need to respect these differences and to appreciate the dignity that all people possess has again and again caused misunderstandings between peoples.

WE RESPOND

As a class produce a talk show. The topic of today's show is: Do the divisions symbolized by the story of the Tower of Babel still affect our lives today? Why or why not?

Each person in the class is to participate in the talk show. Work together to decide who will be the moderator, interviewer, panelists, audience, and reporter.

PROJECT

Show What *you* Know

Use the clues to find the Key Word.

The word has six letters:

- The first letter can be found in *gnat*, but not in *antique*.
- The second letter can be found in *foal*, but not in *fable*.
- The third letter can be found in *psalm*, but not in *palm*.
- The fourth letter can be found in *poems*, but not in *some*.
- The fifth letter can be found in *pear*, but not in *party*.
- The sixth letter can be found in *lawn* but not in *wand*

The word is __G__ __O__ __S__ __p__ __e__ __l__ .

List two things that you know about this word.

Is the Good News about God's work in Jesus.

Itt in the New Testament.

A L U R E I S G D B T

Fast Facts

Custom has it that Noah's ark was built more like a four-sided box than a ship, a good shape for a cargo vessel. It was made of gopherwood (an unidentified wood, not mentioned elsewhere in the Bible) and sealed with pitch (wood tar) to make it watertight. It had one door, which God closed when Noah, his family, and two of every living thing were safely aboard the ark. (See Genesis 7:16.)

DISCIPLE

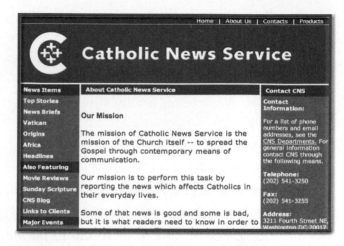

Pray Learn Celebrate Share Choose Live

More *to* Explore

Since 1920, the Catholic News Service has been letting people know what is going on in the world and in the Church. The professional journalists and photographers who work for the Catholic News Service write stories and take pictures that keep people informed about Catholic life today. The latest news is posted regularly at the service's Web site, www.catholicnews.com and is often printed in diocesan newspapers.

DISCIPLE CHALLENGE Why do you think the Catholic News Service is important?

Yes, becaus it keeps people informed on whats goingon in the chatolic life and it also teaches them about Jesus Christ.

Pray Today

Dear Lord,
Help me as I experience misunderstandings with my friends and family.
Give me patience as we work through disagreements.
Help me see things from the point of view of others.
Amen.

Make *it* Happen

It is necessary to respect the differences and appreciate the dignity that all people possess. What are some ways that you can teach this concept to someone younger than yourself?

I can teach it to them by letting then hang out with people that have other personalities orethur **Now, pass it on!** are different them them.

Take Home

Share with your family that the word *gospel* means "good news." This week, urge your family to recognize people and events that share the Good News of Jesus Christ. List some here.

65

see gc-

Abby

CHAPTER TEST

Circle the letter of the correct answer.

1. The _____ are the books of the Bible in which the Good News of Jesus' life and teachings are presented.

   a. covenants **b.** Genesis **c.** Gospels

2. Isaiah was a _____ who spoke to the people on God's behalf and reminded them of the way God wanted them to live.

   a. prophet **b.** shepherd **c.** farmer

3. The story of the Tower of Babel symbolizes the _____ among different groups of people.

   a. covenant **b.** separation **c.** love

4. God promised to send _____ who would restore humanity's friendship with God.

   a. Isaiah **b.** Noah **c.** a Savior

Short Answers

5. What did God do to help humanity after they turned away from him?

   _____

6. The story of Cain and Abel can be understood on several levels. Write one.

   _____

7. What important religious truth is revealed in the story of Noah?

   _____

8. In the story of the Tower of Babel, what does the tower symbolize?

   _____

Write a paragraph to answer this question.

9–10. How did God keep his promise and restore his life and friendship to all humanity?

   _____

   _____

   _____

   _____

The Patriarchs: God Chooses a People

✝ We Gather in Prayer

Leader: Loving God, your psalmist said, "Oh, that today you would hear his voice: Do not harden your hearts." (Psalm 95:7–8)

All: Help us to hear and follow your Word with open hearts. Amen.

Reader 1: For the times when we have deliberately chosen to do what we know is wrong.

All: Lord, have mercy.

Reader 2: For the times we have excluded others because they are not like us.

All: Lord, have mercy.

Reader 3: For the times we have used words to hurt and harm rather than to heal.

All: Lord, have mercy.

Reader 4: For the times we have walked by someone in need.

All: Lord, have mercy.

Leader: Loving God, we believe in you and place our trust in you. Help us strengthen our faith each day.

All: Amen.

St. Theresa's Fall Harvest Drive

The patriarchs are our ancestors in faith.

WE GATHER

✝ *Lord, from generation to generation we praise you.*

What do you know about your ancestors? How can you find out more about them?

WE BELIEVE

The last six verses of Chapter 11 of Genesis introduce us to a new stage in God's relationship with humanity. During this stage God formed a people for himself. We call this formative period *The Age of the Patriarchs*.

A **patriarch** is a father, or founder, of a clan, a group of related families. The four Old Testament patriarchs are Abraham, Isaac, Jacob, and Joseph. Through them God chose a special family for himself. This family is the people of God. Sarah, Rebekah, Rachel, and Leah were important women in God's family. They are called matriarchs. These men and women lived from approximately 1900 B.C. to about 1650 B.C. Their story is told in Chapters 12—50 of the Book of Genesis.

The families of these Old Testament patriarchs and matriarchs lived in tents and made their living primarily by raising flocks of sheep and goats. These people roamed the unoccupied territory between the towns and villages of Canaan and the desert. **Canaan** was an area in western Palestine that included most of present-day Israel.

Although the patriarchs owned no land and had no houses, they usually stayed in one place long enough to grow grain and raise a variety of fruits and vegetables. They also traded with other people for what they needed. They normally traveled on foot, but sometimes they used donkeys for transportation. Their life centered on their families and the clan.

During the period of the patriarchs, Canaan was made up of small independent city-states. A king ruled each city-state. Each city-state was made up of a walled city, usually built on a hill, and the surrounding countryside. Farms and villages dotted the countryside and provided food to the city-state. The walled city itself was the center of industry, crafts, and trade.

Key Words

patriarch a father, or founder, of a clan, a group of related families

Canaan an area in western Palestine that included most of present-day Israel

faith a gift from God that enables us to believe in him and accept all that he has revealed

The inhabitants of Canaan, or Canaanites, had the same background as the patriarchs and their families. They all spoke a similar language. That is why they treated one another as distant cousins rather than as complete strangers.

We, too, think of the families of the patriarchs and matriarchs as our family. They are our ancestors in faith. **Faith** is a gift from God that enables us to believe in him and accept all that he has revealed. "Faith is the realization of what is hoped for and evidence of things not seen." (Hebrews 11:1) Through the trusting relationship of faith, the patriarchs and their families learned what it meant to be a part of God's family. They lived their lives trying to follow God's commands and going where God led them.

These ancestors in faith are a good example of reliance on God during our own journey through life. Because of the gift of faith we, too, are able to believe all that God has revealed to us and to respond positively to it. Faith helps us to freely say yes to God with all our heart and strength. By our yes we follow God's will for us. Through the gift of faith we begin to see our lives and the world around us as God sees them. We start to live the way God wants us to live.

WE RESPOND

One day you will be an ancestor of your family. How would you like to be remembered by future generations of your family?

How will the way you express your faith be a part of your family's memory of you?

God chose Abraham to be the father of his people.

WE GATHER

✝ *Lord, help us to know and do your will.*

🧍 In small groups make a list of people who faced a challenge and never gave up. Their stories might be found in movies, television shows, in the news, on the Internet, or in your neighborhood.

WE BELIEVE

The Book of Genesis describes how God decided to form a people for himself.

📖 Genesis 12:1–7

God looked about him and called Abram. God said, "Go forth from the land of your kinsfolk and from your father's house to a land that I will show you" (Genesis 12:1). This land was the land of Canaan, which God promised to give to Abram and his descendants forever.

As soon as Abram heard God's call, he and his wife, Sarai, gathered their family and property. They started out from the town of Haran in northern Mesopotamia on the long journey to Canaan. This journey symbolized the journey of faith that we make throughout our lives.

In Abram God chose a very unlikely person to begin his people. Abram was seventy-five years old; he was neither famous nor powerful; and, his wife, Sarai, could not have children. Yet when God spoke to him, Abram responded to God. He did not argue with God. Abram had great faith, and trusted completely in God's will. In fact, Abram is our most important Old Testament model of faith.

When Abram and Sarai arrived in Canaan, God tested their faith repeatedly. They went through many difficult situations, and they tried to make the decisions that God wanted them to make. By telling us about these tests, the biblical writer shows us that Abram and Sarai, though chosen by God, struggled like all humans to keep their faith in God.

This testing by God strengthened and purified their faith, and God decided to make a covenant with Abram. God said, "I am God the Almighty. Walk in my presence and be blameless. Between you and me I will establish my covenant, and I will multiply you exceedingly" (Genesis 17:1–2). By the terms of this agreement Abram and his descendants will serve God and follow his ways. In return, God will give Abram a son and make "a great nation" of him (Genesis 12:2). To indicate that they were beginning a new life as a new people, God changed Abram's name to Abraham and Sarai's name to Sarah.

Sometime later, God came to Abraham through three mysterious visitors who appeared at Abraham's tent. One of the visitors predicted that Abraham and Sarah would have a son. When Sarah laughed in disbelief, he asked, "Is anything too marvelous for the LORD to do?" (Genesis 18:14).

As predicted, Isaac, Abraham and Sarah's long-awaited son, was finally born. When Isaac was a young boy, Abraham was again tested by God.

📖 Genesis 22:2–18

God said to Abraham, "Take your son Isaac, your only one, whom you love, and go to the land of Moriah. There you shall offer him up as a holocaust on a height that I will point out to you" (Genesis 22:2).

This was a test of Abraham's faith in God. Abraham did what God asked. Early the next morning he took Isaac some way off, built an altar, and put the boy on it. He was about to sacrifice Isaac to God when a messenger from God called to him, "Do not do the least thing to him. I know now how devoted you are to God, since you did not withhold from me your own beloved son" (Genesis 22:12). Abraham showed his great faith in God, and God blessed him.

This example from Abraham's life shows us that God calls each of us to trust completely in him. We see in these Old Testament stories that God loved his people and wanted them to turn to him.

The Church sees a New Testament parallel in this story: God the Father offered his only Son, Jesus Christ, to save us.

The word *angel* comes from the Greek word meaning "messenger." Angels were created by God as pure spirits with no physical bodies. All through the Bible, we find angels carrying God's messages to his people. We honor the angels today, and we benefit from their powerful help. At every Sunday and feast day Eucharist, we sing the Gloria, the song of the angels at the birth of Christ. In the funeral liturgy, we pray for our loved one, "May the angels lead you into paradise." Each one of us has been given a guardian angel to watch over us. Saint Basil wrote, "Beside each believer stands an angel as protector and shepherd leading him to life."

This week remember to ask your guardian angel for the help that you need in your life.

WE RESPOND

Think about the story of Abraham. How did the different parts of the story make you feel?

Do you think that you could listen to God if he told you to do something very difficult? Why or why not?

God our Father, we place our trust in you.

Detail of *The Story of Jacob and Esau*, by Lorenzo Ghiberti (1378–1455) Baptistery of the Duomo, Florence, Italy

God's people became known as the Israelites.

WE GATHER

✝ *Father in Heaven, bless what is good in us.*

Name the people in your family who are remembered as patriarchs or matriarchs. What do you know about them?

WE BELIEVE

When Abraham died, his son, Isaac, inherited his father's position as patriarch of the family. Isaac married a woman named Rebekah, with whom he had twin sons: Esau, the elder, and Jacob, the younger. The birth of twin sons caused a problem. Which son would someday have Isaac's position in the family? It could not be divided. Only one of the twins could inherit it.

Esau was the first born. It seemed that he should by right inherit Isaac's role. But the matter was not that simple. Before the twins were born, God made it very clear that Jacob was to inherit Isaac's position. God had said to their mother, Rebekah,

"Two nations are in your womb,
    two peoples are quarreling while still
        within you;
But one shall surpass the other,
    and the older shall serve the younger"
(Genesis 25:23).

However, to inherit Isaac's position Jacob must overturn the man-made rules of inheritance. Thus, from the very beginning, the story of Jacob is a story of conflict.

If the choice of Abraham as patriarch was surprising, the choice of Jacob as his successor was even more surprising. Jacob grew up to be something of a trickster. We get our first hint of this side of Jacob's character in Genesis 25:27–34 when he tricked Esau into selling him his birthright for a bowl of lentil stew. A birthright is the natural right to inherit the father's property.

But this was not the end of Jacob's tricks. We read in Genesis 27:1–46 that with his mother's help Jacob pretended to be Esau and tricked his elderly and blind father into giving him the blessing that Esau had the right to. When his father Isaac discovered what had happened, he was outraged. And Esau vowed to get revenge. He wanted to kill his brother, Jacob. So Rebekah told Jacob to flee to the land of Haran.

Yet from all that we read about him, it is clear that Jacob possessed the one quality that was crucial to living out the covenant. This quality was determination, or perseverance. Jacob never gave up.

On his way to Haran Jacob had a dream in which he saw a great staircase reaching to Heaven. In the dream God told Jacob what he told Abraham before him, "I, the LORD, am the God of your forefather Abraham and the God of Isaac; the land on which you are lying I will give to you and your descendants. These shall be as plentiful as the dust of the earth, and through them you shall spread out east and west, north and south. In you and your descendants all the nations of the earth shall find blessing. Know that I am with you; I will protect you wherever you go, and bring you back to this land. I will never leave you until I have done what I promised you" (Genesis 28:13–15).

With these words, God assured Jacob that he would inherit Canaan and that God would always protect him.

Though life in Haran was marked by constant conflict, Jacob prospered. He married, had many children, and grew very rich. This was the biblical writer's way of telling us that God's people were blessed and that they would continue to grow in number. After twenty years Jacob decided to return to Canaan, where he was finally reconciled to his brother and father.

In Genesis 35:9–15 we can read that God renewed the covenant with Jacob. He also changed Jacob's name to Israel. This was the symbolic way to show that God's people had grown to the point that they could actually be distinguished by name. God's people were now called the people of Israel, or the Israelites.

WE RESPOND

Imagine you are an advice columnist. Answer this letter.

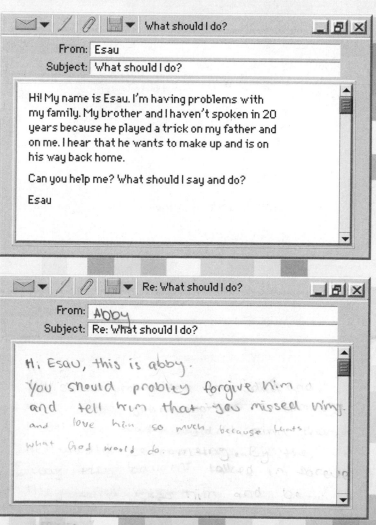

From: Esau
Subject: What should I do?

Hi! My name is Esau. I'm having problems with my family. My brother and I haven't spoken in 20 years because he played a trick on my father and on me. I hear that he wants to make up and is on his way back home.

Can you help me? What should I say and do?

Esau

From: Abby
Subject: Re: What should I do?

Hi Esau, this is abby.
You should probley forgive him and tell him that you missed him. and love him so much because thats what God would do. maing By

73

God cared for the Israelites.

WE GATHER

✝ *God, help me to discover your will for me.*

🏃 With small groups write a skit in which something negative is turned around into a positive outcome. Then act out your skit for the whole class. Ask the class to identify the negative that turned into a positive outcome.

WE BELIEVE

The last of the Old Testament patriarchs is Joseph. His story is told in Genesis 37:1—50:26. Joseph's story is about the way that God's will is achieved. In Joseph's case, God's plan was to provide a temporary home for his people.

Providence is God's plan for and protection of all creation. Through providence God leads his creation toward the perfection for which it was made. In the story of Joseph, providence was symbolized by the fulfillment of dreams. Joseph's only contact with God was through dreams, and these dreams indicated God's plan.

📖 Genesis 37:3–28; 39:1–23; 40:1—46:30

When we first meet Joseph, he and his brothers are on less than friendly terms. Joseph is the son of Rachel and Jacob, and is the favorite of Jacob's twelve sons. Jacob had given Joseph a special long robe such as a king might wear. The other brothers hated Joseph because their father, Jacob, loved him so much.

Joseph also had strange dreams. These dreams predicted that some day Joseph would have authority over his family. These dreams did not make Joseph's brothers very happy. So one day they grabbed him and took his robe. They sold Joseph as a slave to a passing caravan of merchants. The merchants sold Joseph to the chief steward of the **pharaoh**, the king of Egypt.

Twelve Sons of Jacob

1. Reuben
2. Simeon
3. Levi
4. Judah
5. Dan
6. Naphtali
7. Gad
8. Asher
9. Issachar
10. Zebulun
11. Joseph
12. Benjamin

Key Words

providence God's plan for and protection of all creation

pharaoh the king of Egypt

At first Joseph did well in the steward's service, but eventually he was thrown into prison on false charges. In prison Joseph discovered his ability to interpret dreams. This skill brought him to the attention of the pharaoh himself, who had been disturbed by strange dreams. Joseph told the pharaoh that his dreams meant that a period of great abundance would be followed by a time of terrible famine. The pharaoh was delighted by Joseph's explanation of his dreams, and put Joseph in charge of the management of his kingdom. Joseph prepared Egypt for the famine.

When the famine arrived, Jacob and his family in Canaan suffered greatly from hunger. Hearing that there was food in Egypt, Joseph's brothers traveled there to buy grain. This brought them face-to-face with Joseph. They did not recognize Joseph at first and bowed down to him when he entered the room. So Joseph's dreams had come true. Joseph now had authority over his family.

Joseph was eventually reconciled to his brothers. He invited his whole family to move to Egypt. His father, Jacob, accepted the invitation, and, as the story continues, Jacob made the long journey to Egypt. God's purpose had been fulfilled. God's people found a temporary home in Egypt.

WE RESPOND

Think of times when God acted in your life in an unexpected way. Talk with a partner about one of these times.

Thank God for his care and providence.

Show What *you* Know

Unscramble the letters of the **Key Words**. Then put the numbered letters in the boxes to find out who Abraham is.

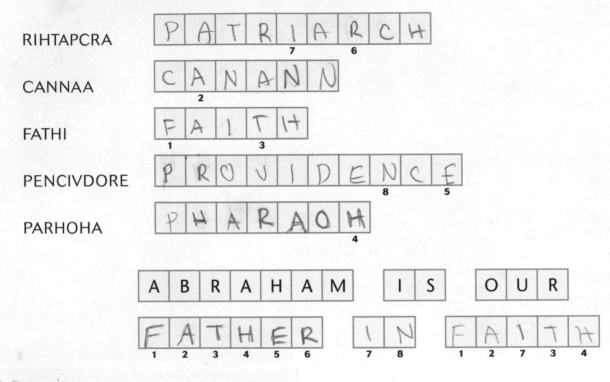

RIHTAPCRA

| P | A | T | R | I | A | R | C | H |

RIHTAPCRA — P A T R I A R C H (7 under R, 6 under C)

CANNAA — C A N A N N (2 under A)

FATHI — F A I T H (1 under F, 3 under T)

PENCIVDORE — P R O V I D E N C E (8 under D, 5 under C)

PARHOHA — P H A R A O H (4 under O)

| A | B | R | A | H | A | M | | I | S | | O | U | R |

| F | A | T | H | E | R | | I | N | | F | A | I | T | H |
| 1 | 2 | 3 | 4 | 5 | 6 | | 7 | 8 | | 1 | 2 | 7 | 3 | 4 |

 ## Pray Today

Blessings are a large part of our daily prayer. This is a custom we received from and share with the Jewish People. There are blessings for meals, families, children, homes, animals, workplaces, times of joy, and times of sorrow, and so on. Share this blessing and pray it with your family:

May the Lord bless and keep you.
May the Lord's face shine upon you,
And be gracious to you.
May the Lord look upon you,
And give you peace.

(add your own family verse)

May the lord bless us all

Amen.

DISCIPLE

Abby

Pray
Learn
Celebrate
Share
Choose
Live

Fast Facts

Joseph and the Amazing Technicolor Dreamcoat is a musical written by the team of Andrew Lloyd Webber and Tim Rice. Loosely based on the story of Joseph in the Bible, this musical was first presented on Broadway in 1982. Its family-friendly storyline, universal themes, and catchy music have made it a continued success. In addition, more than 20,000 schools and amateur theatre groups have successfully put on productions of this musical.

Reality Check

What are some situations in which people can show their trust in God?

- If they have a sick parents.

- If they can't have kids

Now, pass it on!

What Would *you* do?

What advice would you give to a friend that has a "difficult" relationship with a sibling?

I would tell them to talk to them. Your sibling can't be mad at you for forever

Take Home

This week, encourage your family members to go where God leads them. Ask God to lead you and your family to the people and places where your love and care are needed.

77

CHAPTER TEST

Write the letter that best defines each term.

1. __b__ faith

    a. an area in western Palestine that included most of present-day Israel

2. __e__ providence

    b. a gift from God that enables us to believe in him and accept all that he has revealed

    c. the natural right to inherit the father's property

3. __d__ patriarch

    d. a father, or founder, of a clan, a group of related families

4. __a__ Canaan

    e. God's plan for and protection of all creation

Short Answers

5. Who are the patriarchs of the Old Testament?

They were Isaac, Aberman, Josph, Jacob.

6. How is providence symbolized in the story of Joseph?

By the fillfullment of dreams.

7. What quality did Jacob have that enabled him to live out the covenant?

Perseverece and deternation.

8. How was Abraham's faith tested?

To see if he would sacfrice his son for God.

Write a paragraph to answer this question.

9–10. What does the story of each patriarch show about our relationship with God?

They trust God with all there heart. If something dosen't go there way the still trust and follow God. They preach the word of him. they have a strong bond and will do almost anything for him.

"Rejoice in the Lord always.
I shall say it again: rejoice!"

Philippians 4:4

SEASONAL

CHAPTER 6

This chapter presents an overview of the
Liturgical Year.

79

Throughout the liturgical year we celebrate the entire mystery of Christ.

WE GATHER

✝ *Lord, you create all things to give you glory.*

What are some days of the year that are very important to you? Why? How do you show others that these days and times are special to you?

WE BELIEVE

As the Church we have special days and times of the year that are very important to us. One special way we remember these times is in the celebration of the liturgy. The liturgy is the official public prayer of the Church. It includes the celebration of the Eucharist, or Mass, and the other sacraments. The liturgy also includes the Liturgy of the Hours, a prayer, parts of which the Church prays at various times during the day and night.

In the liturgy throughout the year, we remember and rejoice in the saving actions of Jesus Christ. So we call the Church year the *liturgical year*. During the liturgical year we recall and celebrate the whole mystery of Christ. We celebrate the birth of the Son of God, his younger years, his public ministry, his suffering, Death, Resurrection, and Ascension into Heaven. During this year we also venerate, or show devotion to, Mary, the Mother of God, and all the saints.

Advent   The season of Advent begins the liturgical year in late November or early December. Advent is a time of joyful preparation for the coming of Christ. We look forward to Christ's second coming at the end of time. We celebrate that Christ comes into our lives every day. We await Christmas, the celebration of the first coming of the Son of God.

Christmas   The Christmas season begins on Christmas Day with the celebration of the birth of the Son of God. During this entire season we celebrate that God is with us always.

Lent   The season of Lent begins on Ash Wednesday. Lent is the special time when we remember that Jesus suffered, died, and rose to new life to restore our relationship with God. During Lent we work to grow closer to Jesus and one another through prayer, fasting, and penance. We pray for and support all who are preparing for the Sacraments of Christian Initiation. We prepare for the Easter Triduum.

Triduum   The Easter Triduum is the Church's greatest and most important celebration. The word *triduum* means "three days." During these three days, from Holy Thursday evening until Easter Sunday evening, we remember and celebrate Jesus' suffering, Death, and Resurrection in a very special way.

Easter   The season of Easter begins on Easter Sunday evening and continues until Pentecost Sunday. During this season we rejoice in Jesus' Resurrection and in the new life we have in Jesus Christ.

Ordinary Time   The season of Ordinary Time is celebrated in two parts: the first part is between Christmas and Lent, and the second part is between Easter and Advent. During this time we celebrate the life and teachings of Jesus Christ and learn what it means to live as his disciples. On the last Sunday of Ordinary Time, also the last Sunday of the liturgical year, we celebrate the Feast of Christ the King.

The calendar Our calendar of years, months, and days depends upon elements of nature, like the sun and the moon. Many of our liturgical feasts also reflect the cycle of nature.

Our liturgical year is constructed around the dates of the Easter Triduum, which depend each year on the spring equinox and the rising of the full moon. The spring equinox is the day the sun crosses the equator, making day and night of equal length everywhere. Easter Sunday follows the full moon after the spring equinox. This fact alone is a beautiful proclamation of the Resurrection of Christ, whose rising brings light to our darkness.

Astronomers can calculate the date of the spring equinox. They use formulas to do this for years into the future. Looking at their calculations we find that the date of Easter Sunday is always between March 22 and April 25.

Using the date for Easter Sunday, we can construct the liturgical calendar for each year. We can work backward six weeks to determine the beginning of Lent, and forward seven weeks to find the date of Pentecost.

WE RESPOND

The readings we hear, the songs we sing, the colors we see, and the ways we worship help us to celebrate each liturgical season.

 In groups describe some of the ways your parish celebrates each of these seasons of the liturgical year.

Advent

candles, pink & purple,

Christmas

manger, Joy to the world, night mass

Lent

purple, strip the celture

Triduum

Suffn Rised of - Jesus, white also
death

Easter

lambs, white

Ordinary Time

green,

✝ We Respond in Prayer

Leader: Give praise to God, who is rich in mercy and who has favored us in wonderful ways. Blessed be God for ever.

All: Blessed be God for ever.

Leader: Saint Paul urges us to give thanks to God always through Christ, for in him, God has given us everything.

Reader: A reading from the Letter of Saint Paul to the Philippians

"Rejoice in the Lord always. I shall say it again: rejoice! Your kindness should be known to all. The Lord is near. Have no anxiety at all, but in everything, by prayer and petition, with thanksgiving, make your requests known to God."
(Philippians 4:4–6)

The Word of the Lord.

All: Thanks be to God.

Leader: Let us thank God for our blessings and offer our needs to him.

All: Hear us, O Lord.

🎵 Rejoice in the Lord Always

Round 1

Rejoice in the Lord always,
again I say, rejoice!
Rejoice in the Lord always,
again I say, rejoice!

Round 2

Rejoice! Rejoice! Again I say, rejoice!
Rejoice! Rejoice! Again I say, rejoice!

Pray
Learn
Celebrate
Share
Choose
Live

PROJECT DISCIPLE

Celebrate! Design a Web page that explains the liturgical year.

What's the Word?

"There is an appointed time for everything, ...
A time to be born, and a time to die;
*   a time to plant, and a time to uproot the plant."*
(Ecclesiastes 3:1–2)

How does the Church use "appointed times" to recall and celebrate the whole mystery of Christ?

_____

_____

Pray Today

Dear God, Help me to make the most of the seasons of the Church year. In this liturgical year I will recall and celebrate the mystery of Christ. Amen.

Take Home

Plan a family project: make a liturgical calendar for the upcoming liturgical year. Include labels for holy days, liturgical colors and seasons, feasts, and family dates on the calendar. Be creative! Display the completed calendar in a prominent place.

"This is the day the LORD has made;
let us rejoice in it and be glad."

Psalm 118:24

This chapter helps us to understand
the season of Ordinary Time.

85

During the season of Ordinary Time, we celebrate the life and teachings of Jesus Christ.

WE GATHER

✝ *Jesus, help us to keep Sunday holy.*

What is your attitude toward Sunday?
Do you look forward to it? Why or why not?
How is it the same as other days of the week?
How is it different?

WE BELIEVE

Ordinary Time is a season of life and hope. We learn what it means to live as Christ's disciples, and we grow as members of the Church. The color green, which we use during this season, reminds us of the life and hope that come from Christ.

Other seasons during the liturgical year focus on a particular event or period in Jesus' life. During the season of Ordinary Time, we celebrate all that Christ does for us through his birth, life, Death, Resurrection, and Ascension. We recall the life of Jesus Christ and focus on his teachings in a special way.

The season of Ordinary Time lasts thirty three to thirty four weeks. It is called Ordinary Time because the weeks are "ordered," or named in number order. For example, the first week in Ordinary Time is followed by the second week in Ordinary Time, and so on.

We celebrate Ordinary Time twice during the liturgical year. We celebrate first for a short time between the seasons of Christmas and Lent. The first part of Ordinary Time begins in early January and lasts until the Tuesday before Ash Wednesday. The second part of Ordinary Time is between the seasons of Easter and Advent. So it begins in late May or June after Pentecost Sunday, which ends the Easter season, and lasts several months until the evening before the first Sunday of Advent in late November or early December.

The Lord's Day   In the Jewish calendar, Saturday was and still is the Sabbath, the day of rest set apart to honor God in a special way. The Sabbath is a special day to praise God for giving us his creation and for acting in the lives of his people. Saturday is the last day of the week, and the Jewish People rest as God rested on the seventh day after completing his creation. It is Jewish tradition to observe that Sabbath from sundown on Friday to sundown on Saturday.

The early Christians followed many of the Jewish customs of prayer and worship. They prayed the psalms and they kept the Sabbath. Gradually, because Jesus Christ rose on a Sunday, Sunday became the Christian Sabbath. Because Christ rose on a Sunday, the Christians called it "the Lord's Day." On this day they gathered to recall Christ's Death and Resurrection by celebrating the Eucharist.

Today the Church keeps Sunday as our first holy day. We keep the Lord's Day holy by participating in the celebration of the Eucharist, by resting from work and enjoying our families, by remembering our relationship with God and by serving the needs of the community.

Sunday is the most important day to gather with our parishes for the celebration of the Eucharist, the Mass. In the Mass, we

- praise and thank God for his many gifts

- listen to God's Word

- remember Jesus' life, Death, and Resurrection and celebrate Jesus' gift of himself in the Eucharist

- receive the Body and Blood of Christ in Holy Communion

- are joined more closely to Christ and one another in the Church

- are sent out to share Jesus' love, serve others, and work for justice and peace.

In observing the Lord's Day we follow the Jewish custom of celebrating from sundown to sundown. So we begin our celebration on Saturday evening and complete it on Sunday evening. This is why some people participate in the Sunday Mass on Saturday evening.

Receiving the Eucharist

A Procession On the Feast of the Body and Blood of Christ, we celebrate the presence of Jesus Christ with us in the Eucharist in a special way. Many parishes have a procession in honor of Christ's presence in the Eucharist, the Blessed Sacrament. The priest carries the Blessed Sacrament in a special holder called a monstrance. People carry banners and flowers and worship together as they process, or walk, through the city streets or around the area of the parish. In some places flowers are strewn on the streets as the community processes with the Blessed Sacrament. In the church a carpet made of flowers is sometimes laid in the center aisle as a sign of respect and reverence to Jesus in the Blessed Sacrament.

Sundays during Ordinary Time Sundays are the foundation of our liturgical year, and we use them to mark the passing of the weeks of Ordinary Time and the other seasons. Sunday's importance comes from the fact that Jesus' Resurrection was on a Sunday.

During Ordinary Time there are three very important Sundays.

- Trinity Sunday, the first Sunday after Pentecost, is the first Sunday in the second part of Ordinary Time. On this Sunday we celebrate in a special way our belief in the Blessed Trinity: God the Father, God the Son, and God the Holy Spirit.

- The Body and Blood of Christ is the Sunday after Trinity Sunday. This is sometimes called "Corpus Christi Sunday" because the term *Body of Christ* comes from these two Latin words.

- Christ the King is the last Sunday in Ordinary Time. On this day we rejoice that Christ is the King of the universe. He saves us from evil and brings us new life. Through him the Kingdom of God has begun on earth.

WE RESPOND

In groups list some ways that you celebrate the Lord's Day.

- I go to church with my family
- We go eat breakfast
- We do something togher

Have the rest of the class guess what you listed by acting out some of the ways.

✟ We Respond in Prayer

Leader: Lord our God, we bless you. As we come together we ask you in your kindness to fill us with the knowledge of your will so that, pleasing you in all things, we may grow in every good work.

We ask this through Christ our Lord.

All: Amen.

Reader: A reading from the holy Gospel according to Matthew

All: Glory to you, O Lord.

Reader: "You are the light of the world. A city set on a mountain cannot be hidden. Nor do they light a lamp and then put it under a bushel basket; it is set on a lampstand, where it gives light to all in the house. Just so, your light must shine before others, that they may see your good deeds and glorify your heavenly Father." (Matthew 5:14–16)

The Gospel of the Lord.

All: Praise to you, Lord Jesus Christ.

🎵 This Little Light of Mine

This little light of mine,
I'm gonna let it shine. (Repeat 3 times)
Let it shine, let it shine, let it shine.

Ev'rywhere I go,
I'm gonna let it shine. (Repeat 3 times)
Let it shine, let it shine, let it shine.

Jesus gave it to me;
I'm gonna let it shine. (Repeat 3 times)
Let it shine, let it shine, let it shine.

PROJECT DISCIPLE

Pray
Learn
Celebrate
Share
Choose
Live

Picture This

The Chi-Rho symbol is usually associated with the liturgical season of Ordinary Time. It is formed by Greek letters χ(Chi) and ρ(Rho). These are the first two letters in the Greek word *Christ*. Draw the Chi-Rho symbol in the space below. (For reference see the bottom of page 85.)

Chi-Rho

Might be on exam

Celebrate!

Write a "top ten" list about Ordinary Time. 1. will be the most *extraordinary*!

10. green

9. prossion

8. Lifeteen masses

7. 33-34 week

6. Adoration

5. season of life & hope

4. mass

3. Trinity Sunday

2. Body & Blood of Chirst

1. Christ the king

Fast Facts

During Ordinary Time the Church proclaims the Gospels in a three-year Sunday cycle. Each cycle highlights one of these Gospels—(Year A) Matthew, (Year B) Mark, and (Year C) Luke.

Take Home

The Church celebrates Sunday, the Lord's Day, as a holy day. As a family, we can keep the Lord's Day holy by

going to CHURCH

_____

_____

Robox is lico

Grade 6 Unit 1

Abby

20/20

UNIT TEST

Write True or False for the following sentences.
Then change the false sentences to make them true.

1. _True_ Tradition is the Revelation of the Good News of Jesus Christ as lived out in the Church, past and present.

2. _Flase_ An agreement between God and his people is called ~~grace~~.

   covante

3. _True_ The special guidance that the Holy Spirit gave to the human writers of the Bible is called Divine Inspiration.

4. _Flase_ Every human being has an invisible spiritual reality that will never die. This breath of life from God refers to the ~~body~~.

   soul

5. _True_ In the story of Joseph, God's plan for and protection of all creation, which we call providence, is symbolized by the fulfillment of dreams.

6. _False_ The prophet ~~Isaac~~ described a person as the Suffering Servant who would come to free us from sin.

   Isaiah

7. _Flase_ The flood is the sign God gave to Noah to symbolize ~~the covenant between God and all mortal creatures on earth~~.

   the rainbow

8. _True_ The four patriarchs of the Old Testament are Abraham, Isaac, Jacob, and Joseph.

Fill in the circle beside the correct answer.

9. God's making himself known to us is called _____.

   ○ personal sin   ● Divine Revelation   ○ free will

continued on next page   91

10. Evil entered the world through a human act that we call _____.

◉ Original Sin   ⭕ Genesis   ⭕ suffering

11. The first book of the Bible is called *Genesis,* a word meaning _____.

⭕ "Scripture"   ◉ "beginning"   ⭕ "covenant"

12. A _____ is a person who has both the authority over what he or she cares for and the responsibility for seeing that it lives and grows.

⭕ patriarch   ⭕ prophet   ◉ steward

13. Among the _____, or characteristics, of God are that he is eternal, all-knowing, and ever-present.

◉ attributes   ⭕ symbols   ⭕ genealogies

14. To fully restore the friendship with God that was broken by the first humans' disobedience, God promised to send a _____.

⭕ prophet   ◉ Savior   ⭕ covenant

15. God renewed his covenant with Jacob, and changed that patriarch's name to _____.

◉ Israel   ⭕ Isaac   ⭕ Abram

16. In the Old Testament story of _____, the Church sees a parallel to God the Father's offering his only Son, Jesus Christ, to save us.

⭕ Esau and Jacob   ⭕ Cain and Abel   ◉ Abraham and Isaac

Write a paragraph to answer each question.

17–18. Among all the creatures made by God to dwell on earth, humans alone are created with free will. What does this mean and why is it important?

Free will is the abity to know the diffrence between Good and evil, right and wrong. We make our own choices, good or bad. God loves us and wants us to live like him

19–20. The patriarchs of the Old Testament are our ancestors in faith. They freely said yes to God with all their hearts. How can we follow their example?

God gift of faith helps us to freely say yes to God. By our yes we follow Gods will. through the gift of faith our eyes open and we are able to see our livies and the world as God see it.

Building the Covenant Nation

Seasonal Chapters

DEAR FAMILY

In Unit 2 your child will grow as a disciple of Jesus by:

- learning about the enslavement of the Israelites, and God's choice of Moses to lead the people to freedom

- understanding God's guidance of his people as he gave them his law and led them toward the promised land

- appreciating God's people who settled in Canaan, and the stories of Samson and Ruth

- recognizing God's faithfulness to his people, and his guidance of their leaders, Samuel and David

- praying for wisdom as Solomon did, and praying with the psalms.

More to Explore

Visuals can assist with learning. There are DVDs and books that capture some of the biblical events that are in this unit. There are also Internet sites where you can find images of the pyramids or works of art depicting Moses, David, and Goliath. Look for one of these resources to enhance your family's experience of this unit.

Show That You Care

God led his people from slavery to freedom. As people of faith we are to help people who are oppressed or treated unjustly. Talk with your child about the minor, but still painful, "oppressions" that can happen every day, in school or the community. Are there new students who are ignored? Are younger children teased by older students? Do you see children or teachers or crossing guards who are rejected and made fun of? What might your family do to help?

Reality Check

"The importance of the family for the life and well-being of society entails a particular responsibility for society to support and strengthen marriage and the family."
(*Catechism of the Catholic Church*, 2210)

Picture This

Turn to the timeline on pages 96–97 in your child's text. What names and events do you recognize? Ask each family member to share what he or she knows about one of the events or people on the timeline. Have each member identify one person or event to learn more about. Give your 6th grader the responsibility of finding out and sharing what the family wants to know.

Celebrate!

This unit highlights some of the leaders God chose for his people: Moses, Joshua, Deborah, Samson, Samuel, Saul, David, Solomon. Who are the people that lead you as Catholics today? How does their leadership help your family to be better disciples? Pray for those leaders; send a card or an e-mail to thank them and encourage them.

Take Home

Be ready for this unit's Take Home:

Chapter 8: Working to protect human rights

Chapter 9: Praying a psalm together

Chapter 10: Serving the Lord

Chapter 11: Writing a prayer of blessing

Chapter 12: Appreciating God's gift of wisdom

An Enslaved People

✝ We Gather in Prayer

Leader: For followers of Christ, freedom is a gift of love and goodness, and comes from Christ. Let us pray for all those who are not free, who are enslaved, in our world today.

Reader 1: "For freedom Christ set us free; so stand firm and do not submit again to the yoke of slavery." (Galatians 5:1)

Reader 2: For all who are enslaved by the habit of sin and selfishness, let us pray:

All: Lord Jesus Christ, set them free.
(Response to all petitions.)

Reader 3: For all who are enslaved by unsafe working conditions and low pay, let us pray:

Reader 4: For all who are enslaved by addiction, let us pray:

Reader 5: For all who are enslaved by disease and chronic illness, let us pray:

Reader 6: For all who are enslaved by poverty and hunger, let us pray:

Reader 7: For all who are unjustly denied their freedom, let us pray:

♫ Go Down, Moses

When Israel was in Egypt's land,
Let my people go;
Oppressed so hard they could not stand,
Let my people go.

Refrain:
Go down, Moses,
Way down in Egypt's land;
Tell old Pharaoh: Let my people go.

Oh, let us all from bondage flee,
Let my people go;
And let us all in Christ be free,
Let my people go. (Refrain)

Israelites grow and prosper in Egypt

Moses is born and raised by pharaoh's daughter

God reveals himself to Moses

Oppression of the Israelites increases

The first Passover: God leads the Israelites out of Egypt

God speaks with Moses on Mt. Sinai/ Israel is a holy nation

Israelites journey for many years

Pharaoh begins oppression of Israelites

Moses flees Egypt

Moses returns to Egypt to lead the Israelites

Egypt suffers many plagues

Miriam leads rejoicing

Moses dies

God gives Moses the Ten Commandments

Timeline for Chapters 8–12

Egypt became the home of the Israelites.

WE GATHER

✝ *Loving God, protect us.*

What does someone have to do to feel at home in a new town? What difficulties might he or she face? What are some ways we can help people to feel at home?

WE BELIEVE

God led the family of Jacob, or as God had named him, Israel, into Egypt. All twelve of Israel's sons, including Joseph, were reunited. In Egypt they were saved from famine and protected from hardships that they may not have been able to survive. God had provided for his people through Joseph.

Joseph informed the pharaoh, "My father and my brothers have come from the land of Canaan, with their flocks and herds and everything else they own; and they are now in the region of Goshen" (Genesis 47:1). The pharaoh told Joseph that his family could settle there. He said, "the land of Egypt is at your disposal" (Genesis 47:6).

So Jacob's family became honored guests in Egypt. They were given the best land in Goshen, a fertile area in northern Egypt. At the time Egypt was divided into two kingdoms. The southern part of the country was ruled by Egyptian kings. A separate kingdom in northern Egypt was ruled by people who came from regions to the east of Egypt.

Change in Egypt In Goshen, in northern Egypt, Jacob's family prospered and God's people grew in number. At first they lived there in safety and comfort. But in time the Egyptians gained control of the northern kingdom. Two Egyptian kings, who were also brothers, united Egypt. They drove away many rulers and people from foreign countries and kept other people as slaves. Egypt entered a period of tremendous wealth and power. This period is usually called the New Kingdom. It lasted for hundreds of years.

As time passed, Joseph and his generation died. The pharaoh who welcomed the family of Jacob also died, and a new pharaoh came into power. He did not know of Joseph and did not look upon the Israelites as honored guests. In fact, he feared them, saying, "Look how numerous and powerful the Israelite people are growing, more so than we ourselves! Come, let us deal shrewdly with them to stop their increase; otherwise, in time of war they too may join our enemies to fight against us, and so leave our country" (Exodus 1:9–10).

In the Book of Exodus, the second book of the Bible, we find out that eventually the Egyptians made the Israelites their slaves.

96

SETTLING THE LAND

1220 BC   THE JUDGES

THE UNITED KINGDOM

1020 BC   1000 BC   961 BC

Israelites enter and settle Canaan

Deborah the Judge

Samson

Samuel becomes God's prophet and guides Israel

The story of Ruth

God tells Samuel to anoint Saul King of Israel

Saul turns away from God

God chooses David

David defeats Goliath

David becomes King of Israel

Israel becomes a strong kingdom

David dies; Solomon becomes king

Israel achieves peace and prosperity

Temple built in Jerusalem

Solomon turns from God

The pharaoh forced them to build monuments and buildings. He also made some Israelites work long hours in the fields. They were no longer free to worship the one true God and to follow his laws. And their lives became so unbearable that they cried out to God to be rescued from Egypt.

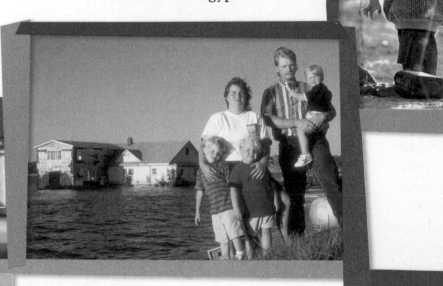

As Catholics...

Throughout history slavery has not only required people to work against their will. It has devalued their human dignity and taken away their freedom. Fortunately most countries have changed their laws and policies to protect people from slavery and forced labor. However, the need to protect the rights of workers remains. The Church teaches us that the opportunity to be employed, to have safe working conditions, and to earn a fair wage are issues of justice.

The work of social justice is to protect the rights and dignity of each person and to make sure that all people have or are given what is due to them. The Church speaks out against any system, private organization, or government that focuses on making a profit at the expense of human dignity and freedom. Instead the Church encourages individuals and groups to bring the Good News of Jesus Christ into society and to work for change in policies and laws so that each person is respected.

What can you do to respect the dignity of workers?

WE RESPOND

Today there are people who need to be rescued from slavery, poverty, homelessness, and hunger.

List some other things from which people need to be rescued.

slavery, portey, hunger, homelessness

What can you do with your parish to help these people?

We can set up a food drive

We can open our homes to them

uptil they a provide for themlfs

97

God chose Moses to lead his people.

WE GATHER

✝ *O Lord, we praise your name.*

In what ways are you free to do and say things? Do people in all parts of the world have these same freedoms?

WE BELIEVE

In the Book of Exodus we find the story of what happened to Jacob's descendants in Egypt. We read of the terrible suffering of the Israelites as slaves of the pharaoh. We learn that out of that suffering God brought freedom and hope. More importantly, in the Book of Exodus we learn about God carrying out his plan to bring his people back to Canaan. The word *exodus* comes from the Greek word for "departure." **Exodus** is the biblical word describing the Israelites' departure from slavery to freedom.

The Israelites were also called Hebrews, since their language was known as Hebrew. The pharaoh noticed that despite all the difficulties in their lives, the number of Hebrews was still growing. He told some of the Hebrew women that all the newly born sons of the Israelites must be killed. But these women did not listen to the pharaoh. They followed God's laws instead. So the pharaoh gave a new command: "Throw into the river every boy that is born to the Hebrews" (Exodus 1:22). Now it was even more difficult for the Hebrew women to protect their baby boys.

In the second chapter of Exodus we read about one woman who saved her son. She made a basket out of reeds from the river. She coated it with tar to prevent it from sinking and then put her son in it. She placed the basket in the shallow water near one of the riverbanks. The pharaoh's daughter found the child and took him home with her. She named the child Moses and raised him as an Egyptian.

This is another biblical story that is filled with symbolism. The same Hebrew word is used for *basket* and *ark*. Moses was saved in the basket just as Noah's family was saved in the ark. As Christians we are saved in the Church through the waters of Baptism.

Life in Midian When Moses was an adult, he visited his fellow Hebrews. One day he saw a Hebrew slave being beaten by an Egyptian, and Moses killed the Egyptian. The pharaoh heard about what Moses had done and wanted him put to death. Moses had to run away to the desert region of Midian. Moses settled there and he married a woman named Zipporah, with whom he had children. There Moses lived the life of a shepherd.

One day while Moses was tending his flocks, God appeared to him in a burning bush. The fire was flaming from the bush but not destroying it. So Moses went over to look more closely. God called out to Moses from the bush and Moses answered, "Here I am" (Exodus 3:4).

Key Word

Exodus the biblical word describing the Israelites' departure from slavery to freedom

God told Moses that this place was holy. God also told Moses that he wanted him to return to Egypt and lead the Hebrews out of slavery. Moses asked God how he would be able to do this, and God told Moses that he would be with him.

Moses asked God what he should say when the Israelites asked him who sent him to them. "God replied, 'I am who am.' Then he added, 'This is what you shall tell the Israelites: I AM sent me to you'" (Exodus 3:14).

This name that God gave was the source of the word *Yahweh*. "I AM" was a name that described God as ever-present to his people. This name was so holy that out of reverence the Israelites did not even speak it. Instead they used the title *Adonai*, which means "my Lord."

In the third chapter of Exodus we read that God once again spoke to Moses. "Go and assemble the elders of the Israelites, and tell them: The LORD, the God of your fathers, the God of Abraham, Isaac and Jacob, has appeared to me and said: I am concerned about you and about the way you are being treated in Egypt; so I have decided to lead you up out of the misery of Egypt into the land of the Canaanites, . . . a land flowing with milk and honey." (Exodus 3:16–17) Moses did as God commanded.

WE RESPOND

Write and illustrate a prayer that expresses gratitude for the many ways God shows love and care for all people.

God thank you for loving me and never giving up on me.

amen

God helped his people.

✝ *Lord, help us to remember that without you we can do nothing.*

🏃 List some tasks that you and your classmates might be put in charge of completing. How would you convince others to help you to complete these tasks?

_____

_____

WE BELIEVE

After God appeared to Moses in the burning bush, Moses returned to Egypt. Moses' brother, Aaron, helped him to explain God's message to the Israelites. Gradually, Moses gained the support of the people.

Moses and Aaron met face-to-face with the pharaoh. They said, "Thus says the LORD, the God of Israel: Let my people go, that they may celebrate a feast to me in the desert" (Exodus 5:1). But the pharaoh refused their request. Worse still, the pharaoh did not give the Israelite slaves the materials they needed for their work.

Soon it became almost impossible for the Israelites to complete their required work. They began to blame Moses for this hardship.

Moses told God how the people were suffering, and God replied, "Now you shall see what I will do to Pharaoh. Forced by my mighty hand, he will send them away; compelled by my outstretched arm, he will drive them from his land" (Exodus 6:1). When Moses told the Israelites what God would do for them, they did not believe him. They were too weary.

God knew that it would be difficult to convince the pharaoh to let the Israelites leave Egypt. So God said to Moses, "I will lay my hand on Egypt and by great acts of judgment I will bring the hosts of my people, the Israelites, out of the land of Egypt, so that the Egyptians may learn that I am the LORD, as I stretch out my hand against Egypt and lead the Israelites out of their midst" (Exodus 7:4–5).

These "great acts of judgment" that God spoke of were the plagues. During biblical times, a major disaster or catastrophe was considered a plague. We read about the plagues in Chapters 7—11 of the Book of Exodus.

Egyptian clay figure (14th Century BC) highlights the terrible destruction of the plague of the frogs.

THE TEN PLAGUES

the river of blood . . . . Exodus 7:17

frogs . . . . Exodus 7:27–28

gnats . . . . Exodus 8:12

flies . . . . Exodus 8:16–17

disease . . . . Exodus 9:1–3

boils . . . . Exodus 9:8–9

hail . . . . Exodus 9:18–19

locusts . . . . Exodus 10:4–5

darkness . . . . Exodus 10:21

death of first born . . . . Exodus 11:4–5

The Plagues A conflict began when Moses and Aaron went to the pharaoh to demand freedom for the Israelites. Moses and Aaron showed the pharaoh a sign of God's power, but the pharaoh and the Egyptians disregarded this sign. A great struggle over the Israelites then began between God and the pharaoh. The ten plagues symbolize this struggle.

The story recounts that at first the pharaoh's magicians were able to duplicate each plague, and the pharaoh refused to recognize Moses' request for the Israelite's freedom. As time went by, however, the pharaoh's magicians could no longer reproduce the plagues. When the Israelites saw the effects of the plagues, they knew that God was protecting them. Their faith in God was strengthened.

The pharaoh considered letting the Israelites leave. He even began to negotiate with Moses and to agree to some of Moses' demands. Yet the pharaoh never completely gave in. Through Moses God continually called the Egyptians to listen to him. However, the pharaoh did not listen to God's warnings and refused to free the Israelites from slavery. Because of his actions the pharaoh was responsible for the suffering of the Egyptian people.

At the end of the ninth plague, the pharaoh seemed to give in to Moses' requests. But again the pharaoh changed his mind. He even refused to see Moses and Aaron. "Then the Lord told Moses, 'One more plague will I bring upon Pharaoh and upon Egypt. After that he will let you depart. In fact, he will not merely let you go; he will drive you away.'" (Exodus 11:1)

WE RESPOND

Imagine that you have been asked to design a banner advertisement for a Web site devoted to people throughout the world whose freedoms are being denied. Design a banner ad that will make people want to visit the Web site and assist in the work of freedom for all.

File Edit View Go Help

Let them have freedom!

Stop standing in silence! People are struggling!

Donte to help!

God guided his people to freedom.

WE GATHER

✝ *God, we are your people.*

What are some ways that these signs protect us:

- traffic signs

  stop crashes

- signs on appliances

  so we don't use them rlong

- signs in school

  follows rules

(Add some other signs) _stop light_
- _makes people step_

WE BELIEVE

When Moses left the pharaoh's presence after the ninth plague, God told him to have every Israelite family prepare for their escape from Egypt. They were to get a lamb and kill it. Then they were to mark the doorframes of their houses with blood from the lamb. This would be a sign that the people inside the house were Israelites, not Egyptians.

After marking the doorframes, the Israelites were to remain inside their houses. They were to cook the lambs and eat them with bitter herbs and unleavened bread. Unleavened bread is made without yeast. It does not need to rise and therefore takes less time to prepare. This unleavened bread symbolized the Israelites' rush to escape.

The Israelites obeyed God's instructions. At midnight God passed over all of Egypt, taking the lives of every firstborn Egyptian, including the son of the pharaoh. This plague even caused the death of all the firstborn animals belonging to the Egyptians. Only the Israelites and their animals were spared. This event was called the **Passover**, since God passed over, or spared, his people.

Every year Jews remember this special night. During the feast of Passover they celebrate a seder by eating the same meal that their ancestors ate on the first Passover. They follow God's command that all descendants of the Israelites observe the feast of Passover. By celebrating this feast, Jews today recall how God spared the lives of their ancestors and brought them out of slavery in Egypt.

Leaving Egypt Horrified by what had happened, the pharaoh summoned Moses and Aaron during the night. He told them to take the Israelites and their possessions out of Egypt immediately. Fearing that the pharaoh would again change his mind, Moses and the Israelites left quickly. The Exodus was finally underway.

Moses led the Israelites toward the Red Sea, the water that separated Egypt from the Arabian Peninsula. During their escape, "The LORD preceded them, in the daytime by means of a column of cloud to show them the way, and at night by means of a column of fire to give them light. Thus they could travel both day and night. Neither the column of cloud by day nor the column of fire by night ever left its place in front of the people" (Exodus 13:21–22).

As soon as the Israelites were gone, the pharaoh changed his mind and sent his army to recapture them. By this time, the Israelites were at the Red Sea, and God again caused a wonder that saved his people.

Exodus 14:10–28

The Egyptian army closed in on the Israelites. God parted the Red Sea, and the Israelites escaped over the dry path God had made through it. But when the Egyptians tried to follow, the waters closed over them, and they drowned.

In this way God brought his people from slavery into freedom. It was the great turning point in the history of God's relationship with his people. As the biblical writer showed us in the story of Noah, God used water to save the people. For the Israelites the salvation of the nation came about as they passed through the waters of the Red Sea. As Christians the waters of the Red Sea symbolize the saving waters of our own Baptism.

WE RESPOND

♫ **Be Not Afraid**

Refrain:
> Be not afraid.
> I go before you always.
> Come, follow me,
> and I will give you rest.

> If you pass through raging waters
>   in the sea,
>   you shall not drown.
> If you walk amid the burning flames,
>   you shall not be harmed.
> If you stand before the pow'r of hell
>   and death is at your side,
>   know that I am with you through it all.

(Refrain)

Passover the event in which God passed over the whole of Egypt, taking the lives of every firstborn Egyptian and sparing the Israelites

P R O J E C T

Pray
Learn
Celebrate
Share
Choose
Live

Show What *you* Know

The Passover and the Exodus were two events that occurred when Jacob's descendants were enslaved in Egypt. Complete the chart to describe the sequence of these events.

The Passover

- the Istrelgts had to sacrfic a lamb and mark doorsteps

- An agnle passed over sprains fle hoomes -with lamb blood.

- Phoph disciele to tet the Isriughts go.

The Exodus

- As soon as they were gone phorph wanted them back

- They were already at the Red Sea by then

- God parted the sea and the Isrights escaped but When the egilphion went throug it closed and they drowned,

What's *the* Word?

"Moses and Aaron went to Pharaoh and said, 'Thus says the LORD, the God of Israel: Let my people go, that they may celebrate a feast to me in the desert.' Pharaoh answered, 'Who is the Lord, that I should heed his plea to let Israel go? I do not know the Lord; even if I did, I would not let Israel go.'" (Exodus 5:1–2)

- Underline the phrase that describes why God wants "Israel" to be set free.
- Why does Pharaoh refuse to let "Israel" go?

  he dosen't know the Lord

Pray
Learn
Celebrate
Share
Choose
Live

Saint Stories

Pierre Toussaint, born in Haiti in 1778, was a slave. He came to New York with the Catholic couple who owned him. They taught him to read and write, which was unusual at the time. They allowed him to become a hairdresser. <u>Pierre encouraged his clients to pray, to trust in God, and to live according to the Gospel.</u> Pierre eventually purchased his freedom. He married a Haitian woman. Together they helped the poor and worked to free slaves. They founded one of the first orphanages and the first Catholic school for children of color. Pierre Toussaint died in 1853. In 1996 Saint John Paul II, as pope, recognized Pierre Toussaint as having lived an outstanding Christian life. The pope declared him Venerable Pierre Toussaint—a step on Pierre's road to becoming a canonized saint.

↳ DISCIPLE CHALLENGE

- Underline the sentence that describes how Pierre used his profession to spread the Gospel.

- What pope recognized that Pierre Toussaint had lived an outstanding Christian life?

  Saint Jhon Paul II

Visit *Lives of the Saints* on **www.webelieveweb.com** to learn about more saints and holy people.

Fast Facts

The term *jubilee* refers to a year-long period observed by Jewish People of ancient times. Every fifty years Jewish slaves were freed, debts were forgiven, and lands were returned to original owners.
(See Leviticus 25:8–55.)

Take Home

Initiate family computer time. Together, visit a news Web site to learn about people in the world being oppressed or enslaved. Consider how your family can support the work of agencies and organizations that work to restore and protect human rights.

Complete the following.

1. When Israel's family first entered Egypt, they were treated as honored guests and given

   the best land, an fertile area.

2. The child Moses was saved from

   pharaoh comand to kill all newborns

3. While Moses was living in Midian and tending his flocks,

   God appered to him in a burning bush.

4. The pharaoh would not let the Israelites leave Egypt, so God

   told Moses, he would send great acats of judgement

Write True or False for the following sentences.
Then change the false sentences to make them true.

5. _Flase_ Goshen was the period of tremendous wealth and power of Egypt.

   new kingdom

6. _True_ The Israelites suffered terribly as slaves of the pharaoh.

7. _Flase_ God revealed his name to the pharaoh.

   Moses

8. _Flase_ After the Passover the Israelites were able to escape from the pharaoh's army.

   when the waters of the Red Sea closed

Write a paragraph to answer this question.

9–10. Why did God free the Israelites from slavery in Egypt?

The Isrealights were Gods people. They beleved and trusted him.

A Free People

✝ We Gather in Prayer

Leader: Like the Israelites, we are on a journey with God. Along the way, there are difficulties, obstacles, and hardships that test our faith and courage. But we follow Jesus, who tells us, "Do not be afraid"(Matthew 14:27).

Side 1: "Send your light and fidelity,
     that they may be my guide

Side 2: And bring me to your holy mountain,
     to the place of your dwelling,

Side 1: That I may come to the altar of God,
     to God, my joy, my delight."

     (Psalm 43:3–4)

Side 2: Glory to the Father, and to the Son,
and to the Holy Spirit.

All: As it was in the beginning, is now,
and will be for ever. Amen.

🎵 Be Not Afraid

You shall cross the barren desert,
     but you shall not die of thirst.
You shall wander far in safety,
     though you do not know the way.
You shall speak your words in foreign
     lands and all will understand.
You shall see the face of God and live.

Refrain:
Be not afraid.
I go before you always.
Come, follow me,
and I will give you rest.

Moses led God's people through the wilderness.

WE GATHER

✝ *God, help us to follow you.*

Can you remember a very long trip you took with your family? Describe some of the events that might have happened along the way.

WE BELIEVE

As we read in Chapter 15 of the Book of Exodus, the Israelites had escaped from Egypt. They were overjoyed that God had saved them. They were beginning their journey to the land of Canaan, the land that God had promised them. Moses and the Israelites sang a song of praise to God. Miriam, the sister of Moses and Aaron, took a tambourine and led a dance of victory. She sang,
"Sing to the LORD, for he is gloriously
    triumphant;
  horse and chariot he has cast into the sea"
(Exodus 15:21).

🧍 Write the lyrics to your own song or poem praising God for something he has done for you.

> Thank You Lord
> Thank You Lord
> for the amazing things you have done
> Leting me live another day
> Praying for my family
> Thank youuu Lord
> Hallelujah

The Israelites faced a long journey through the wilderness of the Sinai Peninsula. The Sinai Peninsula was the triangle of land that connected northeastern Egypt with southern Palestine and northwestern Arabia. The story of the Israelites' wanderings in the wilderness is mainly told in Chapters 16—18 of the Book of Exodus. The Israelites spent many years in the wilderness. It was during this period of wandering that the Israelites made the difficult transition from being slaves under the pharaoh to living as a free people in service of God.

Toward Mount Sinai God was with his people during their time in the wilderness. With God's help Moses led the Israelites toward **Mount Sinai**. This was a mountain peak in the rocky southern part of the Sinai Peninsula. During this journey God tested his people's faithfulness again and again. As we saw in the story of Abraham, God asked his people to show their faith and trust in him. He asked them to stay close to him and to follow his plan. God often asked them to do things that at first did not seem reasonable to them. Yet when they followed God's will, they saw the wisdom of God's plan for them.

The Israelites, however, did not always follow God's will for them. At times they forgot that God had taken them out of slavery. They grumbled against Moses for the hardships of this journey through the wilderness.

Even though the Israelites sometimes doubted God, God demonstrated his faithfulness to his people. He watched over them and worked many miracles. A **miracle** is an extraordinary event that is beyond human power and brought about by God.

For instance, when the people complained that they could not drink the bitter water at Marah, God had Moses change it into drinkable water. When they complained that they had no food, God sent small birds called quail. All through their journey God also provided a bread-like substance called **manna**. This manna, a sweet food that tastes like honey, fell from the desert shrubs. And when the Israelites again grumbled that they had no water, God instructed Moses to strike a certain rock and water miraculously gushed out.

In all of these ways, God listened to his people. He made sure they had what they needed to live and to follow his plan for them. Throughout history God has continued to care for the needs of his people. God listens to us today, helping us to be strong and guiding us to follow his ways.

Along the way to Mount Sinai, Moses was reunited with his family. They had remained in Midian when Moses returned to Egypt. Now with God's help Moses, his family, and all of God's people continued their journey together.

The Exodus and the journey through the desert are clearly signs of God leading his people. We, too, are called by God to follow his plan for us. We may not cross seas and deserts, and we may not lack bread and water. But we do need God's love and guidance on our journey through this life. Just like the Israelites in the desert, we, too, need to trust in God and to believe in his love for us.

mose was the choen one He had a plan for him

The rugged mountain landscape of Mount Sinai, Egypt

Key Words

Mount Sinai a mountain peak in the rocky southern part of the Sinai peninsula

miracle an extraordinary event that is beyond human power and brought about by God

manna a sweet bread-like food that God provided for the Israelites in the desert

WE RESPOND

Look back at the song or poem that you wrote praising God. Reflect on the words and their meaning for you. Share this with a partner.

Now praise God together.
"Give praise with tambourines and dance,
  praise him with flutes and strings.
Give praise with crashing cymbals,
  praise him with sounding cymbals.
Let everything that has breath
  give praise to the LORD!
Hallelujah!" (Psalm 150:4–6)

God gave his people the law.

WE GATHER

✝ *O God, help us to be faithful to your covenant.*

What do friends need to do to keep their friendship strong?

WE BELIEVE

When the Israelites arrived at Mount Sinai, they made their camp. Moses went up to the mountain to pray to God. There God reminded Moses that the Israelites were God's people, special to him. Because of this covenant relationship, the people of Israel "shall be to me a kingdom of priests, a holy nation" (Exodus 19:6). The Israelite people were consecrated to God in a special way. As his people, all of them were to take part in worshiping God and offering sacrifice to him.

When Moses told the Israelites what God had said, they answered together, "Everything the LORD has said, we will do" (Exodus 19:8). On the third day of their stay at Mount Sinai, God appeared to the whole people. Clouds and smoke surrounded Mount Sinai. There was thunder and lightning and the sound of trumpets. The mountain trembled, and God made his presence known.

Then God called Moses to come back up to the top of the mountain. There God gave the Ten Commandments to Moses. The **Ten Commandments** are the laws of God's covenant. If God's people would live by the Ten Commandments, they would keep their covenant relationship with God. He would be their God, and they would be his people. We can find the Ten Commandments in Chapter 20 of the Book of Exodus.

Growing up in a Jewish family, Jesus learned these commandments. He lived by God's laws, and called his followers to obey them, too. As disciples of Christ, we try to show our love for God and for one another by following the Ten Commandments. We try to live in God's love.

110

THE TEN COMMANDMENTS

1. I am the LORD your God: you shall not have strange gods before me.
2. You shall not take the name of the LORD your God in vain.
3. Remember to keep holy the LORD 's Day.
4. Honor your father and your mother.
5. You shall not kill.
6. You shall not commit adultery.
7. You shall not steal.
8. You shall not bear false witness against your neighbor.
9. You shall not covet your neighbor's wife.
10. You shall not covet your neighbor's goods.

God also gave Moses many other laws to help the people live out the covenant. These laws are explained in the final chapters of the Book of Exodus and in the Book of Leviticus, the third book of the Bible.

Sealing the Covenant Moses came down from the mountain and shared with the people all the laws that God had given him. The Israelites agreed to follow these laws. So Moses wrote the laws down. He then set up a stone altar with twelve pillars. The pillars represented the twelve tribes of Israel, the descendants of the twelve sons of Jacob.

Moses then sacrificed some young bulls as a peace offering to God and sealed the covenant. Moses sprinkled some of the blood from the bulls, saying "This is the blood of the covenant which the LORD has made with you in accordance with all these words of his" (Exodus 24:8).

Key Word

Ten Commandments the laws of God's covenant given to Moses on Mount Sinai

After Moses celebrated this ritual with the Israelites, he went back up on the mountain. There he spent forty days and forty nights praying to God. The biblical writer used this number as a reminder of God's covenant with Noah. Throughout Scripture forty was a symbolic number. Noah had spent forty days and forty nights on the ark. And after his baptism at the Jordan River, Jesus spent forty days in the desert. There he prayed and fasted as preparation for his public ministry.

Another symbolic number used throughout Scripture was twelve. There were twelve pillars of the stone altar that Moses set up. And according to Christian interpretation, besides referring to the twelve tribes of Israel, these pillars also symbolized the twelve Apostles. The Apostles were the twelve men with whom Jesus shared his ministry in a special way. Jesus Christ would send them out to spread the Good News that he was the Son of God, sent to save all people.

The New Covenant   Before his Death Jesus had a last meal with his Apostles and some disciples. They were celebrating the Passover meal together. At this meal, which Christians call the Last Supper, Jesus said, "This cup is the new covenant in my blood, which will be shed for you" (Luke 22:20).

As Christians we know that the *new* covenant between God and his people has also been sealed. It has been sealed with Jesus' blood. Jesus Christ offered his own life to save us and to free us from sin. Through this new covenant it is possible for us to share in God's life and friendship. We celebrate the new covenant at each celebration of the Eucharist.

WE RESPOND

What is one way that you can show your love for God and others by following the Ten Commandments? Make a commitment to do so this week.

The people built God a dwelling place.

✝ *O Lord, you alone are God.*

> 👤 When people let other people and things take the place of God, we say they are worshiping a false god. What are some of the false gods in today's world?
>
> iphone, socail media, games

WE BELIEVE

While Moses was on Mount Sinai, God gave him two tablets on which the Ten Commandments were written. God reminded Moses that the Israelites were to worship the one true God, not the false gods that other people thought existed. God gave Moses instructions on the ways the people should worship the one true God. These instructions included plans to make different things that the Israelites needed to use in their worship. Everything they were to make had to be portable because the Israelites still had the long journey to the promised land ahead of them.

Since Moses had been on the mountain for a very long time, the Israelites became restless. They went to Aaron and said, "Come, make us a god who will be our leader; as for the man Moses who brought us out of the land of Egypt, we do not know what has happened to him" (Exodus 32:1). So they constructed a statue of a calf out of their gold jewelry. When it was finished, they set it up in the center of the camp and began to worship it as if it were a god.

When Moses came down from the mountain, he saw the people celebrating around the calf. He was angry because the people were worshiping a false god. They had gone against God's commandment by building an idol. Moses threw down the tablets of the Ten Commandments and they broke. Moses then punished those who were unfaithful to God and begged God to forgive the people.

God called Moses to the mountain one last time. "Then the LORD said to Moses, 'Write down these words, for in accordance with them I have made a covenant with you and with Israel.' So Moses stayed there with the LORD for forty days and forty nights, . . . and he wrote on the tablets the words of the covenant, the ten commandments" (Exodus 34:27–28).

When Moses returned from the mountain with the two new tablets of the commandments, his face was shining from being in God's presence. Moses' face was so bright that the Israelites could not look at Moses. For that reason, Moses wore a veil over his face from then on. He only took it off when he spoke to God.

Building the Dwelling Place Now as God had instructed them through Moses, the Israelites began the great work of making the "dwelling place" for God. They contributed their personal belongings, and made:

- a meeting tent, God's dwelling place, which served as a movable place of worship

- the **ark of the covenant**, a wooden box in which the tablets of the Ten Commandments were kept

- several altars

- various pieces of furniture needed for worship

- vestments for the priests.

Artist interpretation of the way the ark of the covenant might have looked.

The Dwelling Place

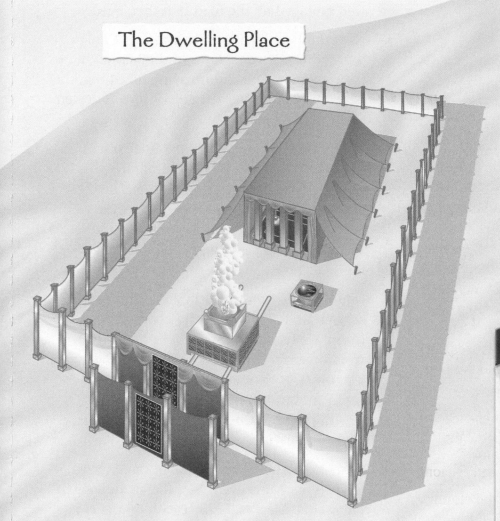

And on the first day of the first month, almost a year after the Israelites had left Egypt, God entered this "dwelling place." The biblical writer symbolized the presence of God by the thunder and lightning that appeared over the tent.

God no longer seemed far away. The Israelites realized that God was always with them, and they were comforted by the visible reminder of his presence. Confident that God was among them, the Israelites continued the long journey to the promised land.

Key Word

ark of the covenant
a wooden box in which the tablets of the Ten Commandments were kept

WE RESPOND

God is present to us at all times and in all places. However, we are sometimes more aware of God in certain places. Sometimes in these places we may feel God with us in a special way. Where are some of these places for you? How often do you visit them? Plan a visit soon to a place that helps you to feel God's presence.

As Catholics...

In our churches, the tabernacle is a beautifully crafted box in which the Blessed Sacrament, or the Eucharist, is reserved for distribution to those who are sick, and also for adoration. *Tabernacle* comes from the Latin word for "tent." The Israelites covered the ark of the covenant with a tent as it traveled with the people. This dwelling place was a sign of God's presence with his people. For us the Blessed Sacrament kept in the tabernacle is more than a sign of the presence of God with us. Christ is really and truly present in the Eucharist.

We genuflect, or kneel briefly on one knee, before the tabernacle as a sign of reverence and worship for Jesus, the Son of God.

Plan to visit your parish church or chapel where the tabernacle is located. Spend time there in prayer before the Blessed Sacrament.

God led his people toward the promised land.

WE GATHER

✝ *God, help us as we journey to you.*

How is your life different now from when you were in fourth grade? What are some of the things that have changed?

WE BELIEVE

The journey of the Israelites to the promised land of Canaan took many years. On this journey God's people grew and changed. From the time that they left Egypt, the biblical writer counted the Israelites' journey as taking forty years. The story of these years is mainly told in the Book of Numbers, the fourth book of the Bible. The Hebrew name for this book means "in the desert." The English meaning refers to two censuses, or head counts of all the people, that took place during the journey to Canaan.

On their journey God made his presence known to the Israelites by the huge cloud that hung over the meeting tent during the day. At night the cloud became fiery, so that the Israelites could see it. When the cloud moved, they followed it. When it did not move, the Israelites remained where they were. The guiding cloud symbolized that God himself was directing their journey.

A Just and Forgiving God As soon as the journey began, the Israelites complained that they had no meat. Out of love for his people, God provided all the food that they needed.

Next the Israelites tried to conquer Canaan without God's consent, and they failed in their attempt. This failure symbolized that the Israelites would succeed only if they followed God's commands.

When the people again complained about the quality of their food—the manna that God provided every day—poisonous snakes appeared among them. Then the people were suddenly sorry for their grumbling and asked Moses to plead with God to remove the snakes.

God then told Moses to make a bronze serpent and set it up in the center of the camp. God said that whoever looked at it would recover from snakebite. In this way the people were reminded to turn to God for safety and to ask his forgiveness for not trusting in him. God was not only just but also all-forgiving.

Saint John, the writer of one of the four Gospels, saw this event as a foreshadowing of the saving effect of Jesus' Death on the cross. "And just as Moses lifted up the serpent in the desert, so must the Son of Man be lifted up, so that everyone who believes in him may have eternal life." (John 3:14–15)

On the Plains of Moab God used the experience in the desert to help his people grow to be more loving and faithful. The Israelites faced many difficult situations during their journey. From these situations they learned more about God and about themselves. Finally the Israelites arrived on the plains of Moab, east of Canaan. Here they met a prophet named Balaam, who predicted the greatness of Israel in the centuries to come.

"I see him, though not now;
  I behold him, though not near:
A star shall advance from Jacob,
  and a staff shall rise from Israel"
(Numbers 24:17).

Though the Israelites had not yet entered Canaan, the time was coming for Moses, who was a very old man, to die. So Moses asked God, "May the LORD, the God of the spirits of all mankind, set over the community a man who shall act as their leader in all things, to guide them in all their actions; that the LORD'S community may not be like sheep without a shepherd" (Numbers 27:16–17).

God told Moses to lay his hand on Joshua, one of his trusted generals, and commission him to lead God's people into Canaan. God's promise would be fulfilled.

Look back over pages 114–115. Highlight the ways God acted in the lives of the Israelites.

WE RESPOND

Look back at your own life. What are some of the ways God has acted in your life?

Pray
Learn
Celebrate
Share
Choose
Live

PROJECT

Show What *you* Know

Design a "desktop wallpaper" summarizing the Israelites' journey through the wilderness. Include Key Words and captions in your design.

What's *the* Word?

"[Jesus] took Peter, John, and James and went up to the mountain to pray. While [Jesus] was praying his face changed in appearance and his clothing became dazzling white. And behold, two men were conversing with him, Moses and Elijah, who appeared in glory and spoke of his exodus that he was going to accomplish in Jerusalem." (Luke 9:28–31)

- Underline the phrase that describes Jesus. ✓
  (Note: This description tells of the Transfiguration of Jesus.)
- Circle what Moses and Elijah were speaking about.
  (Note: Jesus' exodus was his suffering, Death, Resurrection, and Ascension.)

D1SC1PLE

Pray
Learn
Celebrate
Share
Choose
Live

Celebrate! *Read*

Catholics inherited some customs of worship from the Jewish People. One custom was the use of music and songs. Moses' sister Miriam played a tambourine with joy when the people gained their freedom. The Jewish People often praised God with pipes and cymbals, trumpets and horns, lyres and harps. As Catholics, we celebrate with these instruments and many others. Organs, pianos, drums, and guitars—all can help us to "Sing to the LORD a new song" (Psalm 149:1).

↳ **DISCIPLE CHALLENGE** Create a playlist of songs to praise God. *6 songs*

8:26 PM

PLAYLIST

- *spirt & grace*
- *christ be our light*
- *here I am lord,*
- *Amazing grace*
- *soul of my savior*
- *Awesome God*

Fast Facts

Moses is mentioned in the New Testament, more than any other Old Testament person. References to him are found in the Gospels of Matthew, Mark, Luke, and John; in the Acts of the Apostles; these Epistles: Romans, 1 Corinthians, 2 Corinthians, 2 Timothy, Hebrews, and Jude; and in the Book of Revelation.

Take Home

Share these verses from Psalm 119 with your family.

"LORD, teach me the way of your laws;
    I shall observe them with care.
Give me insight to observe your teaching,
    to keep it with all my heart.
Lead me in the path of your commands,
    for that is my delight."
(Psalm 119:33–35)

Abby

-0

CHAPTER TEST

Write the letter that best defines each term.

1. __B__ miracle

2. __D__ manna

3. __A__ Ten Commandments

4. __C__ ark of the covenant

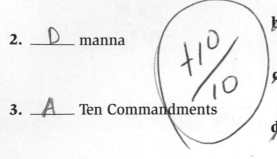

+10/10

a. the laws of God's covenant given to Moses on Mount Sinai

b. an extraordinary event that is beyond human power and brought about by God

c. a wooden box in which the tablets of the Ten Commandments were kept

d. sweet bread-like food that God provided for the Israelites in the desert

e. a meeting tent that served as a movable place of worship

Short Answers

5. How did God demonstrate his faithfulness to his people on their journey to Mount Sinai?

   He watched over them and made mericals happen.

6. Why did the people need the Ten Commandments?

   They were laws they need to follow.

7. List three things that the Israelites made for the "dwelling place" of God.

   1. Vestament.   2. Seval alters   3. The ark of the convants

8. How was God's presence made known to his people during their journey to the promised land?

   He helps them and made his presents known through Moses.

Write a paragraph to answer this question.

9–10. What does the story of the journey of God's people to the promised land tell us about our relationship with God?

   God is always with us. He will forgive us even
   if we don't follly trust him. He loves us.

A Conquering People

10

✝ We Gather in Prayer

†12/18

Leader: Blessed be our God who has shown his people great love. Blessed be God for ever.

All: Blessed be God for ever.

Reader 1: "'Give thanks to the LORD who is good,
   whose love endures forever!'
   Let that be the prayer of the LORD'S redeemed,
      those redeemed from the hand of the foe,
   Those gathered from foreign lands,
      from east and west, from north and south."

Reader 2: "Some had lost their way in a barren desert;
      found no path toward a city to live in.
   They were hungry and thirsty;
      their life was ebbing away."

Reader 3: "In their distress they cried to the LORD,
      who rescued them in their peril,
   Guided them by a direct path
      so they reached a city to live in."

Reader 4: "Let them thank the LORD for such kindness,
      such wondrous deeds for mere mortals.
   For he satisfied the thirsty,
      filled the hungry with good things."

(Psalm 107:1–9)

Leader: Let us pray that all cities
   and towns, may be true cities of God.

♫ City of God

O comfort my people; make gentle your words.
Proclaim to my city the day of her birth.

Refrain:

Let us build the city of God.
May our tears be turned into dancing!
For the Lord, our light and our love,
has turned the night into day!

God's people conquered Canaan.

WE GATHER

✝ *Lord, you alone are our God.*

🏃 Imagine that this year your class has moved to a different school building with the seventh and eighth graders. With a partner decide what you would tell the fifth graders to prepare them for their move up to the new school building next year.

WE BELIEVE

The theme of the Book of Deuteronomy, the fifth book of the Bible, is that God's people must love God and be obedient to him when they enter into and live in the promised land. In Deuteronomy Moses not only said farewell to God's people, but passed his wisdom on to them. Moses told the people: "Hear, O Israel! The LORD is our God, the LORD alone! Therefore, you shall love the LORD, your God, with all your heart, and with all your soul, and with all your strength" (Deuteronomy 6:4–5). These words of Moses became an important prayer which is known as the *Shema*.

Moses told the Israelites, "Take to heart these words which I enjoin on you today. Drill them into your children. Speak of them at home and abroad, whether you are busy or at rest. Bind them at your wrist as a sign and let them be as a pendant on your forehead. Write them on the doorposts of your houses and on your gates" (Deuteronomy 6:6–9).

The Israelites followed Moses' instructions. And through the ages, the Jewish People have continued to make this prayer a part of their everyday lives. God's covenant relationship with the Jewish People remains strong today.

Ancient ram's horn

Bringing the People into Canaan As the Book of Deuteronomy ends, we learn that Moses saw the promised land from a mountain top but did not live to enter it.

he died before

We read in the beginning of the Book of Joshua, the sixth book of the Bible, that God called Joshua to bring the Israelites into their own land. God said to Joshua, "My servant Moses is dead. So prepare to cross the Jordan here, with all the people, into the land I will give the Israelites . . . I command you: be firm and steadfast! Do not fear nor be dismayed, for the LORD, your God, is with you wherever you go" (Joshua 1:2, 9).

The Book of Joshua deals with the Israelites' entry into Canaan. The details are greatly simplified, and the account of conquering and entering Canaan is relatively short. The Book of Joshua is not a day-by-day account of events, but rather the biblical writer's interpretation of the religious significance of these events. According to this book, the Israelites sometimes had to struggle with the Canaanites. In Chapters 1—6 of the Book of Joshua, we find one very famous event in the conquest of Canaan—the fall of Jericho.

The Fall of Jericho Jericho was a well-known city in the center of Canaan, about twenty-three miles northeast of Jerusalem. What was so unusual about this event was the way in which the city was captured. The Israelites did not act like any other army. They did not attempt to batter down the city's walls with special machines. They did not attack the people who were defending the city. And they did not defeat the city's army in battle. Instead, the Israelites followed God's instructions and carried out an unusual plan outside the city walls.

Here is the story of the fall of Jericho.

📖 Joshua 6:1–20

God told Joshua not to attack the city directly but to march around it with his troops. Joshua had his troops do all that God commanded him. They carried the ark of the covenant before them. Seven priests using rams' horns as trumpets led the march. Joshua and his troops did this for six days. On the seventh day they marched around the city seven times. Then the priests blew their horns, and the Israelites shouted loudly. And the walls of Jericho fell down! Then Joshua and the Israelites took over the city of Jericho.

What do you think Joshua thought when he heard God's instructions about Jericho? What would you have thought?

The Israelites conquered this city because they followed the plan of God. In the story God was pictured as a kind of divine warrior who fought on the side of his people and who would bring them victory only if they obeyed him. Even though Joshua was the military leader, it was God who was the real hero in the capture of Jericho. The biblical writer used this story to show that the Israelites believed that God was with them in every part of their lives.

WE RESPOND

🏃 The Book of Joshua emphasizes that God is with his people. Write and illustrate a story that will tell others that God is with them in every part of their lives. Plan your story here.

D.K

God knows everything He helps us throug many sistvations. He tells us when we are wright or wrong.

follow my lead children

$A ← God

121

God's people settled in Canaan.

WE GATHER

✝ *Loving God, help us to see your plan for us.*

🧍 In groups, discuss the different types of decisions people your age have to make at home, among friends, and at school. List some ways that you decide how to make these decisions.

- rember you goods
- ask God
- using my concance O.K

WE BELIEVE

After the Israelites conquered Canaan, the land was distributed among the twelve tribes of Israel. These tribes were the descendants of the twelve sons of Jacob, or Israel. The land was parceled out to each tribe by casting lots. The Hebrews often made decisions by following the ancient practice of casting lots. Lots were coins, sets of specially marked stones, or sticks wrapped in paper. Before the lots were cast, or thrown down, rules about the lots were agreed upon. The rules stated what the lots or the various positions of the lots would represent. The people believed that the outcome of the lots was an expression of God's will.

In the Book of Joshua the biblical writer used the casting of lots to show us that God alone was responsible for the distribution of the land. The land was a gift from God rather than a reward or a human achievement. The Israelites believed that no one except God could ever take the land away from them.

Once the land had been distributed, the tribes met at Shechem, a religious shrine in central Canaan. Here they thanked God for the great blessings he had bestowed on them and renewed their covenant with him. As soon as the ceremonies at Shechem were completed, the Israelites began to settle in Canaan. The story of their settlement in Canaan, which lasted for almost 200 years, can be found in the Book of Judges, the seventh book of the Bible.

As in the Book of Joshua, the biblical writer of the Book of Judges recorded events in a way that helped readers to understand important religious truths. In particular, the writer called attention to the following pattern:

- The Israelites turned away from the one true God and began to worship false gods.

- God allowed other tribes and nations to rule over the Israelites.

- The Israelites cried out to God for help.

- God remembered his covenant and sent a deliverer, in this case a judge, to save the Israelites. This judge was not an officer of the court as in modern times. However, he or she was often a military leader.

- The judge defeated the enemy, often in a great battle, and ruled the land as God directed. Only then did peace return.

This pattern was repeated over and over again during the time of the judges.

Deborah, the Judge One of the first judges the biblical writer described was Deborah. She was one of the great women of the Old Testament. God chose Deborah to remind the Israelites to keep the covenant. She settled legal disputes and offered advice to the people. "She used to sit under Deborah's palm tree, situated between Ramah and Bethel in the mountain region of Ephraim, and there the Israelites came up to her for judgment." (Judges 4:5)

During Deborah's lifetime the Israelites once again began to worship false gods. Due to this failure on their part, Israelite territory was taken over by a Canaanite king and his general. Deborah called on the Israelite commander Barak. Barak had been battling unsuccessfully against the Canaanite general. Deborah ordered Barak to call his troops together at Mount Tabor in the north. She told him that God would give the Israelites a great victory there.

Barak doubted Deborah, but she insisted. Barak told Deborah that he would follow her order as long as she accompanied him and his army to Mount Tabor. So Deborah went with Barak and the army to meet the army of the Canaanites at Mount Tabor. God sent a great thunderstorm that caused the chariots of the Canaanites to get stuck in the mud, and they were defeated. Through God's actions and Deborah's firm faith in him, the land was again free of enemies. And Deborah prayed a great hymn, a canticle, in praise of God.

Bible engraving of Deborah, by Gustave Dore, France

Here is the ending of the Canticle of Deborah: "May all your enemies perish thus, O LORD! but your friends be as the sun rising in its might!" (Judges 5:31).

WE RESPOND

There are people in our lives who help us to stay focused on loving God and one another. Who are some of these people in your life? How do they help you? Let them know that you appreciate all they do for you.

Samson was the most famous judge.

WE GATHER

✝ *Loving God, give us the strength to do your will.*

What are the gifts and talents that people sometimes call their strengths?

How do you use your strengths to help others?

WE BELIEVE

Even though the Israelites had won at Mount Tabor, they again turned from God. Some of God's people found themselves under the rule of the Philistines, who were their enemies. So God sent a special judge to his people. This judge was the only one whose birth was foretold in a very extraordinary way.

An angel of the Lord appeared to a woman in Zorah who had been unable to have any children. The angel said, "Though you are barren and have had no children, yet you will conceive and bear a son" (Judges 13:3). This woman was also told, "As for the son you will conceive and bear, no razor shall touch his head, for this boy is to be consecrated to God from the womb. It is he who will begin the deliverance of Israel from the power of the Philistines" (Judges 13:5).

When the baby was born he was given the name Samson. Samson was blessed by God with great strength. Throughout his life Samson was a Nazirite, a person consecrated to God. As a Nazirite, Samson was supposed to keep special promises, or vows. He was not to drink wine or strong drink, touch anyone or anything that had died, or cut or shave his hair. The spirit of the Lord was with Samson. And as long as Samson kept his vows, God continued to make him strong.

Samson married a Philistine woman, but the Philistines mistreated him and his wife. So a very personal struggle began between Samson and the Philistines. The Philistines went so far as to kill Samson's wife and her family. Samson was enraged by this and took revenge on the Philistines. They began to fear Samson's strength and wanted to capture him. But they were not successful.

Samson and Delilah   Samson then fell in love with another Philistine woman, Delilah. Since the Philistine leaders still wanted to capture Samson, they paid Delilah to find out the secret of Samson's great strength.

At first Samson lied about the key to his strength. This made Delilah very angry. Samson became so afraid of losing her that he told her the truth. He told her that God gave him strength as long as he kept his Nazirite vows. If his hair was shaved, he would no longer have his great strength.

So while Samson was asleep, Delilah had a man shave off Samson's hair. Then she called in the waiting Philistines who blinded Samson. They then took Samson to a prison in one of their cities where they kept him chained and forced him to turn a great stone that ground grain.

While in prison, Samson's hair grew back. One day while the Philistines were having one of their religious festivals to the god of grain, they decided to bring Samson out to mock him. They placed Samson between two columns of their temple. Samson prayed and asked God to give him his strength once again. Then Samson pushed down the columns that were holding up the temple, killing himself and everyone else in it.

The story of Samson symbolized the Israelite nation of his time. Samson's birth, like the birth of Israel, was the result of God's guiding hand.

Samson was dedicated to God, and God was with him, just as God was with the Israelites. Yet instead of using his strength for God, Samson used his strength to take revenge on those who had personally hurt him. But God turned Samson's defeat into the beginning of the downfall of the Philistines. God again allowed the Israelites to be victorious against those who tried to defeat them.

As Catholics...

The vows of a Nazirite play a large part in the story of Samson. Vows are serious promises that people make to God or to each other. The purpose of a vow is usually to help the person who makes the vow to live a life of holiness. For example, during the Sacrament of Matrimony a man and a woman promise to love and honor each other. Similarly, women and men in religious life take vows of chastity, poverty, and obedience. In both cases, the vows help those who make them to focus on living lives dedicated to God and others.

Do you know anyone who has taken vows?

Key Word

Nazirite a person consecrated to God who promised not to drink wine or strong drink, touch anyone or anything that had died, or cut or shave his or her hair

WE RESPOND

Being strong is more than having physical strength. God makes us strong by sharing his life and love with us. What are some ways God does this in our lives?

Write a sentence using each letter of the word *strong* to tell how God shares his life and love with us.

In the **S**acraments God shares his life and love with us.

He **T**urly cares for us

God neve**R** leaves us

G**O**d never turns from you

Nothing is better than God

For **G**ives us

125

Ruth lived a life of self-sacrifice.

WE GATHER

✝ *God, we are your faithful people.*

🏃 In a small group brainstorm synonyms for the word *faithful*. List some synonyms.

- trusting
- loyal
- devoted
- beliving

Discuss some ways people are faithful.

WE BELIEVE

The Book of Ruth is the eighth book of the Bible. It is one of the Bible's most beautiful short stories. The biblical writer shows God's presence in the events of daily life. Even though it is only a few pages long, the story of Ruth teaches us that even in difficult times people can faithfully live out the covenant. They can be good, loyal, and kind. They can follow God's will for them.

The story begins in a time of famine in Israel. An Israelite named Elimelech, his wife Naomi, and their two sons needed to find food. So they traveled eastward from Bethlehem of Judah and crossed the Jordan River into Moab, where people did not believe in the one true God. Elimelech's family settled in Moab because there was no famine there.

Sometime after that, Elimelech died, and each of his sons married a Moabite woman. Then the unexpected happened: the two sons also died. This left Naomi and her daughters-in-law, Orpah and Ruth, sad and in financial trouble. They had no money and Naomi had no relatives in Moab who could help them.

Naomi decided to go back to her homeland. Naomi told her daughters-in-law that they should go back to their own mothers' houses. She prayed that they would marry again and have homes of their own. But Ruth refused to leave her mother-in-law. She said, "Do not ask me to abandon or forsake you! for wherever you go I will go, wherever you lodge I will lodge, your people shall be my people, and your God my God" (Ruth 1:16). Ruth's loyalty and her acceptance of the God of Israel impressed Naomi. The two women went together to Bethlehem.

🎵 Wherever You Go

Wherever you go I shall go.
Wherever you live so shall I live.
Your people will be my people,
and your God will be my God, too.

When it was time for the harvest, Ruth went into a field to gather up grain left behind from the harvest. People without money were allowed to do this, and Ruth needed to feed Naomi and herself. Boaz, who owned the field, noticed her. Boaz was a relative of

Naomi's deceased husband, and he had been told about Ruth's devotion to Naomi. So Boaz told his servants to help and protect Ruth. He even shared some of his own food with her.

When Naomi heard this, she was overjoyed. She hoped that Boaz, as her relative by marriage, would claim some land that she was selling. If he did, then by the law of the Israelites, Boaz would also have the responsibility of taking Ruth as his wife.

Boaz did claim the land and married Ruth. God blessed Boaz and Ruth with a son, who was given the name Obed. "He was the father of Jesse, the father of David" (Ruth 4:17).

In the story of Ruth, the biblical writer shows us that sadness can be turned into joy. We learn that when we bring God's love to one another, God's will is accomplished by our actions. Like Naomi, Ruth, and Boaz, we are called to be part of God's plan by living lives of faithfulness and kindness.

WE RESPOND

Imagine that you have been asked to write a song about faithfulness. What would you name your song? What lyrics would you include? Write them here.

Be Faithful Everyday—

Be faithful to God
Praise him and love him
Be faithful. Be faithful. He is always there for us.

127

Abby

Pray
Learn
Celebrate
Share
Choose
Live

PROJECT

+9/9

Show What *you* Know

Use the clues to complete the chart.

Clue	Your Answer
wife of Elimelech and mother-in-law of Orpah and Ruth	Naomi
appeared to Samson's mother	Angle of the Lord
home of Samson's parents	Zoran
the people who conquered Canaan	Istrelights
refused to leave her mother-in-law	Ruth
the twelve tribes were descendants of his twelve sons	Isreal
"weapons" used to conquer Jericho	Trumpets
Naomi's husband	Elimelen

DISCIPLE CHALLENGE

- Now, circle the first letter of each answer. Use the circled letters to write

  the **Key Word** : N a z i r i t e

- How does this Key Word relate to the story of Samson?

  Samson kept a special prosims to God.

Make *it* Happen

Be part of God's plan by living a life of faithfulness and kindness. This week, I will be part of God's plan by

complemiting all of

my fridends and reading my bible.

Now, pass it on!

Fast Facts

Ruth was the great-grandmother of David. Her son Obed was the father of Jesse, who was the father of David. Therefore, Ruth was an ancestor of Jesus.

Ruth & Naomi,
Malcha Zeldis/© 2014
Artists Rights Society
(ARS), New York

Abby S

DISCIPLE

Pray
Learn
Celebrate
Share
Choose
Live

Saint Stories

Catherine was born in 1347 in Siena, Italy. From a very young age, she lived a life of prayer focused on Christ. Gradually, people began to realize that she had the gift of good judgment. People went to her when they had disputes within their families or among their neighbors. Catherine was concerned about current events and politics, and helped the Church as much as she could. She visited kings and queens and asked them to avoid war. While in Rome working for peace within the Church, Catherine died at the age of thirty-three. She was later canonized a saint and is known as Saint Catherine of Siena.

↳ **DISCIPLE CHALLENGE**

• Underline the sentence that describes how Catherine lived her life.

Visit *Lives of the Saints* on **www.webelieveweb.com** to answer these questions about Saint Catherine of Siena:

• What did Catherine encourage people to do?

  Make peace with one another

• When is her feast day?

  November 25

Reality Check

Like the biblical characters presented in this chapter, we all have unique qualities, or "strengths." List five of your "strengths."

- _Kind_
- _Sharing my thoughts_   - _Creavtives_
- _Loyal_   - _Honest_

↳ **DISCIPLE CHALLENGE** Look over your list. How can you use these strengths to help others?

Take Home

Joshua led the Israelites to the Promised Land. Before Joshua died, he called the Israelites to remember their covenant with God:

"As for me and my household we will serve the LORD" (Joshua 24:15).

As a family, talk about ways you can serve the Lord this week.

Abby S

gc assimate

CHAPTER TEST

**Write True or False for the following sentences.
Then change the false sentences to make them true.**

+13/13

1. _Flase_ The Israelites conquered the city of Jericho with special machines.

   The isreatltes conquered the city of Jericho with trumpets

2. _True_ The land of Canaan was distributed to the twelve tribes of Israel by casting lots.

3. _Flase_ Delilah was chosen by God to remind the Israelites to keep God's covenant, settle legal disputes, and offer other advice.

   Deborah was chosen by God.

4. _Flase_ During the times of the judges, the Israelites stayed faithful to the one true God.

   During the time of the judges, the Israelies tunned away from God and begain worshiping false ones.

Circle the letter of the correct answer.

5. The Book of ___C___ teaches that in difficult times people can live out the covenant.

   a. Deborah   **b.** Naomi   **c.** Ruth

6. A ___A___ was a person consecrated to God who promised vows.

   a. Nazirite   **b.** Philistine   **c.** Moabite

7. The Book of ___A___ emphasizes God's role in the people's entry into the promised land.

   a. Joshua   **b.** Ruth   **c.** Judges

8. God blessed Samson with great ___B___ .

   a. wisdom   **b.** strength   **c.** hair

Write a paragraph to answer this question.

9–10. How does the story of Samson symbolize the Israelite nation of his time?

The Israelites faceed challenges like Samson. Also Samson was faithful and devoted to God the Isreaditos strength came from also being faithul to God and trusting him.

A Royal People

11

✝ We Gather in Prayer

Leader: Jesus, you are the Good Shepherd.
Help us to follow you in all that we say and
do. Be with us as we pray.

Reader 1: "The LORD is my shepherd;
there is nothing I lack.
In green pastures you let me graze;
to safe waters you lead me;
you restore my strength."

All: Jesus, Good Shepherd, lead us in paths of peace.

Reader 2: "You guide me along the right path
for the sake of your name.
Even when I walk through a dark valley,
I fear no harm for you are at my side;
your rod and your staff give me courage."

All: Jesus, Good Shepherd, keep us from
darkness and evil.

Reader 3: "You set a table before me
as my enemies watch;
You anoint my head with oil;
my cup overflows."

All: Jesus, Good Shepherd, thank you for your
Bread of Life.

Reader 4: "Only goodness and love will pursue me
all the days of my life;
I will dwell in the house of the LORD
for years to come."
(Psalm 23:1–6)

All: Jesus, Good Shepherd, show us your
goodness and love!

🎵 The King of Love My Shepherd Is

The King of love my shepherd is,
Whose goodness fails me never;
I nothing lack if I am his,
And he is mine forever.

Where streams of living water flow
With gentle care he leads me,
And where the verdant pastures grow,
With heav'nly food he feeds me.

God called Samuel to serve him.

WE GATHER

✝ *Speak Lord, we are listening.*

What are some events in the history of our country that are often retold?

JFK getting killed, Chirst birth

Why do you think we retell them?

to keep it alive / don't forget

What can we learn from these stories?

we can learn about our nations roots.

WE BELIEVE

The Bible contains many literary forms, or types of writing used to get a message across. Whatever literary form the biblical writer uses, we get to know and encounter God through the events being retold.

As the events being recorded in Scripture changed, so did the literary forms. As Israel grew to become a nation, historical writing began. Historical writing gives an account of a historical event or period in history. The First and Second Books of Samuel, along with some other books in the Bible, represent Scripture's historical books. (See chart, page 27.)

As the First Book of Samuel opens, we read the prayer of a woman named Hannah. Hannah had no children and was praying for a son. She promised God that if he blessed her with a son, she would dedicate the child to God. Hannah did have a son, and she called him Samuel.

To thank God for the gift of her son, Hannah dedicated Samuel to God's service. Samuel was brought to the shrine at Shiloh, which is in central Israel. There he grew up under the watchful eye of an old priest named Eli.

When Samuel was still very young, God called to him while he was sleeping. At first Samuel thought Eli was calling him. However, after

prophet

PROPHET

this happened three times, Eli realized that it was God who was calling Samuel. Eli told Samuel, "Go to sleep, and if you are called, reply, 'Speak, LORD, for your servant is listening'" (1 Samuel 3:9). When God called once more, Samuel answered him in the way Eli had instructed him. Then God spoke to Samuel and told him about the things that he, the Lord, would do.

God was with Samuel, and did not permit "any word of his to be without effect . . . The LORD continued to appear at Shiloh; he manifested himself to Samuel at Shiloh through his word, and Samuel spoke to all Israel" (1 Samuel 3:19, 21). Samuel became God's prophet. A **prophet** is someone who speaks on behalf of God, defends the truth, and works for justice.

> **Key Word**
>
> **prophet** someone who speaks on behalf of God, defends the truth, and works for justice

Desperate Times At this time the situation in Israel was desperate. Many people continued to turn away from God. Israel's enemy, the Philistines, took advantage of Israel's disunity and tried to conquer all of Israel. The Philistines were so successful that they threatened Israel's very existence. The Philistines took so much land from the tribe of Dan that the tribe was forced to find a new home elsewhere. The Philistines even captured the ark of the covenant and paraded it triumphantly through their towns. The ark of the covenant was only given back to the Israelites after those who kept it away from its rightful home experienced terrible hardships.

Besides having enemies, the Israelites were themselves in a state of chaos. For example, the tribe of Benjamin refused to acknowledge that some of their men were criminals and so a civil war broke out. The tribe of Benjamin was almost destroyed.

Worse yet, God himself seemed to have abandoned his people. In the last verse of the Book of Judges we read, "In those days there was no king in Israel; everyone did what he thought best" (Judges 21:25). The biblical writer meant that God, who was considered to be the only king of Israel at this time, did not seem to be with the people.

It was during this time that Samuel was called to gradually take over the leadership of Israel. He brought the ark of the covenant back to a proper resting place. And Samuel offered sacrifice to God, praying for Israel's victory over the Philistines. Indeed, God would never abandon his people. His love for them would never end.

prophet

prophet

PROPHET

WE RESPOND

We are called to love and serve God in different ways. What do you think God is calling you to do? What can you do to answer God's call now and in the future?

Saul became Israel's first king.

WE GATHER

✝ *Lord, help us lead others to you.*

In a small group discuss the reasons why we need leaders. List some characteristics of a good leader.

· Takeing charge · listing to otheres ideas
· Talkeing responbilty for your action
  smart, hardwork'n brave;
                      wise

WE BELIEVE

As Samuel grew older, the Israelites cried out to him for a king. They wanted someone to lead and protect them from their enemies.

For about two hundred years, the twelve tribes of Israel had lived in Canaan. Israel's only king had been the Lord. As God's servants the judges protected the Israelites and led them in loving, obeying, and worshiping God. Now the people wanted to be like other nations. They wanted to be a monarchy. A **monarchy** is a kingdom or empire ruled by one person, either a king or a queen.

At first Samuel was displeased that the people were asking for a king. He believed only God was Israel's king. Although God was also displeased, he told Samuel to let the people have their way. So Israel would now have an earthly king and would become a monarchy.

The First King God revealed his choice of the new king to Samuel. Samuel was told by God to anoint Saul, from the tribe of Benjamin, to govern the people of Israel. This anointing would be a symbol of Saul's consecration to God's service. Samuel poured oil on Saul's head and kissed him. As he

anointed Saul, Samuel said, "The LORD anoints you commander over his heritage. You are to govern the LORD'S people Israel, and to save them from the grasp of their enemies roundabout" (1 Samuel 10:1). Saul became Israel's first king. In the presence of the Lord, the people rejoiced and celebrated.

God spoke to Saul through Samuel. At first Saul followed Samuel's advice and led the people in following God's law. As commander of the Israelite army, Saul won battles against the Philistines. The Israelites were happy that they had a king.

Key Word

monarchy a kingdom or empire ruled by one person, either a king or a queen

As Catholics...

We learn from the Old Testament that being anointed with holy oil set a person apart to serve God as a king, a priest, or a prophet. Anointing is an important part of the life of the Church today. Each year just before the Easter Triduum, the bishop of the diocese blesses three holy oils at a special Mass called the Chrism Mass. These oils are then distributed for use in the celebration of some of the sacraments during the coming year. The oils are:

• the oil of catechumens, used during the Rite of Christian Initiation of Adults and before the celebration of Baptism
• the oil of the sick, used in the Anointing the Sick
• Sacred Chrism, used in Baptism, Confirmation, and Holy Orders.

Find out where the holy oils are kept in your parish church.

Gradually, however, Saul stopped listening to Samuel. He was more concerned with his own interests than those of God's people. Saul began to act on his own, and once he even told his army to stop fighting. This error allowed the Philistines time to regroup, and Israel lost the battle.

As a result of Saul's actions, he no longer ruled with God's blessing. God said to Samuel, "I regret having made Saul king, for he has turned from me and has not kept my command" (1 Samuel 15:11). Therefore God would choose another king. Because God was displeased with Saul, none of Saul's sons would succeed him as king.

Imagine that you have traveled back in time and find yourself living during Saul's reign. You are able to give him advice about being king. What would you tell Saul? With a partner, role-play this scene.

WE RESPOND

Take a moment to listen quietly to God. What is he saying to you today? How will you follow him?

135

God chose David to lead Israel.

WE GATHER

✝ *Thank you God, for loving me for who I am.*

👤 What does the expression "You cannot judge a book by its cover" mean to you? Give some examples that illustrate this expression.

WE BELIEVE

The story of the way God chose Israel's second king is told in Chapter 16 of the First Book of Samuel. God sent Samuel to a man named Jesse who lived in Bethlehem. God told Samuel that he had chosen the next king from among Jesse's sons. So Samuel went to Bethlehem and offered sacrifice there. Then he invited Jesse and his family to the feast that followed the sacrifice.

Jesse and seven of his sons entered the feast, and each of these sons was presented to Samuel. Samuel thought that surely one of these would be the new king. But none of these were acceptable to God. God said to Samuel, "Not as man sees does God see, because man sees the appearance but the LORD looks into the heart" (1 Samuel 16:7).

Then Samuel asked Jesse whether he had any more sons. Jesse told him that he had one more son, David. David was the youngest and was in the fields tending the sheep. Samuel told Jesse to send for David.

David came before Samuel, "then Samuel, with the horn of oil in hand, anointed him in the midst of his brothers; and from that day on, the spirit of the LORD rushed upon David" (1 Samuel 16:13). God had chosen David to eventually replace Saul as Israel's king.

Meanwhile, the spirit of the Lord had left Saul, and he was tormented. So his servants told him about Jesse's son, David, who played the harp. Saul called for David. David played the harp, and his music soothed Saul's spirit. Soon after this, David entered into Saul's service.

David and Goliath Around this time the Philistines were again trying to overcome the Israelites. The Philistine army was gathered on a hill in Judah, and the Israelite army was on a neighboring hill. The Israelites, however, were afraid to attack because the Philistine army was led by a giant of a man named Goliath. Goliath was much taller than all the other men and wore heavy bronze armor. His spear and shield were too heavy for most men to lift. Every day Goliath walked along the valley between the two hills shouting insults at the Israelites and challenging them to come and fight him. But no one accepted Goliath's challenge.

David's three oldest brothers were among the soldiers in the Israelite army. David himself was too young to be in the army. One day Jesse sent David with supplies for his brothers. As David entered the Israelite camp, Goliath began to shout his usual insults. When the Israelites saw Goliath, they fled. David asked, "What will be done for the man who kills this Philistine and frees Israel of the disgrace?" (1 Samuel 17:26).

David's words were reported to Saul, who sent for David. When David arrived, he assured King Saul that he was prepared to fight Goliath. Saul said that David was too young. But David told him that he had often killed a lion or bear when protecting his father's sheep. David said, "The LORD, who delivered me from the claws of the lion and the bear, will also keep me safe from the clutches of this Philistine" (1 Samuel 17:37). Saul then agreed to let David fight Goliath.

When David answered Goliath's challenge, Goliath took one look at him and cursed him. David, however, told Goliath that he came against him in the name of the God of the armies of Israel. David took a smooth stone from his knapsack, put it in his sling, and hurled the stone at Goliath. The stone hit Goliath in the forehead with such force that it knocked him down, and David was able to kill Goliath. When the Philistines saw their leader fall, they ran away. God had indeed saved David and the rest of Israel!

Unlike Saul, David relied on the Lord completely. David's courage came from trusting in God. His faithfulness and military skill would be very important when he became king.

In groups dramatize a TV news segment in which David, Goliath, and Saul are interviewed about the upcoming battle between David and Goliath. Ask each of them the following questions:

- What happened here?

- What is your role in this event?

- What do you think will happen next?

WE RESPOND

What can you learn from the events in the lives of Saul, David, and Goliath?

David was declared the king of Israel.

✝ *God, guide the leaders of the world.*

Name a person you consider to be successful. What qualities does this person have that led to his or her success?

WE BELIEVE

David was from the tribe of Judah, which was a large southern tribe of Israel. After the death of Saul, the people of Judah proclaimed David as their king. Meanwhile, the rest of Israel accepted one of Saul's sons as their king. Saul's son, however, was weak and soon lost his title. Then the elders of the tribes went to David and agreed to make him the king over all of Israel. In around 1000 B.C. David was declared king of Israel by all of the people.

Michaelangelo (1475–1564), *David*

From events we read about in the Bible, David seemed to be an extremely energetic man. He immediately set out to solve Israel's problems. As soon as he became king, he began to plan his attack against the Philistines, the Israelites' main enemy. A born warrior, David soon drove the Philistines from central Israel once and for all. In later battles David forced them out of the rest of the country. He even captured large parts of the Philistines' territory for Israel.

Having conquered the Philistines, David dealt with another important task: taking over the areas in Israel that were still under Canaanite control. In a series of short battles, David captured most of these areas. The rest of the Canaanites simply surrendered to him. As a result, the Israelite takeover of Canaan, begun centuries before under Joshua, was finally completed. Israel became a nation united.

One of the Canaanite cities that David conquered was Jerusalem. The city became the king's private property because he had captured it with his own soldiers. Thus, in biblical writings Jerusalem became known as the City of David.

The City of David David decided to make Jerusalem the capital of all Israel. All the tribes agreed with David's choice because the city was centrally located and was not part of any territory that belonged to the tribes. Jerusalem was to be both the political and religious capital of all of Israel. David brought the ark of the covenant to Jerusalem. As it was brought into the city, David " . . . came dancing before the LORD with abandon, as he and all the Israelites were bringing up the ark of the LORD with shouts of joy and to the sound of the horn" (2 Samuel 6:14–15).

David also set up a government in Jerusalem. He appointed royal officials to run the country. However, he did not burden the people with new taxes. This won him great support from the people.

As a leader, David proved to be brilliant. He was full of ideas. God was with David. Under David's guidance Israel was transformed from a group of weak and disunited tribes into a strong kingdom. And through everything God was present in the lives of the people and in the life of the nation.

Throughout his years, David had been a shepherd, a storyteller, a poet, a musician, a warrior, and a great king. Although David was the greatest king of Israel, he also had weaknesses.

David's love for a beautiful woman named Bathsheba led him to displease God. Bathsheba was the wife of Uriah, one of David's army officers. David wanted to marry Bathsheba, but she was already married. So David arranged to have her husband killed in battle.

The prophet Nathan told David that Uriah's murder had displeased God. And David asked God's forgiveness saying, "I have sinned against the LORD" (2 Samuel 12:13). Then David, who was truly sorry, prayed for God's forgiveness. He did penance before the Lord, and God forgave David.

Once again in learning about the events in the life of God's people, we learn of God's great mercy. God always forgives those who are sorry for their sins.

Complete this profile to describe why you think David is chosen for person of the year in 999 B.C. Then pretend you are person of the year. Design your own profile.

David	_Abby_ (name)
Person of the Year 999 B.C.	Person of the Year A.D. _2024_

Major Accomplishments
He defeted Goliath

Major Accomplishments
· I have become nicer to my sisters

Ways he showed love for God
He realyed on the lord complety,

Ways you showed love for God
I share the Good News of him to my sisters.

Other interesting facts
David was choosen from 3 of his borther to sever

Other interesting facts
I play volleyball

WE RESPOND

How did David use his gifts and talents to give glory to God?

How can you use your gifts and talents to give glory to God this week?

Pray
Learn
Celebrate
Share
Choose
Live

PROJECT

Show What *you* Know

Classified ads found in newspapers or on Web sites are designed to attract offers of, or requests for, jobs, homes, apartments, cars, etc.

Write a classified ad for the Key Words.

> Oh Samula has became Gods prophet.
> He has been choosen because to
> speak on the behalf of God!
> People liked samuail and wanted
> to make a monarcy. They wanted
> him to rule them

What Would *you* do?

There is a new service club at school that does not have many members. Your teacher has praised your leadership skills and has nominated you to lead this club. You

join the club and
gather some other friends
to join it.

Pray Today

As Catholics, we are called to pray for the needs of the Church and the world. Pray the following prayer for civic leaders.

God our Father,
you guide everything in wisdom and love.
Accept the prayers we offer for our nation.
in your goodness,
watch over those in authority,
so that people everywhere may enjoy
freedom, security, and peace.
We ask this through our Lord Jesus Christ.
Amen.

DISCIPLE

Pray
Learn
Celebrate
Share
Choose
Live

Saint Stories

Ignatius Loyola was a courageous and adventurous Spanish soldier who lived during the sixteenth century. During a recovery from an injury, he read a book on the lives of the saints. Ignatius realized that, like the saints, he could be courageous and adventurous for Christ. He eventually became a priest. He founded the Society of Jesus, known as the Jesuits. These men were to serve Christ and the Church.

Ignatius wrote a book called *The Spiritual Exercises* to help people to become more like Christ. His book includes these important questions: "What have I done for Christ? What am I doing for Christ? What am I going to do for Christ?" The Church honors Saint Ignatius Loyola on July 31.

DISCIPLE CHALLENGE

• Circle the phrase that explains why Ignatius founded the Society of Jesus.

• Underline the questions from *The Spiritual Exercises*. Choose one to answer on the lines below.

I am going to be a way better person. I will inclued my friends, be nice to my sibling, and spread the Good. News.

Reality Check

Samuel replied to God's call by saying,

"Speak, for your servant is listening" (1 Samuel 3:10).

What are some ways God "speaks" to you?

☑ In prayer

☑ In everyday occurrences

☑ in signs

DISCIPLE CHALLENGE How do you show that you listen?

Take Home

David asked God to bless his house. (See 2 Samuel 7:29.) As a family, write a prayer to God asking his blessing on your home.

_____

_____

_____

_____

141

CHAPTER TEST

Abby

Write the letter that best identifies the biblical character.

1. ___d___ Saul

2. ___b___ Samuel

3. ___a___ Hannah

4. ___e___ David

a. prayed for a child whom she promised to dedicate to God

b. a leader and prophet of God who felt that only God should be considered Israel's king

c. the father of David

d. the first anointed king of Israel

e. the king of Israel who united and transformed the nation of Israel

10/10

Short Answers

5. How did Israel's enemy, the Philistines, take advantage of Israel's disunity?

   The Philistines took advantage of Israel's disunite by pushing them around, taking land, and stealing the ark of the covenate.

6. What was used to symbolize the consecration of Saul to God's service?

   Holy oil.

7. What is the importance of the story of David and Goliath?

   Unlikes Saul, David relied on the Lord completely. David's couage came from trusting in God. It showss that anyone can do anything when the belie in God.

8. What happened to the nation of Israel during King David's rule?

   The nation or Isreal grew in power, defeated theii enemies and grew there empire by expaing there land.

Write a paragraph to answer this question.

9–10. What meaning do these words have in the story of David?
   "Not as man sees does God see, because man sees the appearance but the LORD looks into the heart." (1 Samuel 16:7)

   God sees differently than we see. Which means we need help to see as God sees. We have a perstiwo that is totaly differens than Gods.

A Prosperous People

12

✞ We Gather in Prayer

Leader: Jesus called the Apostle James a "son of thunder" because of his quick temper! But James became a wise man and taught the meaning of wisdom. Let us listen to his words.

Reader: A reading from the Letter of James

"Who among you is wise and understanding? Let him show his works by a good life in the humility that comes from wisdom. . . . But the wisdom from above is first of all pure, then peaceable, gentle, compliant, full of mercy and good fruits, without inconstancy or insincerity. And the fruit of righteousness is sown in peace for those who cultivate peace." (James 3:13, 17–18)

The Word of the Lord.

All: Thanks be to God.

Leader: Let us pray for wisdom in our lives and in the lives of all people. We will respond, "Lord, hear our prayer."

Reader: For the wisdom to follow the path of goodness,

For the wisdom to be gentle and peaceful with others,

For the wisdom to care for the earth and its creatures,

For the wisdom to be merciful toward those in need,

For the wisdom to be faithful and sincere with our friends,

For the wisdom to include and not exclude others,

For the wisdom to walk the way of peace and righteousness,

Leader: We ask this in your name, Lord Jesus.

All: Amen.

Solomon's reign was a time of peace and prosperity.

WE GATHER

✝ *Christ, help us bring your peace to others.*

Who are some peacemakers you know or know about? How do they work for peace?

WE BELIEVE

After forty years as king, David died and was buried in Jerusalem, the City of David. David's son Solomon succeeded him as king. Under Solomon's rule Israel achieved its greatest peace and prosperity. The story of Solomon's reign as king, which lasted for about forty years, is told in the first eleven chapters of the First Book of Kings and in the first nine chapters of the Second Book of Chronicles.

Solomon did not rule the way his father had. While David was remembered chiefly as a mighty warrior, Solomon was a diplomat.

Solomon's reign was a time of peace. Unlike his father, Solomon did not wage any wars. Rather, he made treaties, or agreements, with other kings and queens. These alliances kept Israel safe from attack and gave the country new business opportunities.

Solomon helped Israel to prosper by his success in overseas trade. During Solomon's time as king, Israel was richer than it had ever been before. For the first time in Israel's history, some of the common people—not just the powerful—began to enjoy a life of plenty.

To showcase Israel's power and success, Solomon began a great building program. This program was designed to strengthen the country's defenses and to beautify its cities, especially Jerusalem.

16th century depiction of the prosperity of Solomon's time.
Solomon with the Treasure of the Temple, Frans Francken II, Flemish, (1581–1642)

The most important of these building projects involved the construction of the Temple in Jerusalem. Other projects included a magnificent palace for the king and another residence for the daughter of the Egyptian pharaoh, whom Solomon married.

With the new emphasis on building, many forms of art began to flourish in Israel. Among the most important were ivory carving, carpentry, stonework, and jewelry making.

Literature was also very important during Solomon's reign. During this time the historical books of the Bible began to be written and compiled. Psalms, proverbs, and other kinds of poetry were also written. In fact, the first steps toward assembling the Bible were taken when Solomon was king.

WE RESPOND

Solomon worked for peace in Israel. In groups, list some ways we work for peace,

- in our homes _helping our parents with taste they need_

- in our school _being a kind student_

- in our neighborhoods _cleaning up after a party_

What would the world be like if everyone worked for peace?

Solomon gained fame for his wisdom.

WE GATHER

✝ *Loving God, grant us wisdom.*

What do you think the difference is between being smart and being wise? Who is the wisest person you know?

WE BELIEVE

We learn from the Bible that Solomon was considered one of the wisest people of his time. When he was a young king, Solomon prayed to God for guidance. God was so pleased with Solomon's faithfulness that he decided to do something special for him. The story of what God did is told in the third chapter of the First Book of Kings.

God appeared to Solomon in a dream and promised him anything that he wished. God told him that he could have riches or power or fame or anything else he desired. Solomon replied, "I am a mere youth, not knowing at all how to act. . . . Give your servant, therefore, an understanding heart to judge your people and to distinguish right from wrong" (1 Kings 3:7, 9).

Delighted by Solomon's reply, God said: "I give you a heart so wise and understanding that there has never been anyone like you up to now, and after you there will come no one to equal you" (1 Kings 3:12). God also promised to give Solomon riches and glory, for which Solomon had not asked. Then God concluded, "And if you follow me by keeping my statutes and commandments, as your father David did, I will give you a long life" (1 Kings 3:14).

Solomon was so grateful that he went to Jerusalem and stood before the ark of the covenant of the Lord. There he offered sacrifice and peace offerings. Then he gave a banquet for all his servants.

Solomon's Wisdom Soon after God granted Solomon wisdom, it was tested by a real-life event. Two women, each having had a child recently, came to Solomon. One woman's child was alive and the other woman's child was dead. Yet both women claimed to be the mother of the baby that was alive. One woman accused the other of switching the babies. The other woman denied the charge, and both women began to argue. How would Solomon possibly determine which woman was telling the truth when there were no witnesses?

In order to test the women, Solomon ordered, "Get me a sword" (1 Kings 3:24). He then instructed a soldier to cut the baby in two and give one half to each woman. Solomon did not want to kill the child. He was just trying to determine who the mother was.

The mother who truly gave birth to this baby pleaded with Solomon not to kill the child but to give the child to the other woman. The mother who had lied told the soldier to divide the child as Solomon had commanded.

Then Solomon ordered the baby to be given to the woman who had pleaded for its life. He saw that she was clearly the mother. All Israel was amazed by Solomon's ability to determine the truth in this case. In fact, they saw God's own wisdom behind Solomon's decision.

Solomon's story helps us understand the importance of wisdom. Wisdom is a gift from God. **Wisdom** is the knowledge and ability to recognize and follow God's will in our lives.

wisdom the knowledge and ability to recognize and follow God's will in our lives

It enables us to see as God sees and to act as God wants us to act. We need God's gift of wisdom to live a good life and to be faithful to our covenant with God.

As Catholics...

God the Holy Spirit is our guide and helper, our advocate who acts on our behalf. The Holy Spirit is always close to us, and we can turn to the Holy Spirit for comfort and guidance. The Holy Spirit strengthens us to live as Christ's disciples and shares seven spiritual gifts with us. The gifts of the Holy Spirit are wisdom, understanding, counsel, fortitude, knowledge, piety, and fear of the Lord. In the Sacrament of Confirmation, we receive the gifts of the Holy Spirit in a special way. These gifts help us to follow Christ's teachings and to give witness to our faith.

What is one gift of the Holy Spirit that you would ask for right now?

WE RESPOND

Wisdom is one of the gifts of the Holy Spirit. It helps us to see and follow God's plan for us. Identify some situations in which people call upon God for wisdom.

They had to choice between something hard. (which friend is actually a good one)

This week ask God for wisdom in everything you do.

The Temple was built in Jerusalem.

WE GATHER

✝ *Holy God, we glorify you.*

Name some national monuments and memorial buildings. Why are they important to people of our country? What meanings do they have for us?

WE BELIEVE

To show his love for God and his desire to be faithful to the covenant, Solomon decided to build a great stone Temple in Jerusalem. This Temple was meant to be the center of worship of the one true God. It was meant to bind all the people to God and to Israel.

The Temple that Solomon built in Jerusalem was a large stone rectangle sitting on an even larger walled stone platform. To create the platform, thousands of workers flattened part of a hill just to the north of Jerusalem.

The Temple itself consisted of two main rooms: the sanctuary, or holy of holies, and the nave. The sanctuary, which was the innermost part of the Temple, was a small raised room reserved exclusively for God. Only the High Priest could enter the holy of holies.

Temple Mount, Jerusalem
Many scholars believe this to be the site of ancient temples.

The sanctuary contained the ark of the covenant which was protected by two huge statues of angels called *cherubim*. In the Old Testament cherubim appeared as God's attendants. They served as symbols of God's presence in the sanctuary, where God was believed to reside invisibly in the ark of the covenant.

The nave of the Temple was a larger room in front of the sanctuary. It contained a small altar for burning incense. The altar had golden candle holders and other sacred objects. The altar was richly decorated with cedar paneling and gold ornaments. A flight of steps and a doorway with a curtain across it led from the nave to the sanctuary.

On three sides of the sanctuary and nave, Solomon built a series of smaller rooms. These were used for storage or were reserved for the priests who worked in the Temple.

In front of the Temple stood the Court of the Priests. It contained a great altar designed for the offering of sacrifices of various kinds. Other equipment included a great bronze bowl in which the priests were to wash themselves before and after offering sacrifices to God.

NAVE

SANCTUARY

An artist's representation of the Temple of Jerusalem.

Finally, a high retaining wall surrounded the whole structure of the Temple and its courts. This wall had elaborate gates and entranceways.

Solomon began to build the Temple about 968 B.C. and completed it eleven years later. Its completion was considered so important that the writer of the First Book of Kings compared it to the founding of the Israelite nation on Mount Sinai.

For the biblical writer the successful completion of the Temple symbolized God's permanent presence among his Chosen People in the promised land. The building of the Temple in Jerusalem was Solomon's greatest achievement.

Beyond the Court of the Priests, was a series of larger walled courts. These courts surrounded the entire Temple. One of them was reserved for male Israelites, one was designed for female Israelites, and one was for visitors who were not Israelites. Walls and columns separated each of these courts from one another.

WE RESPOND

Use the blueprint above to plan a sacred, or holy, space. Design this space in a way that people will feel God's presence there.

The psalms teach us how to pray.

WE GATHER

✝ *God, we will praise you all the days of our lives.*

How important is music in your life? What kinds of music do you like? Why?

WE BELIEVE

Many scholars believe that several sections of the Bible have been completed, or at least begun, during the reigns of David and Solomon. The most important of these writings are the Book of Psalms and the Song of Songs.

The Book of Psalms, also known as the Psalter, is the great collection of Hebrew religious songs. A **psalm** is a poetic prayer designed to be sung or chanted to some kind of musical accompaniment. David is thought to have written many of the psalms. That would make sense because we know that David was a poet and a musician. Other psalms may have been composed by Solomon. And still others were written many centuries later.

As a Jew, Jesus prayed the psalms often. Today the psalms are still prayed by the Jewish People, and the psalms are also an important part of the liturgical life of all Christians. The psalms are intended for use in public worship. They help us to pray and to deepen our relationship with God.

The psalms are found in the Liturgy of the Hours, part of the official prayer of the Church, and in other prayer books. Psalms are found in the missals or song books

that we use in church, and are prayed and sung during the celebration of Mass. The psalms are also a good guide to personal prayer. There are many kinds of psalms. They can be grouped most easily by content or mood. The most important groupings include:

- *Royal Psalms.* These psalms were composed to celebrate various occasions in the reign of a king—a coronation, a wedding, or a victory in battle. Examples include Psalms 2, 21, and 45.

"LORD, the king finds joy in your power;
in your victory how greatly he rejoices!"
(Psalm 21:2)

In Christian tradition the royal psalms are applied to Jesus because he was the Messiah, or Anointed One. For that reason we sometimes called them *messianic psalms*.

- *Hymns praising God and Zion.* These psalms seem to have been composed for use in public worship. They focus on God's power and mighty acts or on the glory of Zion. Zion is another name for the hill on which Jerusalem is built. Examples include Psalms 8, 47, and 84.

"God is king over all the earth;
sing hymns of praise." (Psalm 47:8)

psalm a poetic prayer designed to be sung or chanted to some kind of musical accompaniment

- *Laments*. This is the type of psalm that occurs most frequently in the Psalter. A lament is a poem or song expressing sorrow, mourning, or regret. Laments can come from individuals or whole communities. Examples include Psalms 13, 14, 67–71, 79, 106, 140–143.

"LORD, hear my prayer;
in your faithfulness listen to my pleading;
answer me in your justice." (Psalm 143:1)

- *Wisdom Poems*. These psalms are somewhat different in content and style from the other types of psalms. They are designed to teach rather than to encourage prayer. Examples include Psalms 1, 73, and 128.

"How good God is to the upright,
the Lord, to those who are clean of heart!"
(Psalm 73:1)

The Song of Songs is another important Old Testament book. It is traditionally said to have been composed by Solomon, but no one is exactly certain who wrote it. It is a collection of love poems. In the Song of Songs, the Lord is the one who loves, the Israelites are his beloved, and the covenant between them is described as their marriage. While the psalms contains some of the most beautiful religious songs ever written, the Song of Songs contains some of the most beautiful love poems ever written.

WE RESPOND

🎵 **Psalm 122: Qué Alegría/ I Rejoiced**

Refrain:
I rejoiced when I heard them say,
"Let us go to the house of the Lord.
Let us go to the house of the Lord."

I rejoiced when they said to me,
"We will go to the house of the Lord."
And now inside your gates we
stand, Jerusalem,
we stand, Jerusalem. (Refrain)

Refrain:
Qué alegría cuando me dijeron:
"Vamos a la casa del Señor.
Vamos a la casa del Señor".

Qué alegría cuando me dijeron:
"Vamos a la casa del Señor".
Y ahora en tus portales
entramos ya, Jerusalén,
entramos ya, Jerusalén. (Refrain)

PROJECT

Pray
Learn
Celebrate
Share
Choose
Live

Show What *you* Know

Write the letters found by using the ordered pairs shown.
You will find the Key Words. Write a sentence for each.

✹	P	A	L
♥	D	S	M
✱	W	O	I
	★	◎	✖

1. ___ ___ ___ ___ ___ ___
(★,✹) (✖,✹) (◎,♥) (★,♥) (◎,✹) (✖,♥)

_____

2. ___ ___ ___ ___ ___
(★,✹) (◎,♥) (◎,✹) (✖,✹) (✖,♥)

_____

What's *the* Word?

David gave the following instructions to his son Solomon:

"I am going the way of all mankind. Take courage and be a man. Keep the mandate of the LORD, your God, following his ways and observing his statutes, commands, ordinances, and decrees as they are written in the law of Moses, that you may succeed in whatever you do, wherever you turn" (1 Kings 2:2–3).

• What does David mean when he tells Solomon, "I am going the way of all mankind"?

_____

• Underline the phrase that describes what will happen to Solomon if he follows God and his ways.

Fast Facts

Seventy-three of the one hundred fifty psalms in the Book of Psalms are attributed to David. As a talented musician, he included musical instructions with the psalms he wrote, such as, "with stringed instruments," "with wind instruments," "for flute accompaniment," or "upon an eight-string lyre." David's psalms have many themes, including praise, thanksgiving, and sorrow.

King David as psalmist; illuminated manuscript, France, 13th century

DISCIPLE

Pray Today

Every church building is a house of prayer and a holy place. We show our reverence for this sacred space in many ways. We appreciate the work of the architect who planned this church building. We admire the work of the artists and craftspeople who contributed to its beauty. We thank God for all the people who sacrificed in the past to build this house of prayer. We are grateful for those who take care of the interior of the church, the vestments, and altar vessels.

DISCIPLE CHALLENGE Write a prayer to thank God for all of these people.

_____

_____

_____

_____

_____

Celebrate!

This week at Mass, or the celebration of other sacraments, pay particular attention when psalms are sung. Sing along, and let the presence of God truly enter your heart.

Take Home

Talk about the word *wisdom* with your family. Wisdom is a gift from God, and it enables us to live a good life and to be faithful to God.

Invite your family to share stories or experiences in which people, including your family members, asked God for wisdom.

CHAPTER TEST

Underline the correct answer.

1. Under the rule of (**David/Solomon**) Israel achieved its greatest prosperity and peace in ancient times.

2. In a dream, Solomon asked God for (**glory/wisdom**) to help him rule the Israelites.

3. Solomon built (**a temple/a palace**) to show his love of God and desire to be faithful to the covenant.

4. The (**sanctuary/nave**) of the Temple contained the ark of the covenant.

Choose a word(s) from the box to complete each sentence.

5. _____ are psalms composed to celebrate various occasions in the reign of a king.

6. _____ are psalms designed to teach rather than to encourage prayer.

7. _____ are psalms that express sorrow, mourning, or regret.

8. _____ are psalms that focus on God's power or on the glory of Zion.

Hymns of God and Zion

Wisdom poems

Laments

Royal Psalms

Write a paragraph to answer this question.

9–10. How does the story of Solomon help us to understand the importance of wisdom?

_____

_____

_____

_____

"Then the wolf shall be the guest of the lamb,
and the leopard shall lie down with the kid;
The calf and the young lion shall browse together,
with a little child to guide them."

Isaiah 11:6

SEASONAL
CHAPTER 13

This chapter prepares us to celebrate
the season of Advent.

During Advent, the Church prepares for the celebration of Christmas.

WE GATHER

✝ *Jesus, bring us peace as we prepare to celebrate your birth.*

What does the word *peace* mean to you? How would you describe peace in the world? in your neighborhood? in your school?

WE BELIEVE

The season of Advent is a time of waiting and expectation. We are preparing, celebrating, and anticipating the coming of Christ into the world.

The word *Advent* means "coming," and the four weeks of Advent are a special time of joyous anticipation and preparation.

- We hope for Christ's coming in the future, and we prepare by being faithful to him and living in peace with one another.

- We celebrate Christ's presence in the world today. Jesus comes to us every day in the celebration of the Eucharist, in all the sacraments, and in the love we have for one another. His presence gives us hope and strengthens us to make the world a more just, peaceful place.

- We wait with joyful expectation to celebrate that the only Son of God first came into the world over two thousand years ago in the town of Bethlehem in Judea.

The color violet is a symbol of this waiting and joyful expectation. It also reminds us of the need for penance. During Advent the celebration of the Sacrament of Penance and Reconciliation is an important way to prepare for the coming of Christ.

The prophet Isaiah The powerful voice of Isaiah the prophet rings out in many of our readings during the season of Advent. Isaiah expresses the longings of God's people as they wait for the Savior God has promised to send. Isaiah assures them that the Messiah will come from among God's own people and that he will call the people to choose peace, not war. The Israelites believe that the Messiah will be a just king who will bring them freedom and peace.

During Advent and Christmas we hear the title Emmanuel. This, too, comes from the prophet Isaiah. In the Book of Isaiah we read of *Immanuel*, which is a Hebrew word meaning, "With us is God." Isaiah used this word as a name for the Savior, and he described Immanuel this way:

"For a child is born to us, a son is given us;
　upon his shoulder dominion rests.
They name him Wonder-Counselor, God-Hero,
　Father-Forever, Prince of Peace" (Isaiah 9:5).

The Messiah Isaiah speaks of will have authority. He will be wise and prudent. He will act as a warrior and defender of the people, like God himself. And his Kingdom will be one of peace.

Christians believe that the Savior, promised by God through his prophet Isaiah, has already come. We believe that Jesus Christ is the Messiah. He is our Emmanuel. He is the child and son born to us. Jesus Christ is God the Son who became one of us. He fulfills God's promises. He brings a message of love and respect for all of us, and he shows us how to do the same.

Isaiah used images to tell the people that the Savior would come and call them to turn violence into peace. Some of those images are of a wolf as a guest of a lamb, a cow and a bear as neighbors, a lion eating hay like an ox, and a baby playing in safety by a cobra's den. In groups work to list some images that Isaiah might use today to get across this same message. Then illustrate one image.

John the Baptist   In the early weeks of Advent we hear the words of John the Baptist, often called a New Testament prophet. The writers of all four Gospels describe John with words from the prophet Isaiah.

"A voice of one crying out in the desert:
'Prepare the way of the Lord,
make straight his paths.'" (Mark 1:3)

John fulfills the words of Isaiah. He prepares the people for the coming of the Messiah. He preaches a message of repentance and conversion. He points out Jesus as the Messiah. John's greatest joy is proclaiming that Jesus is the Messiah, the hoped-for Savior, "Behold, the Lamb of God, who takes away the sin of the world" (John 1:29).

We pray these words of John the Baptist at every Eucharist, before we receive the Body and Blood of Christ in Holy Communion. Jesus, the Savior of the world, is no longer a hope. He is truly "Emmanuel," truly God with us.

Isaiah the Prophet

Jesse Tree

John the Baptist

The Jesse Tree   The Jesse Tree is a symbolic way of presenting the story of God's love and action in the lives of his people throughout the centuries. The name comes from Scripture:

> "But a shoot shall sprout from the
> stump of Jesse,
> and from his roots a bud shall
> blossom" (Isaiah 11:1).

The Jesse Tree is a way to connect the season of Advent to God's faithfulness to his people for over four thousand years. God promises Israel that the glory they had during King David's rule will be theirs again. There will be another king from David's family. Jesus was "of the house and family of David." The Jesse Tree is like a family tree that shows Jesus' ancestry.

Traditionally a different symbolic ornament is placed on the Jesse Tree for each of the days of Advent. There is also one for Christmas Day. The chart below lists some people and events that are part of the history of our salvation.

THE JESSE TREE

	People	Theme / Event	Symbolic Ornament
Week 1 of Advent	Abraham	The promise	Field of stars
Week 2 of Advent	Moses	God's leadership	Burning bush
	Israelites	Passover and Exodus	Lamb
	Samuel	The beginning of the kingdom	Crown
Week 3 of Advent	David	A shepherd for the people	Shepherd's crook or harp
	Isaiah	The call to holiness	Fire tongs with hot coal
Week 4 of Advent	John the Baptist	Repentance	Scallop shell
	Mary	The hope of the future	White lily
	Elizabeth (mother of John the Baptist)	Joy	Mother and child
	Joseph	Trust	Carpenter's square or hammer
	Magi	Worship	Star
Christmas Eve	Jesus	Birth of the Messiah	Manger
Christmas	Christ	The Son of God	Chi-Rho symbol

WE RESPOND

How does our preparation during Advent help us to remember the themes and events on the Jesse tree?

Research to find more people and events represented on the Jesse Tree.

✝ We Respond in Prayer

Leader: Our help is in the name of the Lord.

All: Who made heaven and earth.

Leader: In the short days and long nights of Advent, we realize how we are always waiting for deliverance from our God.

Reader: A reading from the Book of the Prophet Jeremiah

"The days are coming, says the LORD, when I will fulfill the promise I made to the house of Israel and Judah. In those days, in that time, I will raise up for David a just shoot; he shall do what is right and just in the land." (Jeremiah 33:14–15)

The Word of the Lord.

All: Thanks be to God.

Leader: Lord our God,
we praise you for your Son, Jesus Christ:
he is Emmanuel, the hope of the peoples,
he is the wisdom that teaches and guides us,
he is the Savior of every nation.
Come, Lord Jesus.

All: Come quickly and do not delay.

🎵 Prepare the Way

Echo each line

Prepare the way for the coming of God!
Make a straight path for the coming of God!
Ev'ry valley will be filled in,
all hills and mountains will be made low;
crooked roads will be straightened out,
all the rough land will be made smooth.
And all the people on the earth
shall see the saving pow'r of God.

PROJECT DISCIPLE

Pray Learn Celebrate Share Choose Live

Celebrate! Complete the sentences about the season.

1. The word *Advent* means "_____."

2. The color _____ is a symbol of waiting and joyful expectation. It also reminds us of the need for _____.

3. There are _____ weeks in the season of Advent.

4. During Advent and Christmas, we hear the title _____, which is a Hebrew word meaning, "With us is God."

5. The _____ is a symbolic way of presenting Jesus' ancestry and the people and events that are part of the history of our salvation.

Make it Happen

This week, invite _____ to
(name)
participate in the celebration of the Sacrament of Penance and Reconciliation with you.

Reality Check

Make a list of actions that you will do during Advent to promote peacemaking.

Week 1 _____

Week 2 _____

Week 3 _____

Week 4 _____

_____

Take Home

Encourage your family to prepare for Advent through good works and prayer. Participate in parish organizations that help to provide supplies, support, or prayer chains for our servicemen and women serving throughout the world. If there is no such program in your parish, you and your family might want to organize one!

"Come, you nations, and adore the Lord.
Today a great light has come upon the earth."

Introductory Rites, Monday after Second Sunday after Christmas

SEASONAL

CHAPTER 14

This chapter addresses the entire
Christmas season.

WE GATHER

✝ *Lord, we thank you for your constant presence.*

How do you show others that you know they are present in your home? in your school? in your parish? in your life?

WE BELIEVE

What we celebrate on Christmas Day, and during the entire Christmas season, is the wonderful gift of Emmanuel, God-with-us. We celebrate that God is with us today and always.

The season of Christmas is a time to rejoice in the Incarnation, the truth that the Son of God became man. We celebrate Christ's presence among us now as well as his first coming into the world over two thousand years ago. We recall that God so loved the world that he sent his only Son to be our Savior.

The Christmas season begins on December 25 and ends with the Feast of the Baptism of the Lord. This feast is usually celebrated around the second week of January. During the Christmas season we have several feasts that help us to celebrate the Son of God's coming into the world and his presence with us today. Here are a few of them.

Saint Stephen On December 26 we remember Saint Stephen, the first martyr for the faith. We read about Stephen's life in the New Testament in the Acts of the Apostles. He spread the Good News of Christ, the Son of God and Savior. Stephen preached in Jerusalem, and many people came to believe and were baptized. This angered the leaders in Jerusalem. They had Stephen taken out of the city and killed. He died praying for those who were about to take his life. Stephen's belief in Jesus, as well as his love for his enemies, is an example for all of us.

Saint John On December 27 we remember Saint John, one of Christ's Apostles. John is credited with writing one of the four Gospels. His Gospel records the life and ministry of Jesus from his very personal view as Jesus' friend and disciple. John proclaimed that in the Son of God the Word became flesh for our salvation.

"And the Word became flesh
and made his dwelling among us,
and we saw his glory,
the glory as of the Father's only Son,
full of grace and truth." (John 1:14)

During the Christmas season we rejoice that the Word is among us, today and always. "The Word among us" and "the Word made flesh" are titles for Christ, but more importantly they are explanations for the Incarnation. In fact, the word *Incarnation* means "becoming flesh."

Holy Innocents On December 28 we remember the children, called the Holy Innocents, who lost their lives near the time of Jesus' birth.

The wise men, or magi, from the East told King Herod about a newborn king of the Jews. Then they traveled on to find this child. They found the child Jesus, praised him, and offered him their gifts.

Herod, afraid that he would lose his power, wanted this newborn king killed. To be sure that this would happen Herod ordered his soldiers to kill all the baby boys in Bethlehem and the surrounding areas who were under two years of age. But the angel of the Lord had appeared to Joseph and told him to flee to Egypt with the newborn Jesus and Mary. So Jesus was saved.

Feast of the Holy Family On the Sunday after Christmas, we honor Jesus, Mary, and Joseph, the Holy Family. We do not know much about Jesus' family life, but what we do know shows us that he grew up in a loving, faith-filled home. Mary, Joseph, and Jesus' relatives followed Jewish traditions, prayed, and celebrated the religious feasts of their time. Jesus was obedient to his parents, and as he grew older he continued to live by the covenant.

On Holy Family Sunday we pray for our own families, and hear readings at Mass that challenge us to be loving and obedient in our own family life. The Church teaches that our families should learn to be like the Holy Family and love and respect one another. All the members contribute to the holiness of the family by the way they live.

Mary, Mother of God On January 1 we celebrate one of Mary's feasts. We say "Hail, holy Mother! The child to whom you gave birth is the King of heaven and earth for ever." We celebrate Mary's role in God's saving action in history. Jesus was truly human and truly divine. He is God the Son, the Second Person of the Blessed Trinity who became man. So Mary is the Mother of God. Mary's love for her son extends to his Church. We honor Mary as the Mother of the Church, too.

Epiphany   On the Sunday between January 2 and January 8 we celebrate the Feast of the Epiphany. We celebrate that God the Father revealed his Son to all nations. On this day we celebrate Jesus' Epiphany, or the showing of Jesus, to the whole world. We hear in the Gospel of Matthew that when Jesus was born in Bethlehem, magi, or wise men, from the east traveled to find him. They arrived in Jerusalem asking, "Where is the newborn king of the Jews? We saw his star at its rising and have come to do him homage" (Matthew 2:2).

During the time of Jesus, many people believed that a new star appeared in the sky at the birth of a new ruler. The magi saw this star from lands far away and came in search of the new king. The magi themselves were not Jewish, but they still wanted to honor Jesus with gifts of gold, frankincense, and myrrh. On Epiphany Sunday we celebrate that Jesus' coming into the world was important to the whole world. The Good News of Jesus Christ is meant for everyone.

Baptism of the Lord   On the Sunday after Epiphany we celebrate Jesus' baptism by John the Baptist at the Jordan River. Even though Jesus is without sin, he asks John to baptize him. John knows that Jesus does not need this baptism with water. He knows that Jesus is the Messiah. Yet Jesus convinces John to baptize him. By his baptism Jesus identifies himself with all of those who struggle to follow God's law and live by the covenant. Jesus shows that he understands what it means to be human.

And it is after Jesus' baptism that his divinity is revealed. The Spirit of God descended on Jesus, "And a voice came from the heavens, saying, 'This is my beloved Son, with whom I am well pleased'" (Matthew 3:17).

The Christmas season begins with the birth of Jesus and ends with his baptism. During the Christmas season, birth and baptism are connected for us, too. We celebrate Jesus, our Savior, born to us on earth, and we celebrate his new life born in us through the Sacrament of Baptism.

WE RESPOND

In groups brainstorm some special ways that you can celebrate the feasts of the Christmas season. As a class share your ideas. Then make a database of the top five and find a way to share your ideas with other classes.

✝ We Respond in Prayer

Leader: Glory to the Father, and to the Son, and to the
Holy Spirit:

All: as it was in the beginning, is now, and will
be for ever. Amen.

Reader: A reading from the Acts of the Apostles

"In truth, I see that God shows no partiality. Rather, in every
nation whoever fears him and acts uprightly is acceptable to
him. You know the word [that] he sent to the Israelites as he
proclaimed peace through Jesus Christ, who is Lord of all,
what has happened all over Judea, beginning in Galilee
after the baptism that John preached, how God anointed
Jesus of Nazareth with the holy Spirit and power. He went
about doing good and healing all those oppressed. . .
for God was with him." (Acts of the Apostles 10:34–38)

The Word of the Lord.

All: Thanks be to God.

Side 1: "Here is my servant whom I uphold,
my chosen one with whom I am pleased,

Side 2: Upon whom I have put my spirit;
he shall bring forth justice to the nations."
(Isaiah 42:1)

🎵 **Psalm 98: All the Ends of the Earth**

Refrain

All the ends of the earth have seen
the saving pow'r of God.
All the ends of the earth have seen
the saving power of God.

The LORD has made his salvation known:
in the sight of the nations
he has revealed his justice.
He has remembered his kindness
and his faithfulness
toward the house of Israel. (Refrain)

PROJECT DISCIPLE

Celebrate!

Across

5. On December 26 we remember this first martyr for the faith.

6. On January 1 we celebrate her role in God's saving action in history.

7. On this feast we celebrate the showing of Jesus to the whole world.

8. On the Sunday after Christmas, we honor Jesus, Mary, and Joseph, the Holy _____.

Down

1. The _____ of the Lord ends the season of Christmas.

2. On December 28 we remember the children, called the Holy _____, who lost their lives near the time of Jesus' birth.

3. On December 27 we remember this Apostle and writer of one of the four Gospels.

4. The season of Christmas is a time to celebrate the _____, the truth that the Son of God became man.

What's the Word?

Read about the birth of Jesus and the visit of the Magi. These accounts are found in the first two chapters of the Gospel of Matthew.

Take Home

The season of Christmas is a time of celebration. What are some Christmas traditions and celebrations that are unique to your family?

_____

_____

_____

The Sacrament of Confirmation

Part 1   I Open My Heart

In fulfillment of Jesus' promise, the Holy Spirit came upon the Apostles at Pentecost. The Apostles were made stronger in faith, and they were then able to proclaim the Good News of Jesus. They began to proclaim the Good News of Jesus to all people.

Look at the picture. In what way is the boy sharing the Good News of Jesus with others? Reflect on and discuss some ways you can share the Good News of Jesus.

I Can Share the Good News

The Sacrament of Confirmation

Part 2   We Come Together for Prayer

Leader: At Pentecost, the Apostles were strengthened in their faith by the Holy Spirit. We receive the Holy Spirit in Baptism, and we celebrate being sealed with the Holy Spirit in Confirmation. Confirmation confirms our union with Christ and strengthens us to actively participate in the work of the Church using the Gifts of the Holy Spirit. Let us pray. Lord, enrich us with the Holy Spirit, so that we too may be strengthened in faith.

Reader 1: Jesus said to his disciples, "I will ask the Father, and he will give you another Advocate to be with you always" (John 14:16).

All: Lord, send out your Spirit upon us. Give us courage to be witnesses to all the world of your love, and reflections of your goodness.

Reader 2: "To each individual the manifestation of the Spirit is given for some benefit. To one is given . . . wisdom; to another . . . knowledge . . . ; to another faith . . . ; to another gifts of healing . . . ; to another mighty deeds; to another prophecy; . . . to another varieties of tongues." (1 Corinthians 12:7–10)

Leader: What gifts have you been given? What is one thing you can do this week to use your gifts to serve God and his people? (*All silently write responses*.) Share your responses with the group.

All: Lord, open our minds and hearts to the gifts you have given us, that through them we may always serve you and your Church. Amen.

Catholic Identity Retreat

The Sacrament of Confirmation

Part 3   I Cherish God's Word

"The fruit of the Spirit is love, joy, peace, patience, kindness, generosity, faithfulness, gentleness, self-control." (Galatians 5:22–23)

READ the Scripture passage. Read slowly. Pay close attention to what you are reading.

REFLECT on what you read. Think about:

- Which of these fruits of the Holy Spirit will you try to develop further?
- Who do you see living one of these fruits of the Holy Spirit?
- Which fruit of the Holy Spirit is a strength that shows through your actions?

SHARE your thoughts and feelings with God in prayer. Let your thoughts and feelings come naturally. Speak to God as a friend.

CONTEMPLATE, or sit quietly and allow the gentle sound of the Holy Spirit to speak to your heart.

The Sacrament of Confirmation

Part 4 I Value My Catholic Faith

In the Sacrament of Confirmation, the bishop extends his hands over the candidates. He prays: "Give them the spirit of wisdom and understanding, the spirit of counsel and fortitude, the spirit of knowledge and piety; fill them with the spirit of the fear of the Lord" (*The Order of Confirmation*, 25).

You will be asked to choose one of the Gifts of the Holy Spirit. With your assigned group, prepare a skit showing how someone you know, or know of, demonstrates that gift of the Holy Spirit in action. After you watch each skit, write some notes about that gift. These notes will help you complete Part 5 of this retreat.

wisdom _____

_____

understanding _____

_____

counsel (right judgment) _____

_____

fortitude (courage) _____

_____

knowledge _____

_____

piety (reverence) _____

_____

fear of the Lord (wonder and awe) _____

_____

Catholic Identity Retreat

The Sacrament of Confirmation

Part 5 I Celebrate Catholic Identity

Work with your group to identify ways the Gifts of the Holy Spirit can help you to be witnesses of Christ at home, in school, and in your parish or neighborhood. Referring to your notes from Part 4 may be helpful. After your group work is complete, write specific actions you will take in each of these areas.

I Will Witness to Christ

In my family:

Among my friends:

In my parish, community, or neighborhood:

With a partner, share one of the things you will do. Make a promise to pray that your partner will be able to carry out his or her action plan.

The Sacrament of Confirmation

Part 6 I Honor My Catholic Identity

Leader: Lord God, on Pentecost you sent your Spirit to the Apostles. Now, as we gather in prayer with the Apostles, with Mary, and with the angels and saints, make complete in us your grace given to us at Baptism. Strengthen us to live as your sons and daughters. Unite us with your Son, Jesus Christ, and let the Gifts of the Holy Spirit help us so that we may bear witness to our faith, through our words and actions. Let us close with a prayer that the Church prays on Pentecost Sunday.

All: O God, who by the mystery of today's great feast
sanctify your whole Church in every people and nation,
pour out, we pray, the gifts of the Holy Spirit
across the face of the earth
and, with the divine grace that was at work
when the Gospel was first proclaimed,
fill now once more the hearts of believers.
Through our Lord Jesus Christ, your Son,
who lives and reigns with you in the unity of the Holy Spirit,
one God, for ever and ever.
Amen.

(Collect, Pentecost Sunday)

Catholic Identity Retreat

Bringing the Retreat Home

The Sacrament of Confirmation

Retreat Recap

Review the pages of your child's *Celebrating Catholic Identity: Liturgy & Sacraments* retreat. Ask your child to tell you about the retreat. Talk about the following:

- We celebrate being sealed with the Holy Spirit in Confirmation.
- Confirmation confirms our union with Christ.
- In Confirmation we are strengthened to live our faith.

Talk about your Confirmation day or one you celebrated with another family member or friend. Share what you remember about that day.

Your Family's Gifts

Together discuss how each member of your family has different abilities, gifts, or strengths. Identify the gift(s) that make each family member unique. Talk about ways to use these gifts in the service of God and others.

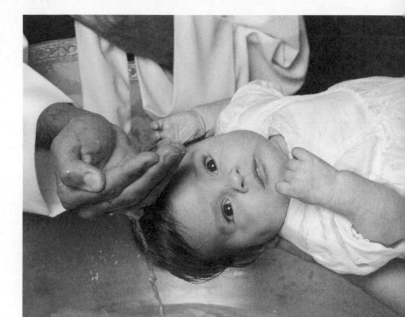

Take a Moment
Your child has learned that Confirmation seals us with the Gift of the Holy Spirit and completes our Baptism. Talk with your child about memories of the day of his or her Baptism, and about your own Baptism. You may wish to mark the anniversary of your child's Baptism by giving him or her a special religious keepsake.

Family Prayer

Pray together the following prayer:

Come, Holy Spirit,
and fill the hearts of our family.
Help us to use our gifts to love and serve
and to follow Christ throughout all our days.
Amen.

For more resources, see the *Catholic Identity Home Companion* at the end of this book.

Why We Believe
As a Catholic Family

What if someone asks us:

- How does a person become fully initiated into the Catholic Church?

The following resources can help us to respond:

There are three Sacraments of Christian Initiation. They are Baptism, Confirmation, and Eucharist. Baptism is the sacrament in which we are freed from sin, become children of God, and are welcomed into the Church. Confirmation is the sacrament in which we are sealed with the Gift of the Holy Spirit and strengthened to witness to our faith. The anointing that takes place in Confirmation confirms and completes the anointing received in Baptism. The Eucharist is the Sacrament of the Body and Blood of Christ in which Jesus is truly present under the appearances of bread and wine. Through the reception of these three sacraments, we become initiated into the Church.

From the beginning of the Church, Baptism, Confirmation, and Eucharist have been the sacraments that lay the foundation for our lives as disciples of Christ. In the Scripture that follows, the "breaking of the bread" in Acts of Apostles 2:41–42 refers to the Eucharist, and the "laying on of hands" in Acts of the Apostles 8:16–17 and 19:5–6 is an essential part of Confirmation.

🌿 What does Scripture say?

The Acts of the Apostles, which teaches us about the early Church, tells us:

"They had only been baptized in the name of the Lord Jesus. Then [the Apostles Peter and John] laid hands on them and they received the holy Spirit." (Acts of the Apostles 8:16–17)

"When they heard this, they were baptized in the name of the Lord Jesus. And when Paul laid [his] hands on them, the holy Spirit came upon them." (Acts of the Apostles 19:5–6)

"Those who accepted his message were baptized, and about three thousand persons were added that day.

They devoted themselves to the teaching of the apostles and to the communal life, to the breaking of the bread and to the prayers." (Acts of the Apostles 2:41–42)

Adults and older children becoming members of the Church receive Baptism, Confirmation, and Eucharist in one celebration, usually at the Easter Vigil. These three sacraments are linked together to bring us into full membership in the Catholic Church.

🌿 What does the Church say?

"The sacraments of Christian initiation—Baptism, Confirmation, and the Eucharist—lay the founda-tions of every Christian life." (CCC, 1212)

"Without Confirmation and Eucharist, Baptism is certainly valid and efficacious, but Christian initia-tion remains incomplete." (CCC, 1306)

Notes:

Redefining the
Covenant People

Seasonal Chapters

PROJECT DISCIPLE

DEAR FAMILY

In Unit 3 your child will grow as a disciple of Jesus by:

- learning the divisions among God's people, and the prophets who proclaimed God's faithfulness
- understanding that the people of Judah struggled to remain faithful to God, and the prophets who brought them comfort and hope from God
- appreciating the role of the prophets who continued to bring God's message to his people
- recognizing that the Jewish People lived and worshipped together, and how the Maccabees defended the Jewish faith
- learning Mary's and Elizabeth's roles in God's plan, and Jesus' Incarnation as the fulfillment of God's promise.

Saint Stories

The angel who brought the news to Mary that she would be the Mother of Jesus is Saint Gabriel the Archangel. Saint Gabriel is the patron saint of communications workers. Saint Clare of Assisi is the patron saint of television, and Saint Isidore of Seville is the patron of computer users and the Internet. Pope John Paul II sent text messages in 2004. Pope Benedict XVI sent texts to World Youth Day participants and opened the first papal Twitter account. Pope Francis regularly "tweets" to his millions of followers on Twitter. There are so many ways to spread the Good News today! How can your family spread the Good News of Jesus this week?

Saint Isidore of Seville

Picture This

Use the timeline on pages 172–175 as a review and a preview. Invite each family member to choose one person or event to look up in the text and then tell about to your entire family. In what ways do these events and people remind us of God's faithfulness?

Reality Check

"The Christian family is a communion of persons, a sign and image of the communion of the Father and the Son in the Holy Spirit."

(*Catechism of the Catholic Church*, 2205)

Pray Today

Throughout the Old Testament, God reveals himself as a faithful God. And God calls us to be faithful to him in return. Thank God for his faithfulness to our ancestors in faith and to your family. Pray that your family will be faithful to God in your decisions, actions and witness—today and every day.

Make it Happen

The prophets reminded God's people of their covenant with God and called them to be faithful. Who are the people in your life who remind you of God's presence and help you to respond to God's love? Have each family member name one person who is a "prophet" for him or her. Then decide on a way to thank these people for helping your family to be disciples of Jesus Christ.

Take Home

Be ready for this unit's Take Home:

Chapter 15: Standing up against injustice

Chapter 16: Respecting God, especially in family life

Chapter 17: Reading/discussing the story of Job

Chapter 18: Setting aside quality time for family

Chapter 19: Answering Jesus' call to discipleship

A Divided People: Israel, the Northern Kingdom

✝ We Gather in Prayer

Leader: The Lord speaks to us in many different ways and through many people. Here is the way he spoke to the prophet Elijah.

Narrator: The prophet Elijah challenged the king and the people to turn away from evil and keep their covenant with God. The queen then ordered the prophet to be killed. Elijah fled. He walked for forty days into the wilderness and took shelter in a cave. Then he heard,

All: "Why are you here, Elijah?"
(1 Kings 19:9)

Narrator: Elijah answered:

Elijah: The Israelites have disobeyed your covenant, "torn down your altars, and put your prophets to the sword. I alone am left, and they seek to take my life"
(1 Kings 19:10).

Narrator: "Then the LORD said,

All: 'Go outside and stand on the mountain before the LORD; the LORD will be passing by.'"
(1 Kings 19:11)

Narrator: A strong and heavy wind was beating at the mountains—

All: "but the LORD was not in the wind.

Narrator: After the wind there was an earthquake—

All: but the LORD was not in the earthquake.

Narrator: After the earthquake there was fire—

All: but the LORD was not in the fire.

Narrator: After the fire there was a tiny whispering sound. When he heard this, Elijah hid his face in his cloak"
(1 Kings 19:11–13).

All: For it was the voice of God.

Leader: Often God speaks to us in stillness. When we are quiet, we can hear God speaking to us in our hearts. Let us pause now in stillness and quiet, and invite the Lord to enter our hearts and minds.
(Silent pause)

God, help us to listen carefully to your voice in the "tiny whispering sound" within our hearts and minds.

All: Amen.

THE DIVIDED KINGDOM (NORTHERN KINGDOM—ISRAEL ■, SOUTHERN KINGDOM—JUDAH ⬚) (All dates approximate)

922 BC   869 BC   842 BC   786 BC   783 BC   735 BC   721 BC   640 BC   612 BC   609 BC

Solomon dies

kingdom
divides in two

Jehu drives
out worship
of false
gods

Jeroboam II
brings
"golden age"

Uzziah restores
Judah to
greatness

Hosea preaches
about love and
faithfulness

Ahaz aligns with
Assyrians for
protection

Assyria conquers
Israel; deports
Israelites as slaves

ten lost tribes

Isaiah of Jerusalem
states God will always
be with his people

Babylon conquers
Assyria; Ninevah falls

Judah loses independence;
becomes part of
Babylonian empire

Josiah after
workers find the
"Book of the Law";
reforms religious
practices

Ahab with Jezebel
worships false gods

Amos addresses
religious and
social problems

Micah condemns false
prophets, greed, and
dishonesty

Timeline for Chapters 15–19

Solomon's kingdom was divided.

WE GATHER

✝ *Lord, may we always do your will.*

What are some reasons why two friends might stop talking to each other?

How would this affect their other friends?

WE BELIEVE

God loves us so much that he gives us the ability to love and care for one another. He also gives us the freedom to choose to love. God wants us to be happy and at peace. He wants what is best for us. However, our choices sometimes may lead us to live in ways that are not good for us.

It seems that this happened to King Solomon, too. Some of Solomon's choices greatly hurt his friendship with God, and this affected all of God's people.

King Solomon, the son of David, was a powerful man who ruled a united Israel. Many projects including the building of the Temple in Jerusalem were completed during his reign. However, Solomon made the people pay heavy taxes and forced them to work long hours on his many projects.

Solomon's heart was slowly turned away from God. He gradually forgot the covenant. He followed the ways of many false gods. He even built altars, burned incense, and offered sacrifices to these false gods.

Since Solomon had chosen to worship false gods and failed to keep the covenant, the kingdom would no longer be his to rule. God said, "I will not do this during your lifetime, however, for the sake of your father David; it is your son whom I will deprive. Nor will I take away the whole kingdom" (1 Kings 11:12–13).

By the time Solomon died in 922 B.C., the Israelites had grown discontent. Solomon's son Rehoboam became the next king. The people asked for lighter taxes and less of a workload. But Rehoboam announced even heavier burdens.

When the ten northern tribes heard this, they refused to accept Rehoboam as king. Instead they followed a man named Jeroboam. The words of the Lord to Solomon were fulfilled, and Solomon's empire was divided into two separate kingdoms. The kingdom made up of the ten northern tribes, with Jeroboam as king, was known as Israel. The kingdom made up of the two southern tribes, with Rehoboam as king, was known as Judah.

🏃 Highlight or underline reasons why Solomon's kingdom divided.

Ezekiel provides words of hope while in exile

Israelites develop wisdom literature

The story of Job

Exiles identify themselves as Jews

A new understanding of the covenant develops

Isaiah of Babylon speaks of the Suffering Servant

Cyrus lets Jews return to their homeland

Esther offers hope and instruction to her people; origin of Purim

Ezra tells people to follow the Law of Moses

Babylonians destroy Jerusalem and Temple

Temple of Jerusalem is rebuilt

Malachi calls people to worship God

Isaiah of Judah calls for social justice

Israelites exiled to Babylon

con't ➤

A People Divided   Jeroboam did not want his people going to Jerusalem, now in the southern kingdom, to offer sacrifices in the Temple. He feared that worshiping with the southern tribes might reunite the people. So he set up places for his people to worship. He provided each place with an altar and a great golden bull. The bulls were meant only to represent the legs of the throne of God, but many of the people worshiped them as gods. By his actions, Jeroboam led the people into idolatry. **Idolatry** means giving worship to a creature or thing instead of to God. Idolatry is forbidden by the First Commandment.

Jeroboam was also appointing false priests. He "made priests from among the people who were not Levites" (1 Kings 12:31). God sent a prophet to warn Jeroboam about his evil ways, but Jeroboam did not listen. And though God had given Jeroboam rule over Israel, Jeroboam was not keeping God's commandments. He did not worship God with all his heart. He led Israel to forget their covenant with the one true God.

In Judah, Rehoboam, too, allowed the people to turn away from their covenant promise. "Judah did evil in the sight of the LORD, and by their sins angered him even more than their fathers had done." (1 Kings 14:22)

The First Commandment calls us to love and honor God above all else. We honor God by our belief in him. We adore God through prayer and worship, by giving thanks and praise to him alone. The commandment also calls us to place our hope and trust in God. Even if we forget God's love and care for us, God's everlasting love for us remains. Unfortunately the kings did not remind their people of this.

Both Jeroboam and Rehoboam led the people away from God. Their northern and southern kingdoms constantly battled with each other, and the divided kingdom continued to decline.

How did the leaders of Israel and Judah fail their people?

WE RESPOND

Solomon's kingdom broke apart, and the people were divided. List some things that divide people today.

_____

_____

_____

In groups discuss ways people can work together to heal relationships and bring people back together. What can you and your classmates do to prevent divisions?

idolatry giving worship to a creature or thing instead of to God

173

175 BC — King orders acceptance of Greek culture and religion

167 BC — The Maccabees lead rebellion to restore Jewish faith

140 BC — Judas Maccabeus cleanses the Temple; origin of Hanukkah

140 BC — Simon Maccabeus gains independence for Judah

Book of Wisdom is written

63 BC — Roman empire takes over Judea; end of kingdom and independence

37 BC — Rome gives power to Herod the Great

The Annunciation

Timeline for Chapters 15–19

Elijah and Elisha proclaimed God's faithfulness.

WE GATHER

✝ *God, help us keep our faith in you.*

Has anyone ever said something that made you stop and think and see things in a different way? In what ways were you, or the way you thought, changed?

The Kings of Israel
The Northern Kingdom

Jeroboam I (jĕr′ ə bō′ əm) ...... 922–901 B.C.
Nadab (nā′ dab) .... 901–900 B.C.
Baasha (bē′ ā shə) .... 900–877 B.C.
Elah (î′ lā) .... 877–876 B.C.
Zimri (zim′ rī) .... 876 B.C.
Omri (ŏm′ rī) .... 876–869 B.C.
Ahab (ê′ hab) .... 869–850 B.C.
Ahaziah (ê ha zī′ ə)............ 850–849 B.C.
Jehoram (jē hō′ rəm) .... 849–842 B.C.
Jehu (jē′ hyoo) .... 842–815 B.C.
Jehoahaz (jē hō′ ə hăz) .... 815–801 B.C.
Jehoash (jē hō′ ăsh) .... 801–786 B.C.
Jeroboam II (jĕr′ ə bō′ əm) ..... 786–746 B.C.
Zechariah (zek ə rī′ ə) .... 746–745 B.C.
Shallum (shal′ lum)............. 745 B.C.
Menahem (mĕn′ ə hĕm) .... 745–738 B.C.
Pekahiah (pē kə hī′ ə) .... 738–737 B.C.
Pekah (pē′ kə) .... 737–732 B.C.
Hoshea (hō shē′ ə) .... 732–721 B.C.

WE BELIEVE

As the kings ignored their responsibilities to the covenant, some of God's people challenged them. The prophets tried to convince the kings and God's people to live justly. But after Jeroboam died, the northern kingdom continued to practice the idolatry which he had introduced. Many of the kings that followed him were not interested in leading the people back to God. They were weak and greedy, and they did not live by the covenant. We find out about these kings in the First Book of Kings and the Second Book of Chronicles.

One of the worst northern kings was Ahab. He did "evil in the sight of the LORD more than any of his predecessors" (1 Kings 16:30). Early in his reign Ahab married a foreign princess named Jezebel. She worshiped a false god named Baal, and King Ahab began to worship Baal, too. Ahab built a temple to Baal in Samaria, the capital city of the northern kingdom. Ahab also used false priests and prophets as advisors.

Broken idol of the false god, Baal.

174

AD (The Year of Our Lord)

Jesus is born — The Holy Family in Nazareth — Relations between Rome and Jews are strained — Religious tensions increase — John baptizes Jesus — Jesus begins his public ministry

Jezebel tried to plant her beliefs in the heart of the people of the northern kingdom. She set up statues of her gods everywhere. Eventually Ahab even allowed Jezebel to kill hundreds of people who believed in the one true God.

Prophets Speak for God God tried to help the people of the kingdom of Israel to stay close to him. He sent prophets to guide the people in his ways. Because they experienced God's love and presence in their own lives, the prophets clearly saw the wrongs that were taking place in their communities. The prophets told the people to stop and think about the way they were living. They called the people to be faithful to God just as God was faithful to them.

The first prophet whom God sent to the northern kingdom was Elijah. Elijah lived during the reign of King Ahab. The name Elijah means "Yahweh is my God." Elijah's message called the people to faith in the one true God.

Elijah eventually anointed Elisha to do God's work, too. Elijah threw his cloak over Elisha as a sign that he was called to the mission of a prophet. So Elisha had the spirit of God upon him, just as Elijah did. These two prophets spoke God's words to many and urged the people to live in justice and faithfulness.

The deeds of Elijah and Elisha are recorded in the First and Second Book of Kings. All of their works show that the power of a prophet comes from the one true God. Their words and actions show that God is loving and faithful to his people, even when they are not faithful to him.

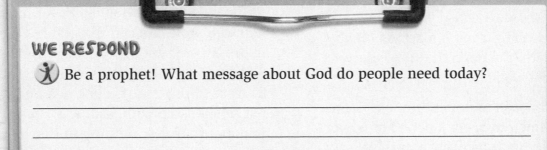

WE RESPOND

Be a prophet! What message about God do people need today?

_____

_____

_____

_____

How would you deliver this message in a way that will make people stop and think about it? In groups, share your responses.

The Assyrians destroyed the northern kingdom.

WE GATHER

✝ *Lord, help us to be strong in our faith.*

What are some ways that one person can influence another? How can people resist bad influences?

WE BELIEVE

In 850 B.C. King Ahab died in battle. He had not been a good influence on God's people. He had led them away from their covenant with God. Ahab was first succeeded by one of his sons and then by another. These young leaders tried to get Israel, the northern kingdom, to worship the one true God. However, they had very little success because their mother, Jezebel, was still too powerful.

In 842 B.C., Jezebel and most of Ahab's family were killed by Jehu, a general. Jehu also destroyed the places where false gods were worshiped, killed the false priests and officials, and established himself as king. Because of Jehu the northern kingdom was freed from the worship of false gods.

In 801 B.C. Jehoash took the throne as king. His reign seemed to begin a period of power and prosperity unknown since the days of Solomon. Under Jehoash's son, Jeroboam II, Israel even regained lost land in the north and established peace with the southern kingdom of Judah. To all appearances Jeroboam II's reign was another "golden age."

Problems in Israel Unfortunately, what seemed to be a time of success and prosperity was not one for all the people. While some people in Israel were wealthy, many others were poor. Most Israelites lived a hard life, and the government did little or nothing to make life easier. Economic differences, which had not previously existed, now became a problem. Many people of all economic levels grew greedier and acted in evil ways.

Along with these social injustices, there were also religious problems. Though the great religious centers were filled with worshipers, the faith of the people was still influenced by the worship of false gods. The real meaning of the covenant was forgotten. Many people no longer fulfilled their promises to God. In fact, the faith of the Israelite people was almost completely lost.

Faith is a gift from God. And even today we can lose faith if we do not turn to God to strengthen our faith. When we follow the example of Christ, and ask the Holy Spirit for help, our faith can grow. We can respond to God's love in our lives. Spending time in prayer, studying Scripture, celebrating the sacraments, and living as Jesus' disciples all strengthen our belief and our relationship with God. It is always important to keep our faith in God strong.

The Downfall of Israel After Jeroboam II's death in 746 B.C., Israel's power and prosperity vanished. This downfall was due to the rise of a new power—the nation of Assyria. Assyria was centered on the city of Nineveh on the Tigris River in Mesopotamia.

Assyria had slowly been building its empire and was getting ready to make Israel a part of this empire.

In 724 B.C. the king of Assyria attacked Israel and took over the countryside. He took the king of Israel prisoner and occupied all the land except for Samaria, the capital city. Then in 721 B.C. Samaria finally fell to Assyria. Great numbers of Israelites were sent away, or deported, to Mesopotamia and other places to live as slaves. The Assyrians filled the northern kingdom with people from other lands, and Israel became a province of the Assyrian empire. The Israelites who were deported— over twenty-seven thousand in all—were never heard from again. They became known as the ten lost tribes of Israel. Thus, the northern kingdom of Israel became just another part of the Assyrian empire.

The experience of God's people shows us that sinfulness does not lead to life. Faithfulness to God and to one another is necessary for living as God calls us to live.

WE RESPOND

List some ways that your parish shows faithfulness to God and one another.

_____

_____

_____

As a class discuss ways that people your age can participate in these parish activities.

Other prophets brought God's message to Israel.

WE GATHER

✝ *God, help us hear your voice.*

Sometimes even helpful, or constructive, criticism is difficult to accept. Think of a situation where you might have to give someone constructive criticism.

WE BELIEVE

In encouraging the people to change their lives, prophets often had to point out the ways God's people failed to show him love. This was not always easy for the people to accept.

Elijah and Elisha were prophets who tried to help the people of the northern kingdom to turn back to God. Though Elijah and Elisha left no written records of their own, a number of other northern prophets did. Amos was a prophet who left such records. His message can be found in the Book of Amos, one of the prophetic books of the Old Testament.

Amos was a shepherd who lived during the middle of the reign of Jeroboam II. Though Amos was from the southern kingdom of Judah, God called him to preach in the northern kingdom. As we have seen, the reign of Jeroboam II seemed like a time of prosperity. In reality, however, many social and religious problems existed. Amos addressed these problems fearlessly.

The message Amos delivered to Israel was difficult yet necessary for the people to hear. Amos told them that they were heartless, greedy, and dishonest. He accused them of turning their backs on God. He pointed out that they had forgotten those who were poor and orphaned, unjustly taxed widows and farmers, and committed crimes and other social injustices. Amos challenged people who claimed they served God, while in their hearts they worshiped the gods of luxury, wealth, and idleness.

The Call to Justice

Amos told the people that God was not impressed by their religious practices when he saw that they were not living justly. Amos warned that if people were going to make offerings to God,

"then let justice surge like water,
 and goodness like an unfailing stream"
(Amos 5:24).

Amos insisted that Israel's only hope of salvation was to act justly. He called the people of Israel to remember that their actions must show what was in their hearts. He proclaimed,

"Seek good and not evil,
 that you may live;
Then truly will the LORD, the God of hosts,
 be with you as you claim!" (Amos 5:14).

Just like God's people thousands of years ago, we are called to act justly and stand up for what is fair and right. We all share in the work of social justice. The Church calls each of us to follow Christ's example of faith in God the Father and outreach to those who are oppressed, neglected, or in need in any way. We cannot separate love for God and love for neighbor.

Unfortunately many people ignored Amos' message and refused to act justly. Amos saw no clear sign that the people of Israel would change their ways. For that reason Amos declared that Israel would be punished, and he predicted the kingdom's final destruction. His words later proved true when Assyria took over Israel.

What was Amos' message to God's people?

The Message of Hosea Another northern prophet, Hosea, lived around the time of Amos. His message is preserved in the Book of Hosea, another Old Testament prophetic book.

Hosea's story was about his love for and marriage to a woman named Gomer. Gomer was not faithful to him, just as Israel was not faithful to God. Though Hosea was horrified by Gomer's unfaithfulness, Hosea loved her so much that he could not give her up. Hosea told the people that God felt the same way about Israel: God refused to abandon Israel even though its people had been unfaithful to him.

For Hosea, Israel's lack of faith showed up in their idolatry and in their injustices against the poor. He told them that their promise of faithfulness to God was empty unless they could show their love by the way they lived.

How can we follow Hosea's message today?

As Catholics...

We need prophets today in our Church and in our world. Through their words and actions, prophets offer us constructive criticism about the ways we are following the Gospel. They remind us that justice, peace, and love of neighbor—especially those who are poor and oppressed—must be part of our Christian way of life. Such people in our modern times include Saint Teresa of Calcutta, Saint John Paul II, Dorothy Day, César Chavez, Dr. Martin Luther King, Jr., and Sister Thea Bowman.

Choose one of these people to research. Discover why we call that person a prophet for today.

WE RESPOND

Plan a short commercial that encourages people to stay faithful to God.

PROJECT

Show What *you* Know

Complete the flow chart to show the effects of the practice of idolatry during the following reigns.

Idolatry
Definition:

_____

_____

_____

Solomon

_____

_____

Jeroboam and Rehoboam

_____

_____

Ahab

_____

_____

Fast Facts Dr. Martin Luther King Jr. was inspired by the prophet Amos' call for social justice. King quoted Amos in his famous "I Have a Dream" speech. (See Amos 5:24.) The quote is the centerpiece of the Civil Rights Memorial in Montgomery, Alabama. This memorial honors those who lost their lives from 1954 to 1968 while working against racism and for social justice.

Question Corner

Which prophet would you like to learn more about?

❏ Elijah   ❏ Amos

❏ Elisha   ❏ Hosea

Why?

_____

_____

DISCIPLE

More to Explore

In 1943, the bishops of the United States founded Catholic Relief Services (CRS) to assist people outside of the United States who are in need in any way. CRS follows the teaching and example of Jesus Christ by trying to stop human suffering and poverty, by working for the development of people, and by encouraging peace and justice. CRS aids those who are in need of food, health care, homes, and education. It helps people to make their communities safer and to find better places to live. CRS also educates Catholics in the United States about the responsibilities of caring for all members of the human family.

DISCIPLE CHALLENGE

• Whose example does CRS follow?

_____

• What does CRS do for Catholics in the United States?

_____

Visit Catholic Relief Services Web site (www.crs.org) to answer these questions:

• In how many countries does CRS operate?

_____

• What kind of work did CRS do in Europe when CRS was first founded?

_____

What Would you do?

What if you were asked to encourage others to be faithful to God? What would you say?

_____

_____

_____

Now, pass it on!

Take Home

Just like God's people thousands of years ago, we are called to act justly and stand up for what is fair and right. As a family, decide on one way you will stand up against injustices that you see around you.

_____

_____

_____

CHAPTER TEST

Write the name of the prophet described.

1. _____ preached a message about the people of Israel being unfaithful to God.

2. _____ preached a message to address the social and religious problems that existed in the northern kingdom.

3. _____ was the first prophet God sent to the northern kingdom to call the people to have faith in the one true God.

4. _____ was anointed and had a cloak thrown over him to show that he was called by God to the mission of a prophet.

Jezebel

Elisha

Hosea

Elijah

Amos

Write True or False for the following sentences.
Then change the false sentences to make them true.

5. _____ God sent Israel prophets to keep them close to him and to guide them.

   _____

6. _____ Judah was the kingdom of the ten northern tribes where Jeroboam was king.

   _____

7. _____ Assyria was the kingdom of the two southern tribes where Rehoboam was king.

   _____

8. _____ God refused to abandon Israel even though its people were unfaithful to him.

   _____

Write a paragraph to answer these questions.

9–10. What is idolatry? Why is it forbidden by the First Commandment?

_____

_____

_____

_____

A Divided People: Judah, the Southern Kingdom

16

✝ We Gather in Prayer

Leader: As God's people, we are called to faith in the one true God who is ever faithful.

Side 1: "Praise the LORD, all you nations! Give glory, all you peoples!

Side 2: The LORD'S love for us is strong; the LORD is faithful forever."

(Psalm 117:1–2)

Side 1: Glory to the Father, and to the Son, and to the Holy Spirit:

Side 2: as it was in the beginning, is now, and will be for ever. Amen.

♫ Though the Mountains May Fall

Though the mountains may fall
and the hills turn to dust,
yet the love of the Lord will stand
as a shelter for all who will call on his name.
Sing the praise and the glory of God.

Judah struggled to remain faithful to God.

WE GATHER

✝ *Holy Spirit, guide us to be faithful.*

Name someone you know or have heard of who has made a difference in the lives of other people. Explain your choice.

WE BELIEVE

Each person who ruled the people of God had the responsibility to help them stay close to God. Some took this responsibility very seriously, and others did not. Rehoboam, the king of Judah, and his successor Abijah, permitted the worship of false gods and practices against God's law. This greatly affected the attitude of God's people in Judah.

However, Asa, the next king, was different. During Asa's reign only followers of the one true God were allowed to be officials in the government. Asa also worked to free Judah from practices against the one true God. In the words of the writer of the Second Book of Chronicles, Asa ordered the people of Judah "to seek the LORD, the God of their fathers, and to observe the law and its commands" (2 Chronicles 14:3). Asa's son Jehoshaphat also firmly believed in God and acted to bring the people back to faithfulness to God.

Unfortunately, through the wife of the next king, the worship of the false god Baal was introduced into Jerusalem. Yet despite all that took place during each king's reign, the people's faith in God never completely failed.

When Uzziah became king, he restored Judah to a greatness unknown since the days of Solomon. Both the northern and southern kingdoms experienced revivals of power and prosperity. However, only the southern kingdom, Judah, remained faithful to God.

Threats to Prosperity About 735 B.C., the king of Israel and the king of Syria invited the king of Judah to join their alliance against the

The Kings of Judah The Southern Kingdom	
Rehoboam (rē ə bō′əm)	922–915 B.C.
Abijah (ə bī′jə)	915–913 B.C.
Asa (ā′sə)	913–873 B.C.
Jehoshaphat (jē hŏsh′ə phăt)	873–849 B.C.
Jehoram (jē hō′rəm)	849 B.C.
Ahaziah (ā həz ī′ə)	842 B.C.
Athaliah (ăth ə lī′ə)	842–837 B.C.
Joash (jō′ăsh)	837–800 B.C.
Amaziah (ăm ə zī′ə)	800–783 B.C.
Uzziah (ŭ zī′ə)	783–742 B.C.
Jotham (jō′thəm)	742–735 B.C.
Ahaz (ā′hăz)	735–715 B.C.
Hezekiah (hez ə kī′ə)	715–687 B.C.
Manasseh (mə năs′ə)	687–642 B.C.
Amon (ā′mən)	642–640 B.C.
Josiah (jō sī′ə)	640–609 B.C.
Jehoahaz (jĕ hō′ə hăz)	609 B.C.
Jehoiakim (jē hoi′ək′ĭm)	609–598 B.C.
Jehoiachin (jē hoi′ək′ĭn)	598–597 B.C.
Zedekiah (zĕd ə kī ə)	597–587 B.C.

Assyrians. And when the king of Judah refused, there was a real threat of war with Israel and Syria.

When the next king, Ahaz, began his reign, he feared an invasion from Syria and Israel. In order to protect Judah from this, Ahaz asked the Assyrians for help. The king of Assyria agreed to protect Judah, and soon the Assyrian armies conquered Israel and Syria. However, to get Assyria's help Ahaz had to pay a price. Judah had to give up its independence and pledge loyalty to Assyria.

The Prophet Isaiah Mistreated by the Assyrians, the people of Judah questioned God's power and doubted him. God wanted his people to stay close to him, so he sent a great prophet to reassure them. We call this prophet Isaiah of Jerusalem. Like Amos before him, Isaiah spoke out against all forms of idolatry and injustice. His message is recorded in Chapters 1—39 of the Book of Isaiah. This was the first of three different messages that were recorded in this prophetic book of the Old Testament.

Isaiah reminded the king and the people of God's love for them. He told them how to be faithful to God. Isaiah was one of King Ahaz's advisors. Isaiah did not think the king should rely on Assyria, and he warned the king that the people would suffer because of the Assyrians. He preached that Judah and Israel would lose their freedom. King Ahaz refused to listen to the prophet.

The Assyrians forced the people of Judah to recognize Assyria's false gods. Ahaz felt that he had no choice but to obey Assyria. The Assyrians even set up a huge altar in the Temple in Jerusalem. And as a result, the people practiced idolatry once again. The Assyrians also made the people of Judah pay heavy taxes. Poverty, suffering, and injustice began to spread in Judah just as they had in the northern kingdom of Israel.

Despite the prophet's words, Ahaz and the people turned away from God and from their covenant with him, and "the LORD had brought Judah low because of Ahaz, . . . who let Judah go its own way and proved utterly faithless to the LORD" (2 Chronicles 28:19). Yet, Isaiah insisted that God's punishment was not meant to destroy Judah, but to make it pure and faithful again. Isaiah's message was one of hope and comfort to the people of Judah.

WE RESPOND

Talk about why it is important for world leaders to make just decisions for their people and to treat neighboring countries with respect.

In this space, write a prayer for world leaders.

_____

_____

_____

_____

Prophets brought Judah hope and comfort.

WE GATHER

✝ *O God, we place our hope in you.*

👤 Think of times when someone's just actions might cause people to dislike him or her. Discuss in small groups.

WE BELIEVE

The actions of the prophet Isaiah were not always easy to accept. He called kings to act justly on behalf of God's people. King Ahaz did not listen to Isaiah. However, King Hezekiah, his successor, did. He stopped practices against the one true God, removed foreign idols from the Temple, and closed local shrines where the false gods and goddesses were worshiped.

Hezekiah also tried to help the poor and those who were suffering because of the many injustices in Judah. Twice Hezekiah tried to free Judah from the Assyrians. Although he failed both times, he still prevented the Assyrians from completely destroying Judah. More importantly, Hezekiah managed to keep the people of Judah faithful to the worship of the one true God. "This Hezekiah did in all Judah. He did what was good, upright and faithful before the LORD, his God. Everything that he undertook, for the service of the house of God or for the law and commandments, was to do the will of his God. He did this wholeheartedly, and he prospered."
(2 Chronicles 31:20–21)

👤 Hezekiah knew that God wanted all people to live in justice and peace. In small groups list some ways your class can make your school a more just and peaceful place.

_____

_____

_____

Isaiah's Message Isaiah told Hezekiah that Jerusalem would not be taken nor Judah destroyed. God would use foreign nations to make Judah pure and once again faithful to his commands. However, the power of these nations would be subject to God's will. Out of his great love for his people, God would not allow these nations to destroy them.

Isaiah pointed out that even if events went against his people, God, who always kept his promises, would be with them. God would bring new life out of death and destruction.

"God indeed is my savior;
   I am confident and unafraid.

My strength and my courage is the LORD,
   and he has been my savior." (Isaiah 12:2)

For Isaiah, faith was complete trust in God's plan and wisdom. Isaiah brought hope and comfort to the people of Judah. He told them that in his mercy God would spare a remnant of the people. A *remnant* is a small piece left over from something larger. This remnant, or small group of God's people, would survive and live just and holy lives as God's faithful community.

Micah the Prophet Micah was another prophet who preached in Judah. Micah had a deep understanding of people and their relationship with God. His messages are recorded in the Old Testament in a prophetic book that bears his name—the Book of Micah.

Micah began his work around the time of Isaiah of Jerusalem. Micah spoke out against false prophets. False prophets tried to become popular by telling their listeners only what they wanted to hear. Unfortunately, Micah's message was difficult for people to accept, so they often ignored or rejected his words.

Micah was angered by the sinful actions of God's people. He had particularly harsh words for the greed, dishonesty, and corruption of those around him. Micah preached that goodness lies in the practice of social justice and in faithfulness to the one true God. It was not enough, he said, to perform elaborate religious ceremonies without faith or to say one thing and believe another. God was not interested in such false worship. Micah told the people that God required them,

"Only to do the right and to love goodness, and to walk humbly with your God"
(Micah 6:8).

The prophet Micah saw the terrible effects of sin at work in both the northern and southern kingdoms. For that reason he warned of the eventual destruction of both kingdoms. But Micah assured the people that God would not abandon his chosen people nor allow them to be destroyed. God would welcome his people back and forgive their sins. He would restore them through the work of a new David.

As Christians we believe that this promise of a new David has been fulfilled in Jesus Christ. Jesus Christ, the Son of God, did what was right, loved goodness, and was humble before God his Father. He spoke out against injustices and, in a way no one else could, brought the people back to God.

WE RESPOND

If Micah or Isaiah were living today, what issues and concerns would they be preaching about? As followers of Jesus Christ, how can we address their issues and concerns? Write your answers on the chart below.

The Prophet's Message Today	Our Response as Followers of Jesus Christ
_____	_____
_____	_____
_____	_____
_____	_____
_____	_____
_____	_____

The kingdom of Judah came to an end.

✝ *Jesus, help us never to turn away from you.*

The verb *reform* can mean to improve something by correcting an error. It can also mean to get rid of abuses or wrong practices. As a noun the word *reform* often means a change for the better or a correction of abuses. In groups discuss ways you may have heard the word *reform* being used or situations in which it could be used.

WE BELIEVE

When Josiah became king of Judah in 640 B.C., the Assyrian empire was falling apart. Josiah helped Judah to slowly regain its independence. However, Josiah was remembered for something much more important. While some of his workers were repairing the Temple, they found a copy of "the book of the law." This was probably an early version of the Book of Deuteronomy.

When Josiah read the book, he was surprised to discover how different the worship of his day was from that of the time of Moses. Thus, Josiah began a reform of religious practices in Judah. Josiah banned all false practices. Even local places of worship to the one true God were closed, and their priests were brought to the Temple.

The prophet Zephaniah appeared early in Josiah's reign. His message is in the Book of Zephaniah. Like Isaiah before him, Zephaniah condemned the worship of false gods. He welcomed Josiah's reforms. The prophet urged the people to change their ways and to return to the faith of Moses. Zephaniah said that God, in his great love, would allow a faithful remnant to at last enjoy the peace, prosperity, and justice that the covenant promised.

Why was Josiah's rule important to Judah?

Babylon Conquers Judah   In 609 B.C., Josiah died in a battle against the king of Egypt. Judah once again lost its independence and now had to pledge loyalty to Egypt. This did not last for long, however.

We can read in the Book of Nahum that Assyria was eventually conquered. The king of Babylon destroyed Nineveh, the capital of Assyria. He also attacked and defeated Egypt. So Judah now became a part of the Babylonian empire. As a result, the king of Judah, had to pledge loyalty to Babylon. The king did not remain faithful to God. He encouraged idolatry. Violence and social injustice flourished and many people turned their backs on God.

When the king of Judah was disloyal to the king of Babylon, revenge was taken on Judah. Babylon invaded Judah in 598 B.C. The king of Babylon ruined the crop and pasture lands, and captured Jerusalem in 597 B.C. He forced the new king of Judah, the royal family, the court officials, and many other people to leave Judah and go to Babylon. This was the first step of the exile, or forced removal, of God's people from their own land.

The king of Babylon also carried off as much of Judah's wealth as he could. He left Zedekiah in charge of Judah. Later Zedekiah rebelled against the king. In 594 B.C. the king of Babylon invaded Judah a second time. Once again he ruined farm lands, deported more of the people to Babylon, and carried off more of Judah's wealth. Despite these losses, Zedekiah continued to resist the king of Babylon. But in 587 B.C. the king of Babylon invaded Judah a third time. He destroyed Jerusalem, including the Temple, and deported even more people to Babylon. The people of Judah were in exile. This was the end of Judah, the southern kingdom, and its proud line of kings descended from David.

WE RESPOND

Think about the messages of Isaiah, Micah, and Zephaniah. Then pretend you are a prophet calling the people of Judah to turn back to God. What is your message to them? Write some notes here.

_____

_____

_____

In small groups deliver your speeches to one another.

Prophets called the people to faithfulness.

WE GATHER

✝ *God, help us to show your love to others.*

How do you serve God and your parish community now? How do you think God will call you to serve in the future?

WE BELIEVE

Prophets served God by constantly calling the people to change their ways and to rely on God, especially during the difficult times. One of these prophets was Habakkuk, who appeared between 605 and 597 B.C. His message can still be read in the Book of Habakkuk. The prophet questioned God's ways saying,

"Why do you let me see ruin;
  why must I look at misery?"
(Habakkuk 1:3).

In reply, God told him that Babylon was an instrument for purifying Judah of its sins. However, God added that those who were faithful to him and just to their neighbors would continue to remain in his love.

God calls each of us to be cleansed of our sins and strengthened to be faithful to him. It is in the Sacrament of Baptism that we are first freed from sin. We sometimes fail to follow God's laws and then it is in the Sacrament of Penance that we are forgiven our sins. Our promise to perform a penance shows that we are sorry for turning away from God and not loving others. We try to focus on loving God and the things that are important in our lives as Christians. Part of reconciling with God is our firm purpose to rely on God and not to sin again.

The Prophet Jeremiah Another prophet named Jeremiah lived from around 650 B.C. until just after 583 B.C. These were very troubled times. They affected Jeremiah deeply and caused him to struggle with his vocation. A **vocation** is God's call to serve him. In Jeremiah's case, it was a call to be God's prophet.

God is with each of us too, as we work to serve God and others.

Jeremiah resisted God's call at first, saying,
  "I know not how to speak; I am too
      young."
But God replied,
"Have no fear . . .
because I am with you . . ."
Then God touched Jeremiah's mouth and said,
"See, I place my words in your mouth!"
(Jeremiah 1:6, 8, 9). Thereafter, Jeremiah was dedicated to God's service.

In 627 B.C. after "the book of the law" had been found, King Josiah called the people to follow their covenant relationship with God. Jeremiah supported the king, but Jeremiah soon had doubts about these reforms. He saw people openly perform religious ceremonies, but they did not have an inner understanding of the covenant and how it called them to live justly. The people simply did not have their hearts in God's service. Jeremiah wept at this unfaithfulness.

Jeremiah warned the people of awful consequences for failing to live by the covenant. He told the people of Judah that nothing would remain, not even a remnant, *unless* they started to live according to the covenant. "Only if you thoroughly reform your ways and your deeds; if each of you deals justly with his neighbor . . . will I remain with you in this place, in the land which I gave your fathers long ago and forever" (Jeremiah 7:5, 7).

When the people heard Jeremiah's threatening prediction, they accused him of blasphemy. **Blasphemy** is a thought, word, or act that refers to God without respect or reverence. Jeremiah was rejected, attacked, and imprisoned. Still, Jeremiah continued to speak out against the sins of the nation. He begged God to let him abandon his vocation. But God told Jeremiah to remain faithful, for God would be with him.

In 587 B.C., just before the final destruction of Jerusalem, Jeremiah advised the people not to resist the Babylonian invaders. He said, "Serve the king of Babylon that you may live; else this city will become a heap of ruins" (Jeremiah 27:17). Jeremiah urged the people to do this so that Jerusalem and its Temple might be spared from complete destruction. The people were very angry and did not accept that the Babylonians were part of God's plan. Thus, the people did not listen to Jeremiah. They did not realize what was about to happen to Jerusalem and to the Temple.

How is the message of Jeremiah similar to that of other prophets?

Baruch Assures the People The prophetic writing in the Book of Baruch was similar to that of Jeremiah. It was written to bring comfort to people who had lost their homeland. It stressed belief in the one true God, faithfulness to the Law of Moses, repentance, and hope.

Key Words

vocation God's call to serve him in a special way

blasphemy a thought, word, or act that refers to God without respect or reverence

As Catholics...

A vocation is God's call to serve him, and it is a way of living our faith. As baptized Christians we all share a common vocation. We are called to grow in holiness and to become more like Jesus Christ. We are called to bring the Good News of Jesus to others so that they, too, will love and follow him.

God also calls each person to serve him in a particular way. There are specific ways to follow our vocation: as members of the lay faithful, as religious brothers or sisters, or as priests or deacons.

Like Jeremiah, we may be unsure of God's call. But the Holy Spirit will guide us as we pray and find out more about the different vocations. Family, friends, and teachers also help us to discover how God is calling us to serve him.

In groups identify the vocations of different people in your lives.

WE RESPOND

Jeremiah asks that each of us treat our "neighbors" justly. Who are our neighbors? With a partner list some ways that we can work for justice for all people.

_____

_____

_____

Act out some of your ideas for the class. Have the members of your class try to guess your works of justice.

PROJECT

Show What *you* Know

Write an online profile for Jeremiah. Include the Key Words in your profile.

Fast Facts

The prophet Isaiah's words of peace (see Isaiah 2:4) are inscribed in a granite wall in a park across the street from the United Nations in New York City. Ralph J. Bunche Park, named for the African-American diplomat and winner of the 1950 Nobel Peace Prize, is the site of the Isaiah Wall.

What's *the* Word?

"Then I [Isaiah] heard the voice of the Lord saying, 'Whom shall I send? Who will go for us?' 'Here I am;' I said; 'send me!' And he [God] replied: 'Go and say this to the people:
   Listen carefully, but you shall not understand!
   Look intently, but you shall know nothing!'"
(Isaiah 6:8–9)

↳ DISCIPLE CHALLENGE

- Underline the sentences that tell how Isaiah responds to God's call.
- What does the prophet Isaiah say to the people?

_____

_____

DISCIPLE

Pray
Learn
Celebrate
Share
Choose
Live

More to Explore

One way that the Church has carried on the mission of the prophets has been through encyclicals. Encyclicals are teachings that the popes have sent in letter form to the whole Church. Encyclicals help us to understand world events and how we can help society by living out the Gospel. In 1963, Pope John XXIII wrote an encyclical about the right of all people to live in peace and freedom. In 1995, Pope John Paul II wrote an encyclical on the value of human life. In 2007, Pope Benedict XVI wrote an encyclical on true Christian hope. In 2013, Pope Francis published an encyclical about the virtue of faith, begun by Pope Benedict XVI. Like the writings of the prophets, these letters from the popes give us words of wisdom for our times. They call us to live as faithful followers of Jesus Christ.

↳ **DISCIPLE CHALLENGE**

• What kind of writing is an encyclical?

_____

• Who writes encyclicals for the whole Church?

_____

Find out more about encyclicals.

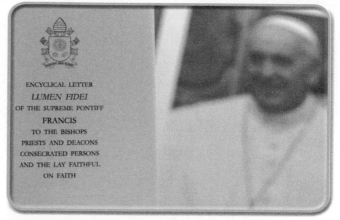

An English edition of Pope Francis's first encyclical, titled *Lumen Fidei*, is displayed next to a portrait of the pontiff during the press conference for the release of the encyclical on July 5, 2013, at the Vatican.

Emblem of the papacy

Question Corner

Have you ever made a difference in someone's life?

❏ Yes   ❏ No

Has someone made a difference in your life?

❏ Yes   ❏ No

↳ **DISCIPLE CHALLENGE** Pray that as Jesus' disciple you can make a difference in the future.

Take Home

Plan a family discussion. Talk about the ways you use the name of God. Talk about the ways you can bring greater respect for God into your thoughts, words, and actions.

Now, pass it on!

CHAPTER TEST

Circle the letter of the correct answer.

1. _____ began a reform of religious practices in Judah, banning all false practices.

   a. Ahaz   **b.** Manasseh   **c.** Josiah

2. The life of the prophet _____ was tragic and his message was not often accepted, but he never lost hope. He knew that God was always with his people.

   a. Jeremiah   **b.** Jehoiakim   **c.** Josiah

3. _____ is a thought, word, or act that refers to God without respect or reverence.

   a. Blasphemy   **b.** Vocation   **c.** Remnant

4. God sent the prophet _____ to keep the people of Judah close to him. His message was one of hope and comfort to the people.

   a. Ahaz   **b.** Isaiah   **c.** Hezekiah

Short Answers

5. What was Jeremiah's vocation?

   _____

6. What was stressed in the prophetic writing in the Book of Baruch?

   _____

7. What happened to Judah after it became part of the Babylonian empire?

   _____

8. What did Micah say about goodness?

   _____

Write a paragraph to answer this question.

9–10. What did Isaiah say about a remnant of God's people?

_____

_____

_____

_____

The Exile and the Journey Home

✝ We Gather in Prayer

Leader: There are many people in our world who live in exile, who have been sent away from their home or country. Let us pray for them.

Reader 1: For those who are homeless in our towns and cities, let us pray.

All: Lord, help us to help them.

Reader 2: For those in prison, especially for those who are unjustly accused, and for their families, let us pray.

All: Lord, help us to help them.

Reader 3: For refugees from war, famine, and oppression, let us pray.

All: Lord, help us to help them.

Reader 4: For all children without homes, let us pray.

All: Lord, help us to help them.

Reader 5: For all those in hospitals, let us pray.

All: Lord, help us to help them.

Reader 6: For those who are dying, that they may reach their heavenly home in peace, let us pray.

All: Lord, help us to help them.

Leader: Let us pray.
Lord, we remember all who are in exile today,
all who are kept from their homes by war, poverty, and illness.
May we find ways to help them in prayer and action.
We ask this in your name, Lord Jesus.

All: Amen.

195

Prophets continued to share God's message.

WE GATHER

✝ *God, save your people and grant us your salvation.*

What are some different ways that people show their sorrow? Think of a time when you felt sorrow and shared it with someone.

WE BELIEVE

The destruction of Jerusalem was a frightening and sorrowful experience for God's people. They mourned for their nation, their Temple, and the people who had been lost. The Book of Lamentations expresses what the people were feeling during this time. A **lamentation** is a sorrow that is expressed in the form of a poem.

The Book of Lamentations contains five such poems. These poems describe in detail the destruction of Judah and the suffering and grief of the people. The biblical writer of Lamentations, most likely the prophet Jeremiah, knew that only firm faith in God's love could comfort the people.

The prophet Ezekiel had a message very similar to Jeremiah's. Ezekiel was a priest and almost certainly was one of the Israelites exiled to Babylon in 597 B.C. Called to be God's prophet in 593 B.C., he carried out his twenty-year ministry among the Israelites exiled in far-off Babylon. His message is found in the Book of Ezekiel.

Ezekiel called the people back to God and condemned all forms of social injustice, idolatry, and superstition. **Superstition** is the false belief that living creatures or things possess powers that in fact they do not have.

Superstitions take away from the honor we owe the all-knowing and all-powerful God.

These Old Testament messages apply to us today. We, too, are called to trust in God and his desire for our well being. We are called to follow Christ's example of complete confidence in God the Father's blessings for us.

The Message of Ezekiel In powerful language Ezekiel described a vision that he had. In this vision the glory of God abandoned Jerusalem. The glory of God first left the holy of holies, then the Temple itself, and finally the city of Jerusalem. Ezekiel declared that, by their actions, the people had rejected God. Now as Ezekiel's vision showed, God rejected Jerusalem and the Temple as his dwelling place.

lamentation a sorrow that is expressed in the form of a poem

superstition the false belief that living creatures or things possess powers that in fact they do not have

196

Ezekiel's message went further than Jeremiah's by declaring that the people had been unfaithful to God from the very beginning. Ezekiel delivered these stinging words of God to the people. "Can your heart remain firm, will your hands be strong, in the days when I deal with you? I, the LORD, have spoken, and I will act. I will disperse you among the nations and scatter you over foreign lands, so that I may purge your uncleanness." (Ezekiel 22:14–15) These words of Ezekiel came true after the final destruction of Jerusalem in 587 B.C.

During the time of the exile, Ezekiel began to offer words of hope and comfort to the people. He told them that God had said, "I will give you a new heart and place a new spirit within you" (Ezekiel 36:26).

Ezekiel described a new exodus and desert experience. Ezekiel said that God would purify those who remained true to him. He would shepherd them triumphantly back to their homes in the promised land. There Israel would live forever in peace. Prosperity and justice would prevail under the guidance of the one true God. God would again choose Jerusalem as his dwelling place. He would give the city a new name meaning "The LORD is here" (Ezekiel 48:35).

WE RESPOND

How do you think the people in exile received Ezekiel's message of hope and comfort?

Imagine that Ezekiel had not spoken this message, but had painted a picture or made a sculpture to symbolize the return to the promised land. What might this look like? Design your own work to assure others that God brings comfort and hope.

Babylonian ruins in the Middle East.

God's people in exile were given hope.

WE GATHER

✝ *God, my God, in you we hope.*

How did you first learn about God's unfailing love? Has your understanding of it changed as you have grown older? How has your faith grown?

WE BELIEVE

As exiles in Babylon, God's people were afraid and confused, but this experience also helped them to grow. The way they understood themselves and their relationship with God changed. For the first time the exiles identified themselves as Jews and called their religion *Judaism.* More importantly, they began to realize just how unfaithful they had been to God.

The Jewish People asked themselves what their covenant with God involved. They began to see that it was not birth in the promised land or citizenship in an independent Judah that made a person one of God's people. Rather, being one of God's people meant truly following his will, having absolute faith in him, and making a personal commitment to follow the covenant. For the Jews this was a new understanding of their relationship with God. This understanding of faith still influences Jewish faith and practices today.

The Babylonians treated the exiles quite well, and the Jews were able to remain a community. The Babylonians gave them fertile land on which to live and allowed the exiles to go freely about their lives. As a result, many of the exiles became quite wealthy, and some were even appointed to important positions at the royal court. In these ways God continued to protect his people and to set in place his plan for their future.

Isaiah in Babylon Late in the exile another prophet appeared in Babylon. He was known as Isaiah of Babylon, and his clear message of hope to the people of Israel can be read in the Book of Isaiah. It is found in Chapters 40—55. His message is the second prophetic message in the Book of Isaiah.

198

Like faith, hope is a gift from God. **Hope** enables us to trust in God's promise to be with us always. Hope enables us to be confident in God's love and care for us.

Isaiah called the people to be faithful to God and to have hope. He reminded them that God remained as faithful and loving as he was to his people when they were in Egypt. He proclaimed that God was about to save them in an even greater way than he had when their ancestors crossed to freedom at the Red Sea.

But Isaiah said that salvation would come only through the suffering of a servant of the Lord. This servant would be without sin.

"Through his suffering, my servant shall justify many,
   and their guilt he shall bear . . .
And he shall take away the sins of many,
   and win pardon for their offenses."
(Isaiah 53:11, 12)

The writers of the New Testament understand these passages to be fulfilled in Jesus Christ. He is the sinless servant who "did not come to be served but to serve and to give his life as a ransom for many" (Matthew 20:28).

As Christians we believe that God showed us his great love by sending his only Son to us. In Jesus Christ God's love is made present to us, so our hope is in Christ. Hope helps us to rely not on our own strength, but on the strength of God the Holy Spirit—sent to us by the Father and the Son.

Key Word

hope a gift from God that enables us to trust in God's promise to be with us always; it enables us to be confident in God's love and care for us

As Catholics...

We believe that Jesus Christ is the Suffering Servant about whom Isaiah spoke. Christ is the Messiah, or Anointed One for whom the people waited and yearned. At Jesus' baptism, the Father made it known that Jesus was his Son. The Holy Spirit came upon him, anointing him as priest, prophet, and king.

We call Jesus a priest because he offered the perfect sacrifice that no one else could. Jesus offered himself to save us. Jesus was a prophet because he delivered God's message of love and forgiveness. He spoke out for truth and justice. Jesus showed himself to be a king by the care he gave to all his people. Jesus lived among the people as one of them. He came to serve, not to be served. Jesus' reign, or rule, makes God's love present and active in the lives of his people.

As baptized members of the Church, we share in Jesus' role as priest, prophet, and king. How can we serve others by what we say and do?

WE RESPOND

Pretend that you are in Babylon listening to Isaiah preach. With a group role-play the situation. Have one person be Isaiah and deliver God's message. Have others ask Isaiah questions about this message and about the way God would save them.

God's people searched for wisdom.

WE GATHER

✝ *God, grant us wisdom.*

Think about communities in your neighborhood, city, or state. How do the customs of many countries influence the people in these communities?

WE BELIEVE

During the years of the Babylonian captivity, and throughout their long history, the Jews met people who had different beliefs and customs. Some Jewish people became particularly attracted to the tradition of writing about wisdom.

The Jewish People went on to write a body of wisdom literature of their own. Some of this material is contained in the wisdom books of the Old Testament. The wisdom books give practical guidance on how to live. Some of these books use proverbs to teach. A **proverb** is a brief saying that gives wise advice. It makes a clear point that can be easily remembered.

The Wisdom Literature of the Old Testament

Book of Job	This book reminds us that suffering is a part of life for all people. Those who are innocent and faithful to God suffer, too, and are brought to a deeper trust in God.
Book of Psalms	This book is a collection of poetic prayers and songs known as psalms. These psalms help us to give worship to God. They are an important part of the Church's liturgy.
Book of Proverbs	This book gives advice on how to live. It covers a wide range of topics, from the simplest everyday concerns to the most complicated thoughts about God and our faith.
Book of Ecclesiastes	This book teaches us that riches, pleasure, and even wisdom, only bring happiness for a while. God alone can provide lasting happiness.
Song of Songs	This book is a collection of love poems that use symbolic language to help us understand God's love for us and our covenant relationship with him.
Book of Wisdom	This book is designed to urge people to live a good and holy life. For that reason it argues *against* greed, selfishness, and idolatry, and *for* faith in the one true God.
Book of Sirach (or Ecclesiasticus)	This book deals with growing in faith and teaches that we can grow in faith by living a good and holy life.

The Book of Job One of the most famous examples of wisdom literature is the Book of Job. It tells the story of what happened to Job, a wealthy and powerful man.

Job had a wonderful wife, a large family, many relatives and servants, and a great number of possessions. He was also a good and just man of God. Suddenly, everything went wrong for Job. He lost his children and his possessions. Worse yet, a dreadful disease took hold of his body, and he began to feel desperate. Throughout his unexplainable suffering he remained faithful to God and said "We accept good things from God; and should we not accept evil?" (Job 2:10).

When Job cried out to God during his sufferings, God reminded Job that human beings did not always understand God's purposes. Suffering, the Lord explained, also came to those who were faithful to God. Job accepted this explanation, and he was suddenly filled with a deeper trust in God. Eventually the Lord rewarded his faithful follower and everything that Job had lost was given back to him in a double measure.

What does the story of Job teach us? Do you know people who suffer yet remain faithful to God?

Key Word

proverb a brief saying that gives wise advice

WE RESPOND

As a class start a book of proverbs that is a how-to manual for living a good and just life. What will you call your book of wisdom?

The long return to Judah happened in three stages.

WE GATHER

✝ *Jesus, be our guide.*

Think about a project that you have completed. What were the different stages that you went through before the project was finally accomplished?

WE BELIEVE

Throughout history God shows that his love is everlasting. We see God's constant love for his people, Israel, as he planned the stages of their return to the land that he had promised them.

In 539 B.C. the Persians came down from the mountains of what is now Iran and Afghanistan and took over the Babylonian empire. A year later, the Jews in exile received unbelievable news. Cyrus, the Persian king, had decided to let them return to their homeland. They would be free to rebuild the Temple and practice their faith in peace. Though Judah would still belong to Persia and have a Persian governor, the Jews would be allowed to govern themselves in local and religious matters. This news was greeted with joyous celebrations, and Cyrus became an instant hero.

First Stage of the Return to Judah Returning to Judah and rebuilding the nation would

not be an easy task. It would have to be accomplished in stages. In 538 B.C. Cyrus appointed a prominent descendant of David to lead a group of Jews back to Judah. This group began the rebuilding of the Jewish nation.

Then Cyrus unexpectedly died in battle. And the rebuilding project was delayed and work on the Temple was stopped. Still, the exile was over and Jews were in their homeland again.

Around 520 B.C. the voices of two new prophets, Haggai and Zechariah, were heard. They cried out to those who had returned to stop concentrating only on their own interest and to rebuild the Temple. They wanted the unfinished work to be completed. We can still read their stirring arguments in the Book of Haggai and in the Book of Zechariah, Chapters 1—8.

By this time a strong new ruler was reorganizing the Persian empire. He appointed two prominent Jews to lead a large Jewish expedition back to Judah. With the help of the rousing calls of Haggai and Zechariah, this group succeeded in rebuilding the Temple and resettling a large part of the land. The incomplete Temple was dedicated in 520 B.C., and the Temple was finally finished around 515 B.C. In this manner God completed the first stage of his plan to reestablish the exiled Jews in their homeland: Jews occupied the land, and the Temple was restored.

Second Stage of the Return to Judah

About seventy years after the Temple was rebuilt, Judah was again in danger. Foreign people were trying to take Jewish land in the south and southeast. Nehemiah was sent to protect the city from these attacks by rebuilding the walls of Jerusalem. His work moved God's plan for his people forward. God completed the second stage of the return: Judah was freed from foreign attack. This part of the history of Judah can be read about in the Book of Nehemiah.

Third Stage of the Return to Judah

Nehemiah's mission had been a military one, but another Jew, Ezra, wanted to reform the religious and social practices in Judah. Ezra obtained Persian permission to lead a group of Jewish exiles back to Judah. The Book of Ezra records what happened. To carry out his task, Ezra brought along a copy of the law that was transcribed in Babylon about 560 B.C. He ordered it to be read publicly in Jerusalem. At first the people were very enthusiastic. Then Ezra told them that they should be following the Law of Moses or the Torah, and that they had failed in doing so too many times. The **Torah** is the Hebrew name for the first five books of the Old Testament.

In a dramatic scene in the Temple Ezra wept publicly and recalled the people's sins against God. The people were so moved that they repented and agreed to follow God's law. In this way God accomplished the last stage of the return to Judah: The people submitted fully to God's law.

Though Judah remained a Persian province until 331 B.C., the people were serving God, not the Persian king.

Key Word

Torah the Hebrew name for the first five books of the Old Testament

WE RESPOND

We, too, are called to follow God's law. We do this when we live by the teachings of Jesus Christ.

With a partner brainstorm different ways that we, as members of the Church, can say and do the things that Jesus Christ taught us to do.

_____

_____

_____

Choose one thing that you will do this week to show that you follow Jesus' teaching.

Pray Learn Celebrate Share Choose Live

PROJECT

Show What *you* Know

Write a summary of the Israelites' experiences during the exile in Babylon and the journey home. Be sure to use the Key Words in your summary.

Celebrate!

Psalms are an important part of the Church's liturgy. They help us to give worship to God. During Mass, when are psalms proclaimed?

❏ the Introductory Rites

❏ the Liturgy of the Word

❏ the Liturgy of the Eucharist

❏ the Concluding Rites

Picture This

The anchor was one of the most popular early Christian symbols of hope. The anchor as a symbol of hope is based on Scripture. (See Hebrews 6:18–19.) Think of your own symbol of hope and draw it in the space below.

DISCIPLE

Pray
Learn
Celebrate
Share
Choose
Live

Saint Stories

Saint Bonaventure was born in 1221 in Tuscany, Italy. At a young age he joined the Franciscans, a religious community founded by Saint Francis of Assisi. He moved to Paris, France, where he studied at the university. He wrote about God and became known for his great love of God. He kept a large crucifix on his desk. He said that he learned of all the beautiful things he wrote about God from Jesus, his only teacher. He also wrote a biography of Saint Francis of Assisi. Bonaventure's books made him famous, but he remained humble. In 1273, Bonaventure was made a cardinal. His knowledge and wisdom helped the pope and bishops. Saint Bonaventure University in Olean, New York, was named in honor of the saint. His feast day is July 15.

↳ DISCIPLE CHALLENGE

- Underline the sentence that describes the source of Bonaventure's writing.
- Circle the name of the religious community that Bonaventure joined.

Visit *Lives of the Saints* on **www.webelieveweb.com** to find out more about other saints and holy people.

Devereux Hall on the campus of St. Bonaventure University, Olean, New York

What's *the* Word?

The Book of Proverbs, one of the wisdom books of the Old Testament, gives advice on how to live. Read the following passage and explain its meaning.

"Rich and poor have a common bond:
the LORD is the maker of all." (Proverbs 22:2)

_____

_____

_____

_____

Take Home

As a family, read the story of Job found on page 201. Talk about Job's sufferings and his faithfulness. What situation in today's world reminds you of the story of Job?

_____

_____

_____

CHAPTER TEST

Write the letter that best defines each term.

1. _____ hope

2. _____ lamentation

3. _____ proverb

4. _____ superstition

a. false belief that living creatures or things possess powers that in fact they do not have

b. the Hebrew name for the first five books of the Old Testament

c. a gift from God that enables us to trust in God's promise to be with us always

d. a sorrow expressed in the form of a poem

e. a brief saying that gives wise advice

Short Answers

5. How are the messages of the prophets Ezekiel and Jeremiah similar?

_____

6. Name one important change that took place while God's people were exiled in Babylon.

_____

7. What was the outcome of the third stage in God's plan for the return of the exiled people to Judah?

_____

8. Name three wisdom books of the Old Testament that give practical guidance on how to live.

_____

Write a paragraph to answer this question.

9–10. According to Isaiah of Babylon, how will God save his people?

_____

_____

_____

_____

A Strong People

18

✝ We Gather in Prayer

Leader: The wise walk in the ways of the Lord. They listen to the messages that God sends them.

Let us listen to these words of wisdom from Scripture.

Reader 1: "He who walks honestly walks securely, but he whose ways are crooked will fare badly."
(Proverbs 10:9)

All: Lord, give us wisdom to speak and act with honesty.

Reader 2: "Hatred stirs up disputes, but love covers all offenses."
(Proverbs 10:12)

All: Lord, give us wisdom to grow in love for all people.

Reader 3: "Better a little with virtue, than a large income with injustice."
(Proverbs 16:8)

All: Lord, give us wisdom to act justly and with compassion.

Reader 4: "He sins who despises the hungry; but happy is he who is kind to the poor!"
(Proverbs 14:21)

All: Lord, give us wisdom to find and serve you in all our brothers and sisters.

Reader 5: "A faithful friend is a sturdy shelter; he who finds one finds a treasure."
(Sirach 6:14)

All: Lord, give us wisdom to be faithful and true friends to others.

Reader 6: "A cheerful glance brings joy to the heart; good news invigorates the bones."
(Proverbs 15:30)

All: Lord, give us wisdom to understand the Good News that you send to us. Let it fill us with joy!

Leader: Lord, teach us your ways. Help us grow in grace and truth. Let us pray:

All: Give us the peace of mind to accept what cannot be changed. Give us the courage to change what can be changed. And give us the wisdom to know the one from the other. Amen.

The Jews lived and worshiped together.

WE GATHER

✝ *We will go up to the house of the Lord.*

Think of a book, television show, or movie that contains an important message for people.
What is the message?
How is the message communicated?

WE BELIEVE

As we have seen, each of the prophets had a message for God's people. Through the prophets, God showed the people love and concern. Ezra was a priest who also helped God's people. He called them back to faithfulness to God's laws.

The prophets supported Ezra's reforms. One of these prophets was known as Isaiah of Judah. His message, the third prophetic message in the Book of Isaiah, can still be read in Chapters 56—66 of that book.

Like Ezra, Isaiah focused on true worship. However, Isaiah made a connection between worship and the fair and just treatment of others. Isaiah linked praising God and social justice. Isaiah called the people to care for the needs of all those who suffered. Worship, he said, must lead people to act with justice or it is meaningless. Isaiah told the people that since they had been faithful to God during their exile in Babylon, God would restore them to their former glory, and they would be a light to all nations. Isaiah said,
"Rise up in splendor! Your light has come,
   the glory of the Lord shines upon you."
(Isaiah 60:1)

Other Biblical Writings The Book of Malachi is a short prophetic book, and is the message of a person who goes by the title Malachi, meaning "my messenger." He called the people to worship God and to be just. He foresaw a day when God would come to judge his people. He mentioned a messenger who would prepare the way for repentance and true worship. We read about such a messenger in the Gospel of Matthew when John the Baptist appears in Judea:

"A voice of one crying out in the desert,
'Prepare the way of the Lord,
   make straight his paths.'" (Matthew 3:3)

The Book of Obadiah reminds us that God is just. This book was written at a time when the Jewish People were having problems with the Edomites. Edom was a small area to the southeast of Judah. The people living in Edom worshiped false gods. During the Jewish return from Babylon, the Edomites started to settle in southern Judah and this caused God's people many problems. The Book of Obadiah presents the hope for the survival of the Jewish People and the return of the kingdom begun by David.

The Book of Joel uses images to show the people the need for true repentance.
"Rend your hearts, not your garments,
   and return to the LORD, your God" (Joel 2:13),
the prophet insists. He tells the people that only in this way will Israel be restored to God's favor.

The Book of Daniel gives insight into the long years of Babylonian exile and Persian domination. Stories about Daniel and his companions convey a religious message. These stories express hope and tell of the importance of behavior that is acceptable to the Lord. They show that God's people are able to be faithful to their religious traditions even in a foreign land. They also demonstrate that God is always at work protecting his people, whatever happens to them.

The Book of Esther, like the Book of Daniel, is a kind of historical romance. It is a mixture of fact and fiction designed to offer hope and instruction to a defeated people.

Mordecai wrote a letter to Jews everywhere telling them of these events. He asked them to mark this day when God delivered the Jews from destruction. This day would be celebrated by a new festival—the feast of Purim. Jews today continue to celebrate this feast recalling that through God's help Esther saved God's people.

WE RESPOND

Throughout history God has worked through his people. What are some ways that God works through people

in your family?

_____

_____

in your parish?

_____

_____

in your city or town?

_____

_____

in your state or country?

_____

_____

in the world?

_____

_____

Esther appeals to the king of Persia. A page from the Megillat—The Book of Esther, 18th century.

Esther was a virtuous Jewish girl. She was also married to the king of Persia. The king appointed Esther's guardian, Mordecai, to a high office. When Mordecai displeased Haman, a Persian nobleman, Haman plotted to destroy Mordecai and all the other Jews in the Persian empire. Haman convinced the king that the Jews were traitors because they lived apart and worshiped the one true God. The king agreed that the Jews should be killed and the day of this terrible event would be decided by casting lots, or in Hebrew, *purim*.

Mordecai begged Esther for help. Esther prayed and fasted and, then at great risk to herself, appealed to the king to save the Jews. God heard Esther's prayer. The king spared the Jews.

God continued to work through his people.

WE GATHER

✝ *God, help us to see your work in our lives.*

What are some favorite stories from your childhood? Are they about people you know and things that happened, or are they from books that you have read?

Why did you enjoy these stories?

WE BELIEVE

Storytelling is an important way that the biblical writers help people to understand their relationship with God. The stories in the Bible are sometimes a part of historical or prophetic books. Other times the story is recorded in a specific book of the Bible— often bearing the name of a character in the story. Either way the stories contain symbolic, interesting characters who deal with the issue of God's providence. Providence is God's constant care for and protection of his people.

The Story of Tobit   Tobit was a wealthy Jew living in Nineveh, Assyria. His story is recorded in the Book of Tobit. When Tobit had financial losses and then became blind, he prayed that God would let him die because he was so miserable. Tobit sent his son Tobiah to Media, a Persian province, to collect a large sum of money that was owed to him.

Meanwhile, a young woman named Sarah lived in Media. She too was very sad. Every one of the seven husbands that she had married had died. God decided to send the angel Raphael in disguise to help Tobit, Tobiah, and Sarah.

Raphael helped Tobiah recover his father's money and arranged for Tobiah to marry Sarah. Then Tobiah, Sarah, and Raphael returned to Nineveh. There Raphael showed

Tobiah how to cure his father's blindness. Finally Raphael revealed his true identity and returned to Heaven. Tobit then sang a beautiful hymn. His song began,
"Blessed be God who lives forever,
    because his kingdom lasts for all ages"
(Tobit 13:1).
Tobit's hymn praised God for his providence.

In what ways is God present in our lives? In what ways do we praise God for his care and concern for us?

Detail of *Judith*, by Giorgione (1476–1510)

The Story of Judith   Providence is also the principal theme of the Book of Judith. As her story opens, the Jews had refused to help Assyria fight against its enemies. Thus, the king of Assyria had sent his commander-in-chief to punish the Jewish People. The Jews fought for thirty-four days protecting themselves, but eventually were ready to surrender.

In the story Judith quickly offered to rescue the Jews from danger. Her offer was accepted. After fasting and praying for God's help, Judith went to the Assyrian camp. There Judith was the last to leave a banquet at which the Assyrian commander had had too much to drink.

210

The story goes on to portray Judith as a great heroine whose brave actions rescued the Jews. So through Judith's courage, God saved his people from their enemies.

The Story of Jonah   One of the most interesting writings of the time is the short story that makes up the Book of Jonah. The story of Jonah is also known as a *parable*. A **parable** is a short story that has a message. A parable is usually about something familiar, but it is told to make a point about something else.

In the story, Jonah was called to be one of God's prophets. But he flatly refused to carry God's message of doom to the sinful city of Nineveh. Instead Jonah sailed off on a ship because he did not believe that the people of Nineveh would listen to him. While he was at sea, there was a great storm. Thinking he was bad luck, the crew threw Jonah overboard and he was swallowed by a huge fish. After three days, the fish coughed up Jonah safe and sound onto dry land. Then God sent him back to Nineveh to complete his mission.

Jonah's story is very symbolic. As Christians, it reminds us of the Resurrection. Just as God wanted Jonah to deliver a message, God sent Jesus Christ to bring his life and love to all people. And just as Jonah spent three days in the belly of the fish, Jesus Christ rose from the dead after three days in the tomb.

The people of Nineveh listened to Jonah's message and repented and God spared the city. This unexpected turn of events made Jonah angry. He complained that God should have punished the wicked people of Nineveh. God reminded Jonah that these people were also God's creation.

This story conveys a message: God extends his mercy to all who truly repent. It reminds us not to be narrow-minded but to have a tolerant attitude toward all people.

As Catholics...

Jesus often used parables in his teaching. His parables compare one thing to another or identify one thing by an example of another. For instance, Jesus used examples from nature, farming, feasts, and everyday work to describe the Kingdom of God— the power of God's love coming into the world and into our lives. Jesus also told parables to help his disciples understand God's mercy and God's justice.

With your family select one parable from Chapter 13 of the Gospel of Matthew and discuss what you think it means.

parable short story that has a message

WE RESPOND

Make a mural that illustrates the meaning of one of the stories from the Books of Tobit, Judith, and Jonah. Write a caption to explain the importance of the story today.

The Maccabees defended the Jewish faith.

WE GATHER

✝ *Jesus, our faith is in you.*

🧍 Throughout history, territories and even countries, passed from one group of people to another. Often national holidays were set up to remember these events. Make a list of these kinds of holidays. Which one is your favorite?

WE BELIEVE

The rule of Judah changed hands several times. At various times, Judah was part of different kingdoms. In 323 B.C. Judah, which was part of Palestine, came under Syrian-Mesopotamian rule. However, none of Judah's traditional political and religious arrangements changed. The Jews continued to live as they had under the Persians.

In 175 B.C., the king of Syria-Mesopotamia was warned about the Roman empire trying to take over his land. So he decided that his kingdom should be more united. He required that everyone accept the Greek culture and practice the Greek religion.

This policy split the Jewish community in Palestine. Some Jews favored the introduction of Greek culture; they were called Hellenists, or the Greek party. Others disagreed; they were the Hasidim, or the Pious party. When the king saw that his policy was being resisted, he began to persecute the Hasidim. He also captured Jerusalem, removed the high priest, and damaged the Temple.

This caused a rebellion in 167 B.C. It was led by a man called Mattathias. The events of this rebellion were recorded in the First and Second Books of Maccabees. In 166 B.C. Judas Maccabeus took charge of the revolt. The Hasidim joined Judas in rebellion against the Syrian armies and won many battles. Judas and his followers recaptured Jerusalem.

In 164 B.C. Judas cleansed the Temple and rededicated it to the worship of God. The Temple menorah, or lamp stand, was lit once again. Judas asked the people to remember this event with a festival. The festival was called the "the feast of lights" because a one-day's supply of oil in the menorah lasted for eight days. This was the origin of the festival of Hanukkah, which Jews still celebrate today. They celebrate the deeds of the people of God who refused to give up their faith.

When Judas died in battle in 160 B.C., his brother Jonathan led the people. For seventeen years they were successful in their struggle against Syria, which had been weakened by a civil war. Then Jonathan died, and his brother Simon took his place as the leader of the rebellion against the Syrian armies.

Simon took advantage of the Syrian weakness and negotiated independence for Judah. He became the country's first Jewish king since 587 B.C. Simon was also the high priest. Judah was strengthened because Simon had both civil and religious authority.

The writers of the books of Maccabees have shown us that God's providence again saved his people. The heroism and diplomacy of many men and women helped God's people survive. They could again live their faith and their covenant with God.

WE RESPOND

During the time of the Maccabees how did God provide for his people?

Illustrate ways that God provides for people today.

Judea lost its independence to Roman rule.

WE GATHER

✝ *Holy Spirit, enlighten all leaders.*

Which countries today are ruled by kings or queens? What kind of decisions do these kings and queens make for the people in their countries?

WE BELIEVE

In 134 B.C. Simon Maccabeus was killed and his son, John Hyrcanus, became king. John acquired a great deal of land in the south.

Because he was also the high priest, he insisted that the people living there worship the one true God and give up their false religious practices.

During John's reign there was disunity and fighting among the Pious party, the Hasidim. They questioned whether John had the right to the office of high priest. So different groups within the Hasidim formed. However, most Jews continued to worship at the Temple and did not join any of these groups.

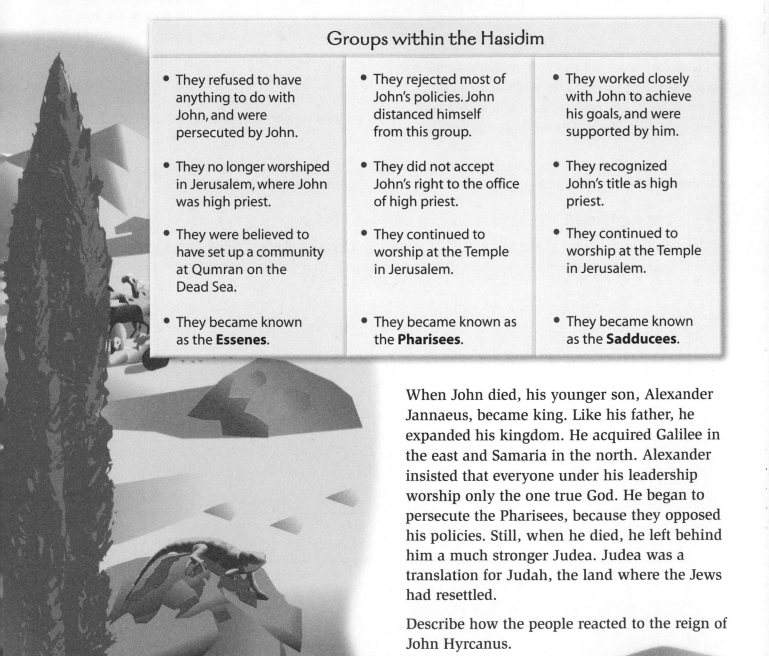

Groups within the Hasidim

• They refused to have anything to do with John, and were persecuted by John.	• They rejected most of John's policies. John distanced himself from this group.	• They worked closely with John to achieve his goals, and were supported by him.
• They no longer worshiped in Jerusalem, where John was high priest.	• They did not accept John's right to the office of high priest.	• They recognized John's title as high priest.
• They were believed to have set up a community at Qumran on the Dead Sea.	• They continued to worship at the Temple in Jerusalem.	• They continued to worship at the Temple in Jerusalem.
• They became known as the **Essenes**.	• They became known as the **Pharisees**.	• They became known as the **Sadducees**.

When John died, his younger son, Alexander Jannaeus, became king. Like his father, he expanded his kingdom. He acquired Galilee in the east and Samaria in the north. Alexander insisted that everyone under his leadership worship only the one true God. He began to persecute the Pharisees, because they opposed his policies. Still, when he died, he left behind him a much stronger Judea. Judea was a translation for Judah, the land where the Jews had resettled.

Describe how the people reacted to the reign of John Hyrcanus.

Rome Casts Its Long Shadow Over Judea

When Alexander Jannaeus died his wife, Alexandra, took over the leadership of Judea, and his oldest son became the high priest. This displeased his younger son, who selfishly wanted to be both king and high priest himself. When Alexandra died, a civil war broke out between the two brothers. Rome sensed the trouble in Judea and decided to get involved.

In 63 B.C. the Senate, the governing body in Rome, decided to send its most able general, Pompey the Great, to settle matters in the East. By this time Syria-Mesopotamia had fallen apart, and Rome had extended its territory into Asia Minor and elsewhere. Pompey made what remained of Syria-Mesopotamia a Roman province. He filled it with Roman troops. He also tried to end the civil war in Judea. Pompey invaded Judea, captured Jerusalem, and brought the kingdom of Judea under Roman rule. This marked the end of the kingdom, as well as the end of Jewish independence for over two thousand years.

The next thirty-three years or so saw a confused struggle for power, not only in Judea but also in Rome. During these conflicts, many Jews and many Romans, including Pompey himself, were killed.

Herod Rules in Judea

When peace returned in 30 B.C., Judea found itself under Roman rule. Rome gave power in Judea to a complete outsider, a man known to history as Herod the Great. Herod was a descendant of one of the families from the southern lands that had been forced by John Hyrcanus to accept the one true God. For that reason many Jews doubted whether Herod was a Jew at all.

Herod's main concern, however, was not to convince the Jews about his faithfulness to God, but to survive in a dangerous world. So Herod tried to please the all-powerful Rome, now governed by the emperor Caesar Augustus. To do this Herod stopped all local attempts to free Judea from Rome's control. He changed the office of the high priesthood from one of inheritance to one of appointment. He encouraged Greek and Roman culture in all parts of his territory. Herod also put to death all who challenged his authority, even members of his own family. The Romans were so happy with the way Herod was ruling that they made him king of Judea.

In order to have the money for his programs and to pay the huge amounts of money demanded by Rome, Herod also imposed heavy taxes on the people of Judea. Thus he was hated by many Jews and admired by most Romans.

Why was Herod hated by the Jews and admired by the Romans?

WE RESPOND

What can leaders do to show respect for the religious beliefs of their citizens? How can we show that we respect the religious beliefs of others?

215

PROJECT

Pray Learn Celebrate Share Choose Live

Show What *you* Know Use the clues to complete the chart.

Clue	Your Answer
Jewish feast recalling that through God's help Esther saved God's people	
the country defeated by the actions of Judith	
the angel that helped Tobit, Tobiah, and Sarah	
he became king of Judah (Judea) when his father, John Hyrcanus, died	
the place of exile that is the setting of the Book of Daniel	
Hanukkah is "the feast of _____"	
Hasidim group that was persecuted by John Hyrcanus, and believed to have set up a community at Qumran on the Dead Sea	

↳ **DISCIPLE CHALLENGE** Look over your answers.

• Then, circle the first letter of each answer.

• Use the circled letters to write the **Key Word**:

___ ___ ___ ___ ___ ___ ___

The story of Jonah is a parable. What is its message?

_____

_____

Question Corner

You may have heard the saying, "When the going gets tough, the tough get going!" What helps you get "going" when the "going is tough"? Check all that apply.

❑ determination

❑ family and friends

❑ faith in God

❑ _____

Fast Facts

The phrase, "the whole megillah," comes from the Jewish feast of Purim. *Megillah* is the Hebrew word for "scroll." The scroll containing the Book of Esther is read in its entirety in the synagogue on Purim. So the phrase "the whole megillah" has come to mean a long, complicated story.

DISCIPLE

Pray
Learn
Celebrate
Share
Choose
Live

Saint Stories

Saint Genevieve was born in the fifth century in a small village near Paris. When she was fifteen she dedicated her life to God. After the death of her parents, she lived with her godmother in Paris. There she prayed every day and worked hard to care for those in need. Genevieve grew closer to Jesus and wanted to share his goodness with others. She became well known for her courage, faith, and just ways. Once she convinced the people of Paris to trust in God and remain in the city when an enemy attack was feared. She had them fast and pray to show their faith. Paris was spared! She is the patron saint of Paris. Her feast day is January 3.

↳ DISCIPLE CHALLENGE

- Underline the phrase that describes the characteristics for which Genevieve became well known.

- Circle the name of the city for which Genevieve is patron saint.

Visit *Lives of the Saints* on **www.webelieveweb.com** to find out more about other saints and holy people.

What Would you do?

Daniel, Esther, and Tobit remained faithful to God in lands where people did not know God. What if you lived among people that did not share your faith? How would you continue to live your faith and remember your relationship with God?

_____

_____

_____

Take Home

Within a home, everyone's schedule may be so full that it can be difficult to find enough time to eat a meal together, let alone sit down to talk.

This week, plan some "family time" to do something together. Attend Mass together and share a meal afterward. Make time to really "connect" with one another.

Underline the correct answer.

1. The prophet (**Isaiah/Malachi**) foresaw a day when God would come to judge his people, and mentioned a messenger who would prepare the way for repentance and true worship.

2. The Book of (**Obadiah/Daniel**) contains stories that express hope and tell of the importance of behavior that is acceptable to the Lord.

3. The Book of (**Tobit/Judith**) describes how on one occasion God rescued the Jews from their enemies through one person's courage.

4. The writers of the Books of the (**Maccabees/Romans**) show us that God's providence saved his people, and allowed them to again follow their faith.

Short Answers

5. What does the Jewish feast of Purim celebrate?

_____

6. What is God's providence?

_____

7. How did Judea lose its independence to Roman rule?

_____

8. What does the Jewish feast of Hanukkah celebrate?

_____

Write a paragraph to answer this question.

9–10. Why is the story of Jonah considered to be a parable? How is it symbolic of the Resurrection of Christ?

_____

_____

_____

_____

God Fulfills His Promise

✝ We Gather in Prayer

🎵 Christ, Be Our Light

Refrain:

Christ, be our light!
Shine in our hearts.
Shine through the darkness.
Christ, be our light!
Shine in your church gathered today.

Longing for light, we wait in darkness.
Longing for truth, we turn to you.
Make us your own, your holy people,
light for the world to see. (Refrain)

Reader: The words of Isaiah the prophet are repeated as Saint Mark writes about the mission of John the Baptist.

A reading from the holy Gospel according to Mark

All: Glory to you, Lord.

Reader: "Behold, I am sending my messenger
    ahead of you;
    he will prepare your way.
A voice of one crying out in the desert:
    'Prepare the way of the Lord,
        make straight his paths.'"
(Mark 1:2–3)

The Gospel of the Lord.

All: Praise to you, Lord Jesus Christ.

Refrain:

Christ, be our light!
Shine in our hearts.
Shine through the darkness.
Christ, be our light!
Shine in your church gathered today.

Longing for peace, our world is troubled.
Longing for hope, many despair.
Your word alone has pow'r to save us.
Make us your living voice. (Refrain)

A painting from the *Annunciation Series*, by Maria Pia Marrella, 1995.

Mary is blessed by God.

WE GATHER

✝ *Hail Mary, full of grace, pray for us.*

What is the most important thing that has happened to you?

What do you consider the most important event in history? Why?

WE BELIEVE

During the last year or two of King Herod's reign over Judea, the most important event in the history of salvation took place. The world was changed when an angel of God was sent to the town of Nazareth in Galilee. The angel gave a message to a young girl named Mary, who was engaged to Joseph. Joseph was a descendant of King David. Joseph's ancestry could be traced back through the generations to Abraham, the father of God's Chosen People.

The angel said to Mary, "Hail, favored one! The Lord is with you" (Luke 1:28). When the angel saw that Mary was frightened, he continued, "Do not be afraid, Mary, for you have found favor with God. Behold, you will conceive in your womb and bear a son, and you shall name him Jesus. He will be great and will be called Son of the Most High, and the Lord God will give him the throne of David his father, and he will rule over the house of Jacob forever, and of his kingdom there will be no end" (Luke 1:30–33).

Mary did not understand how all of this would happen to her. She was not even married yet. But the angel explained, "The holy Spirit will come upon you, and the power of the Most High will overshadow you. Therefore the child to be born will be called holy, the Son of God" (Luke 1:35).

Take a moment to imagine how Mary must have felt.

The angel also told Mary that her relative Elizabeth would conceive a child. Elizabeth had never been able to have a child, and she was now very old. But the angel said that nothing was impossible with God.

Mary spoke to the angel saying, "Behold, I am the handmaid of the Lord. May it be done to me according to your word" (Luke 1:38). Mary's words showed her complete faith in God and her choice to accept and follow God's plan. The fulfillment of all that God had promised through the prophets had now begun. The long-awaited Messiah, the Savior of all people, would soon come into the world.

Joseph and Mary Mary was blessed by God. The child that she had conceived was the Son of God. Through Mary, God the Son, the Second Person of the Blessed Trinity, would become one of us. Joseph was unaware that this was part of God's plan. So Joseph was going to leave Mary quietly. Then an angel of the Lord came to Joseph in a dream. The angel said, "Joseph, son of David, do not be afraid to take Mary your wife into your home. For it is through the holy Spirit that this child has been conceived in her. She will bear a son and you are to name him Jesus, because he will save his people from their sins" (Matthew 1:20–21).

When Joseph woke up he realized what had been revealed to him. Like Mary, Joseph did what the Lord asked of him. He welcomed Mary into his home. He protected her and cared for her and for the son that she was now carrying within her.

What did the angel tell Joseph? How did Joseph respond? How do you think he felt?

WE RESPOND

Imagine that you have been asked to announce the coming of God's Son. Design a television news alert, a press release, or an Internet banner advertisement to share the Good News. Share your design with a partner; then discuss how you think people would react to the news.

Mary and Elizabeth had special roles in God's plan.

WE GATHER

✝ *We proclaim the greatness of the Lord.*

Talk about some ways that your family shares good news.

WE BELIEVE

Throughout the history of the Jewish People, God had called many women to help his people to grow strong and faithful. Now he called Mary and Elizabeth. God had special work for these two women. They had important roles in God's plan to save his people.

After the angel's visit to her, Mary began her journey to see her relatives Elizabeth and Zechariah. Zechariah had been visited by an angel, too. The angel told Zechariah that his wife, Elizabeth, would have a child and the child should be named John. Because Zechariah did not believe that this could happen, he lost his ability to speak. The angel told him that he would not speak again until his son was born.

When Mary arrived at Zechariah's house she greeted Elizabeth. The child that Elizabeth was carrying moved within her in the presence of Mary and her unborn child. Filled with the Holy Spirit and recognizing the presence of God, Elizabeth said, "Most blessed are you among women, and blessed is the fruit of your womb. And how does this happen to me, that the mother of my Lord should come to me? For at the moment the sound of your greeting reached my ears, the infant in my womb leaped for joy. Blessed are you who believed that what was spoken to you by the Lord would be fulfilled" (Luke 1:42–45).

What do Elizabeth's words tell us about Mary?

The Visitation, Franco-Flemish school, 15th century

Mary responded to Elizabeth's joyful words. As a servant of the Lord, Mary praised God in a song. Like Miriam and Hannah before her, Mary showed her joy and wonder at the fact that God had chosen her to bring about the fulfillment of his promises. Here is part of Mary's song of praise to God, or her canticle. The whole song, known as the *Magnificat*, can be found on page 326.

"My soul proclaims the greatness of the Lord;
    my spirit rejoices in God my savior.
For he has looked upon his handmaid's
        lowliness;
    behold, from now on will all ages call me
    blessed.
The Mighty One has done great things for
    me, and holy is his name." (Luke 1:46–49)

Mary stayed with Elizabeth and Zechariah for about three months. Then she traveled home again.

John's Birth   When Elizabeth gave birth to a son, she, Zechariah, and all their relatives and friends rejoiced. When it was time to name the child, everyone thought that he would be called Zechariah. But his father wrote on a tablet "John is his name" (Luke 1:63). It was then that Zechariah was able to speak again. All his relatives and neighbors wondered "'What, then, will this child be?' For surely the hand of the Lord was with him" (Luke 1:66).

Then Zechariah, filled with the Holy Spirit, spoke. Here is part of his prophesy.

"Blessed be the Lord, the God of Israel,
    for he has visited and brought redemption
        to his people . . .
And you, child, will be called prophet of the
    Most High,
    for you will go before the Lord to prepare
    his ways,

to give his people knowledge of salvation
    through the forgiveness of their sins . . .
    to guide our feet into the path of peace."
(Luke 1:68 76–77, 79)

Zechariah's prophesy is called *The Canticle of Zechariah* and can be found on page 328.

Elizabeth and Zechariah's child, John, only a baby now, would grow strong in body and spirit. John, too, would have an important part in the fulfillment of God's promise to his people. Like the prophets before him, John would prepare the way for the coming of the Messiah.

WE RESPOND

Sing together this contemporary version of the canticles of Mary and Zechariah.

🎵 Luke 1: Magnificat/Benedictus

With joyful heart I sing God's praise,
and love my Savior all my days.
God chooses me in lowliness
to be the one forever blessed.
God raised me up for all to see,
and holy is God's name to me.

To God of Israel be praise,
who saves us all from sinful ways.
From David's house and family
a Savior comes to set us free.
Our enemies we need not fear,
the prophets said, "The Lord is near!"

God the Son became man.

✝ *Jesus, save us.*

What are important things that parents can pass on to their children?

WE BELIEVE

Mary and Joseph began their life together in Nazareth, a town in Galilee. There they waited for the child to be born. They prepared for his birth and for the life that they would share with him.

God had spoken to each of them about this child. The event that was about to take place was beyond Mary and Joseph's understanding. The child who was about to be born of Mary was the Son of God.

At this time in Judea, a census, or count of the people, was being taken. Joseph and Mary went up to Bethlehem of Judea, the city of King David's birth. Joseph and Mary went there because all men had to enroll their families in the city of their ancestors, and Joseph was a descendant of David. Mary, too, was of the house of David.

It was in Bethlehem that Mary gave birth to her son. Thus, the words of the prophet Micah were fulfilled. Bethlehem is the birthplace of the "one who is to be ruler in Israel" (Micah 5:1).

Following the instructions of the angel in Joseph's dream, Mary and Joseph named the child Jesus. This name means "God saves." God the Son became one of us.
"And the Word became flesh
and made his dwelling among us."
(John 1:14)

This mystery is called the Incarnation. The **Incarnation** is the truth that the Son of God, the Second Person of the Blessed Trinity, became man.

This child of Mary, conceived by the power of the Holy Spirit, came to save people from all that would keep them from the love of God. Jesus is the Savior sent to fulfill God's promise. Jesus is true God and true man, and so he shares God's life and love with all people.

The Presentation in the Temple   Mary and Joseph followed the laws of their Jewish faith, and so they traveled to Jerusalem to present Jesus in the Temple. There they met a holy man named Simeon. "It had been revealed to him by the holy Spirit that he should not see death before he had seen the Messiah of the Lord." (Luke 2:26) When Simeon saw Jesus, he took the baby in his arms and said,

"Now, Master, you may let your servant go
   in peace, according to your word,
for my eyes have seen your salvation,
   which you prepared in sight of all the
      peoples,
a light for revelation to the Gentiles,
   and glory for your people Israel"
(Luke 2:29–32).

A prophetess named Anna witnessed all of this and gave thanks to God. She spoke about this child to all who were waiting for the fulfillment of God's promise of salvation.

Mary, Joseph, and Jesus settled in Nazareth, and Jesus grew up there with his relatives and friends. There he played, studied, and learned much from his mother and foster father. Jesus heard about his Jewish ancestors, their faith, and the ways to live out God's covenant. With his family and friends he celebrated the Jewish feasts. And on certain feasts his family traveled to the Temple in Jerusalem.

Incarnation the truth that the Son of God, the Second Person of the Blessed Trinity, became man

Luke 2:41–52

The Finding in the Temple Each year Mary and Joseph went to Jerusalem to celebrate the feast of Passover. When Jesus was twelve years old, he went up to Jerusalem with them. As they were returning home to Nazareth, Jesus remained behind in Jerusalem. But Mary and Joseph did not know this. They thought he was among their relatives and acquaintances. When they could not find him, they went back to Jerusalem to look for him.

They found him three days later, listening and questioning the teachers. People were astounded by his knowledge and understanding. His parents were astounded, too, but they were very anxious. Jesus said that they should have known that he was in his Father's house. "But they did not understand what he said to them. He went down with them and came to Nazareth, and was obedient to them; and his mother kept all these things in her heart. And Jesus advanced [in] wisdom and age and favor before God and man" (Luke 2:50–52).

This is one of the few accounts we have of Jesus' early years. We learn from it that Jesus was a faithful, obedient Jewish child. We also see that he had deep understanding and knowledge of God. In his Father's house, meaning the house of God, Jesus did his Father's work. This would be a theme throughout Jesus' life.

How do you think Mary and Joseph felt when they could not find Jesus? Why?

WE RESPOND

Role-play the story of Mary, Joseph, and Jesus during their visit to Jerusalem to celebrate Passover as found in Luke 2:41–52. Characters will include: a narrator, Mary, Joseph, Jesus (12 years old), friends and relatives, and teachers in the Temple.

Write your own script and present your play.

John prepared the way for Jesus.

WE GATHER

✝ *Glory to the Father, and to the Son, and to the Holy Spirit.*

What are some reasons that groups of people do not get along? What can happen because of these conflicts?

WE BELIEVE

From the Gospels we do not learn much about Jesus' life until he was about thirty years old. During these "hidden" years, as they are called, things changed in Judea.

When Herod the Great, king of Judea, died his relatives could not agree on his successor. So Caesar Augustus in Rome was called upon to settle the argument. He used this opportunity to weaken Judea by dividing Herod's territories among his sons Archelaus, Philip, and Herod Antipas. None of Herod's children were pleased with this division of their father's territory.

When Archelaus turned out to be a terrible leader, Augustus removed him and decided that Rome would rule this part of Herod's old kingdom. Caesar Augustus set up a procurator, a kind of deputy governor. For about forty years, Philip and Herod Antipas continued to lead their territories. But Rome was slowly taking over complete control of Judea, which the Romans called Palestine.

Judea was a divided country. In Judea the Jews were only a part of the population now. Some regions were ruled directly by Rome, and others were governed by Jewish princes who were reporting to the Romans. Therefore, relations between Rome and the Jews were very strained. In fact, many of the Jews came to distrust and dislike the Romans. Rome worried about the possibility of new revolts by the Jews.

Religious tensions were also a problem in Judea at this time. The Jews were fearful that they would not be allowed to keep the Law of Moses. They feared that the Romans would interfere with their worship and observance of the covenant with God. Religious divisions, problems between the rich and the poor, and many other social injustices were widespread. It was in these troubled times that " . . . the word of God came to John the son of Zechariah in the desert" (Luke 3:2).

John began to preach and to prophesy throughout the land. He urged the people to repent and to ask God for forgiveness. He encouraged them to change their lives and to get ready for the coming of the Messiah, the Anointed One, the one foretold by the prophets. Since people came to be baptized by him in the Jordan River, he was known as John the Baptist.

Jesus' Baptism from the TV mini series, *Jesus of Nazareth* (1977).

This baptism by John showed people's willingness to change their lives. "And the crowds asked him, 'What then should we do?' He said to them in reply, 'Whoever has two cloaks should share with the person who has none. And whoever has food should do likewise.' Even tax collectors came to be baptized and they said to him, 'Teacher, what should we do?' He answered them, 'Stop collecting more than what is prescribed.' Soldiers also asked him, 'And what is it that we should do?' He told them, 'Do not practice extortion, do not falsely accuse anyone, and be satisfied with your wages.'" (Luke 3:10–14)

John told the people, "I am baptizing you with water, but one mightier than I is coming . . . He will baptize you with the holy Spirit and fire" (Luke 3:16).

It was about this time that Jesus left Nazareth and went to the Jordan River to hear John preach and to be baptized by him. "After all the people had been baptized and Jesus also had been baptized and was praying, heaven was opened and the holy Spirit descended upon him in bodily form like a dove. And a voice came from heaven, 'You are my beloved Son; with you I am well pleased.'" (Luke 3:21–22)

Truly, Jesus is the one who is beloved by God. He is the one who offers us himself and who shows us how to love. Like John, we can prepare the way for people to welcome Jesus, too. By Baptism, each of us is called to live as one of Jesus' disciples. When we do what is right and treat others fairly and with justice, we are showing what it is to be a follower of Jesus.

WE RESPOND

Can you prepare the way for Jesus today? What will you say? What will you do? Write some ways here. Role-play one of them.

_____

_____

_____

_____

_____

Pray Learn Celebrate Share Choose Live

PROJECT

Show What *you* Know

Who am I? Write the letter that best describes the biblical character.

a. Anna

b. Elizabeth

c. John

d. Simeon

e. Zechariah

1. _____ I preached and encouraged the people to repent and to ask God for forgiveness.

2. _____ I lost my ability to speak when I did not believe the angel's announcement that I would have a son.

3. _____ I am a holy man. The Holy Spirit revealed to me that I would not see death until I had seen the Messiah of the Lord.

4. _____ I saw the presentation of Jesus in the Temple, and I spoke of him as the fulfillment of God's promise of salvation.

5. _____ I expressed joy when I recognized the presence of the God in an unborn child.

What's *the* Word?

"The angel said to them, 'Do not be afraid; for behold, I proclaim to you good news of great joy that will be for all the people. For today in the city of David a savior has been born for you who is Messiah and Lord. And this will be a sign for you: you will find an infant in swaddling clothes and lying in a manger.'" (Luke 2:10–12)

- Circle another name for Bethlehem in the passage.
- Why do you think the birth of Jesus involves so many visits from angels (to Mary, Joseph, Zechariah), and, in this passage, the shepherds?

_____

Fast Facts The accounts of Jesus' birth and childhood are called the *infancy narratives*. The infancy narratives are found in the first two chapters of the Gospels of Matthew and Luke.

DISCIPLE

Pray
Learn
Celebrate
Share
Choose
Live

More to Explore

The Liturgy of the Hours, part of the public prayer of the Church, helps us to praise God throughout the entire day. It is made up of psalms, readings from Scripture and Church teachings, hymns, and prayers. It is celebrated at various times during the day and night. At Morning Prayer, the Canticle of Zechariah is always prayed. In this canticle, Jesus is referred to as "the daybreak from on high." At Evening Prayer, the Canticle of Mary is always prayed. In this prayer we, along with Mary, praise God for all he has done for us. The Liturgy of the Hours reminds us that God is always active and present in our lives.

DISCIPLE CHALLENGE

- Underline the phrase that tells the purpose of the Liturgy of the Hours.
- Circle the phrase that describes Jesus in the Canticle of Zechariah.
- Find out more about the Liturgy of the Hours.

Pray Today

In 2005, Pope Benedict XVI presented the *Compendium of the Catechism of the Catholic Church.* He urged Catholics to learn the common prayers of the Church in Latin. Visit the *Latin Hall* on **www.weliveourfaith.com** to learn and listen to prayers of the Church in Latin.

Celebrate!

Every Sunday at Mass during the Profession of Faith, we profess our belief in the Incarnation—the truth that the Son of God, the Second Person of the Blessed Trinity became man. This week at Mass, listen closely as the words of the Creed are professed.

Take Home

When we do what is right and treat others fairly, we are showing what it is to be a follower of Jesus. Talk about our call to live as disciples, and ask your family members to share ideas for living out this call.

CHAPTER TEST

Circle the letter of the correct answer.

1. _____ told Mary that her relative Elizabeth was with child.

   a. Anna   **b.** An angel   **c.** Zechariah

2. _____ prepared the people for the Messiah.

   a. Elijah   **b.** Zechariah   **c.** John

3. Zechariah lost his ability to speak because he was _____.

   a. old   **b.** sick   **c.** unbelieving

4. _____ was a descendant of King David.

   a. Joseph   **b.** Simeon   **c.** Zechariah

Short Answers

5. What role did angels play in the coming of the Messiah?

   _____

6. Why was Jesus born in Bethlehem?

   _____

7. What is the Incarnation?

   _____

8. Why is the story of the finding of Jesus in the Temple important?

   _____

Write a paragraph to answer this question.

9–10. How was Mary blessed by God?

   _____

   _____

   _____

   _____

Our hope is the God
of mercy and forgiveness.

SEASONAL

CHAPTER 20

This chapter offers preparation for
the season of Lent.

231

The season of Lent is a period of preparation for Easter.

WE GATHER

✝ *Jesus, help us to follow in your way.*

Have you ever been on a trip away from home? Where did you go? Was this a vacation trip or was it taken for another reason? What did you learn from your travels?

WE BELIEVE

The entire season of Lent is like a pilgrimage. A pilgrimage is a trip taken to a shrine or sacred place. As Christians, a pilgrimage is a prayer journey that helps us follow Christ more closely. During Lent we focus on following Christ and thinking about the relationship that we began with him at Baptism. In Baptism we are united to Christ and to all others who are baptized. Through the waters of Baptism we die with Christ only to rise to new life with him.

Lent is a journey during which we prepare to celebrate at Easter Christ's dying and rising to new life. The entire Church takes part in this preparation through our worship and by the way we live. This season is the final time of preparation for those who will celebrate the Sacraments of Christian Initiation at Easter. These three sacraments—Baptism, Confirmation, and the Eucharist—are called the Easter Sacraments. Those who receive them will share in Jesus' Death and Resurrection and have new life in Christ. We pray for them, support them, and welcome them into our parish.

On Ash Wednesday Catholics and other Christians can receive ashes, a sign of both sorrow and hope.

232

The season of Lent begins on Ash Wednesday and ends many weeks later on Holy Thursday evening. Absence and simplicity describe the season of Lent. There are signs of this absence in our churches and in our liturgy. During the liturgy, alleluia is not said or sung nor are bells rung. Dark purple is the color used in worship, and green plants and flowers may be removed from the churches. All of these changes remind us of our need to recommit ourselves to Christ and to the Church.

They help us to prepare to renew our baptismal promises at Easter and to celebrate the new life Christ has won for us by his Cross and Resurrection.

The way we live during this season is also a sign of absence and simplicity. We are called to follow the Lenten practices of prayer, fasting, and almsgiving, or practicing works of compassion. The word *alms* comes from a Greek word meaning "compassion." Almsgiving can be the giving of time, money, or goods to those in need. Prayer, fasting, and almsgiving are always part of Christian living. However, during Lent they take on special meaning as we prepare to renew our Baptism.

Prayer

During Lent we focus on God's mercy and forgiveness. We call out to God to remember us and strengthen us to live by his laws. Lent is a good time to spend extra time in conversation with God. We may devote more time to personal prayer and to prayer with our parish community.

The Church prays especially for those who are preparing to receive the Sacraments of Christian Initiation. Many parishes gather for the Stations of the Cross and have special celebrations of the Sacrament of Penance.

Fasting

Fasting is a way to cleanse our bodies of harmful things and our hearts and minds of things that keep us from loving God and others. Fasting is also a form of penance. Doing penance helps us to turn to God and to focus on the things that are important in our lives as Christians. Doing penance is a way to show that we are sorry for our sins.

One way to fast is to give up things we enjoy, like a favorite food or activity. Catholics of a certain age are called to fast from food on Ash Wednesday and Good Friday. They are also called to give up meat on these days and on all the Fridays during Lent.

Almsgiving

During Lent we also show special concern for those in need. We follow Jesus' example of providing for the hungry and caring for the sick. We try to help other people to get the things they need and make sure that people have what is rightfully theirs.

Many parishes have food and clothing drives during this time of year. Families may participate in these drives and also volunteer at soup kitchens, visit those who are sick, and practice other works of mercy.

Stations of the Cross   In Lent, as always, we are traveling toward the happiness of living forever with God. We have many opportunities to follow in the footsteps of Jesus. One of the most famous places to follow Jesus is the land where he once walked, or the Holy Land. Through the centuries, Christians have made pilgrimages to the Holy Land. They have walked in the footsteps of Jesus along the way of the cross. Since most people could not travel to the Holy Land, Stations of the Cross began to be placed in parish churches. In this way, everyone could follow Jesus on his path from Death to Resurrection. Everyone could be a pilgrim.

Following the Stations of the Cross became a devotion that takes place often during the season of Lent. The word *station* comes from a Latin word meaning "stopping point." In a parish the stations are usually fourteen statues, pictures, or crosses placed along the walls of the church. At each station we stop, we remember, and we pray.

At each station we usually pray this way:

We adore you, O Christ,
   and we bless you.
Because by your holy cross,
   you have redeemed the world.

WE RESPOND

Break into pairs or small groups and choose one station. Using various art materials design your station and write a meditation or prayer about that station. Use this space to brainstorm your ideas.

Stations of the Cross

1. Jesus is condemned to die.
2. Jesus takes up his cross.
3. Jesus falls the first time.
4. Jesus meets his mother.
5. Simon helps Jesus carry his cross.
6. Veronica wipes the face of Jesus.
7. Jesus falls the second time.
8. Jesus meets the women of Jerusalem.
9. Jesus falls the third time.
10. Jesus is stripped of his garments.
11. Jesus is nailed to the cross.
12. Jesus dies on the cross.
13. Jesus is taken down from the cross.
14. Jesus is laid in the tomb.

✝ We Respond in Prayer

Leader: Blessed are you, Lord, God of all creation:
All: you make us hunger and thirst for holiness.

Leader: Blessed are you, Lord, God of all creation:
All: you call us to true fasting:

Leader: to set free the oppressed,
to share our bread with the hungry,
to shelter the homeless and to clothe the naked.

All: Blessed be God for ever.

Reader: A reading from the Letter of Saint Paul to the Philippians

"Whatever is true, whatever is honorable, whatever is just,
whatever is pure, whatever is lovely, whatever is gracious,
if there is any excellence and if there is anything worthy
of praise, think about these things." (Philippians 4:8)

The word of the Lord.

All: Thanks be to God.

Leader: Let us now ask forgiveness of one another and of God.

All: I confess to almighty God
and to you, my brothers and sisters,
that I have greatly sinned,
in my thoughts and in my words,
in what I have done and in what I have failed to do,
through my fault, through my fault,
through my most grievous fault;
therefore I ask blessed Mary ever-Virgin,
all the Angels and Saints,
and you, my brothers and sisters,
to pray for me to the Lord our God.
Amen.

LENT

235

PROJECT DISCIPLE

Celebrate! You have been asked to mentor a student who is younger than you. How would you explain the season of Lent to this student?

Pray Today

One traditional Lenten practice is prayer. Choose one of the seven Penitential Psalms (Psalms 6, 32, 38, 51, 102, 130, and 143) to pray during the season of Lent. Or pray one on each Friday of Lent. The message of these psalms is repentance. As you pray each psalm ask God for his help and forgiveness.

Now, pass it on!

Fast Facts

The Fourth Sunday of Lent is called Laetare Sunday. *Laetare* means "rejoice" in Latin. On Laetare Sunday, the opening prayer of the Mass and the prayer over the gifts during the Liturgy of the Eucharist speak of joy in anticipation of Easter. Rose-colored vestments may be worn by the priest to celebrate this Mass, and flowers may adorn the altar.

Laetare Rejoice

Take Home

As a family, make time to develop good spiritual habits during the Lenten season. For example: encourage daily family prayer, daily examination of conscience, weekly Bible readings, participating in the Sacrament of Penance, and the Sacrament of the Eucharist.
List other ideas here:

_____

_____

"Rejoice, O earth, in shining splendor,
radiant in the brightness of your King!
Christ has conquered! Glory fills you!
Darkness vanishes for ever!"

The Exsultet, the Easter Vigil

SEASONAL

CHAPTER 21

This chapter includes the three days from Holy
Thursday evening until Easter Sunday.

The Easter Triduum is also known as the Christian Passover.

WE GATHER

✝ *Jesus, take us with you into new life.*

Think about times when people count on a map to guide them in getting someplace. What would their experience be like without a map?

WE BELIEVE

The Easter Triduum guides us on a journey. We journey with Jesus Christ from Death to new life. When we celebrate the Easter Triduum, we are celebrating the most important three days of the year for Christians. These three days extend from the evening of Holy Thursday to the evening of Easter Sunday. They are counted as our Jewish ancestors in faith count their days—from sundown to sundown.

The liturgical celebrations of these three days are seen as one connected liturgy in which we celebrate Christ's passing from Death to new life. These days focus on the whole Paschal Mystery of Christ—his suffering, Death, Resurrection, and Ascension. Paschal comes from the word *pasch* which means "Passover." So the Paschal Mystery is the mystery of Christ's sacrifice of himself and of his passing over from Death to life.

Holy Thursday The Evening Mass of the Lord's Supper is not simply a reenactment of the events of the Last Supper when Jesus gathered to celebrate Passover with his disciples. It is a celebration of the new Passover, Christ's Body and Blood that he shared then and still shares with us today in the Eucharist. It is a celebration of the love and service Christ calls us to everyday.

During this Mass a ceremony of the washing of the feet takes place. This action commits us to follow the example of Jesus' love and service. He washed his disciples' feet as a sign of his love for them.

On Holy Thursday one way that we show our love and service for others is by contributing to a special collection for those who are in need.

Good Friday On this day we recall Jesus' suffering and Death. The celebration often takes place in the afternoon around three o'clock P.M.

We hear the Passion of Christ read from the Gospel of John, and we offer ten General Intercessions that include prayers for the whole world. We also show reverence to the cross, for upon it hung the Savior of the world. The cross is the sign of Christ's Death and of the victory he wins for us by his Death. The cross is a symbol of the salvation Jesus Christ offers to the world.

Because the Liturgy of the Eucharist is not celebrated on Good Friday, a short communion service takes place and then all depart in silence.

Holy Saturday During the day we spend time thinking and praying. We remember that Jesus died to save all people and we thank God for this gift. We pray especially for those who will celebrate the Easter Sacraments. On Sundays and very important feast days, the Church begins the liturgical celebration on the night before with a vigil.

On Holy Saturday evening we gather with our parish for the celebration of the Easter Vigil.

The Easter Vigil is the most important vigil of the year and it is the highpoint of the Triduum. It begins after sundown on the Saturday before Easter Sunday. It is a time of watchful waiting. Two beautiful symbols of our faith are a central part of this night: light and water.

Throughout the history of salvation, fire has been a symbol of the presence of God. On the night of the Easter Vigil, a fire is made outdoors or in the back of the Church. The priest prepares the Paschal candle by marking the year on it. Then the Paschal candle is lit from this new fire and the priest says, "May the light of Christ, rising in glory, dispel the darkness of our hearts and minds." The fire represents the fire of the burning bush, and the Paschal candle reminds us of the pillar of fire that accompanied the Israelites on their journey out of Egypt. The Paschal candle is more, though. It is a symbol of the risen Christ among us. It is a reminder of our own passing with Christ from Death to life, from darkness to light.

The Paschal candle is carried into the dark church with great reverence. The deacon or priest sings "Christ our light" three times. The assembly responds "Thanks be to God" each time. Often those assembled light small candles from the Paschal candle, and the light of Christ spreads throughout the whole assembly.

Then the deacon or a parish member chants the Exsultet, or Easter Proclamation. To *exult* means to "rejoice with great joy and triumph." The Exsultet is a proclamation of our Easter faith. It is like a map of the celebration of Easter. The Exsultet proclaims God's plan, and notes that we are part of that plan.

"This is our passover feast," we hear. We also hear, "This is the night when first you saved our fathers: you freed the people of Israel from their slavery."

The waters of the Red Sea remind us of the waters of Baptism. Most importantly, we hear,

"This is the night when
    Jesus Christ
    broke the chains of death
    and rose triumphant
        from the grave."

This is the most beautiful and exciting night of the year! It is fitting that on this night new members of the Church are baptized, confirmed, and receive the Eucharist for the first time.

Water is another symbol that is very important to the Easter Vigil. It is important to the newly baptized and to all of us who renew our baptismal promises and are sprinkled with water. It is a symbol of our new Easter life. We, too, are risen with Christ.

Easter Sunday   Our joy continues at the Easter Sunday Eucharist as we pray:

"May the risen Lord
breathe on our minds
    and open our eyes
that we may know him in the
    breaking of bread,
and follow him in his risen life."

WE RESPOND

What can you do to help others to believe and experience the new life that comes from Christ?

How can you spread the light of Christ in your home? your school? your parish? the world?

✝ We Respond in Prayer

Leader: Let us rejoice in the Resurrection of Jesus.

🎵 **Resucitó/He Is Risen**

Refrain

Resucitó, resucitó, resucitó, aleluya.
Aleluya, aleluya, aleluya, resucitó.
(He is risen, alleluia.)

Leader: Let us pray the great Easter Proclamation.

Group 1: "Rejoice, heavenly powers! Sing, choirs of angels!
Exult, all creation around God's throne!
Jesus Christ, our King, is risen!
Sound the trumpet of salvation!"

All: (*Sing Refrain.*)

Group 2: "Rejoice, O earth, in shining splendor,
radiant in the brightness of your King!
Christ has conquered! Glory fills you!
Darkness vanishes for ever!"

All: (*Sing Refrain.*)

Group 3: "Rejoice, O Mother Church! Exult in glory!
The risen Savior shines upon you!
Let this place resound with joy,
echoing the mighty song of all God's people!"

All: (*Sing Refrain.*)

Group 4: "Most blessed of all nights, chosen by
God to see Christ rising from the dead!

Of this night scripture says:
'The night will be as clear as day:
it will become my light, my joy.'"

All: (*Sing Refrain.*)

Pray Learn Celebrate Share Choose Live

PROJECT DISCIPLE

Celebrate!

Write the day of the Triduum (HT = Holy Thursday, GF = Good Friday, HSE = Holy Saturday Evening) that corresponds to each statement.

1. _____ The priest prepares the Paschal Candle by marking the year on it, and the candle is lit and carried into the dark church with great reverence.

2. _____ Around 3P.M. a celebration often takes place at which we recall Jesus' suffering and Death.

3. _____ At an evening Mass we celebrate the events of the Last Supper—when Jesus gathered to celebrate Passover with his disciples.

4. _____ During Mass a ceremony of the washing of feet takes place.

5. _____ A short communion service takes place because the Liturgy of the Eucharist is not celebrated.

6. _____ New members of the Church are baptized, confirmed, and receive the Eucharist for the first time.

7. _____ The Easter Vigil is celebrated after sundown.

8. _____ We hear the Passion of Christ read from the Gospel of John, offer ten general intercessions for the whole world, and show reverence to the cross.

What's the Word?

"You call me 'teacher' and 'master,' and rightly so, for indeed I am. If I, therefore, the master and teacher, have washed your feet, you ought to wash one another's feet. I have given you a model to follow, so that as I have done for you, you should also do." (John 13:13–15)

↳ **DISCIPLE CHALLENGE**

- Circle the names the disciples use for Jesus.
- Why does Jesus ask his disciples to wash one another's feet?

Take Home

One of the most ancient traditions of the Catholic Church is the veneration of the cross on Good Friday. The cross is the sign not only of Christ's Death, but also of the victory Christ won for all humankind by his Death. Place a cross or crucifix in a prominent place in your home. Remember to always treat this symbol of our faith with reverence.

Grade 6 Unit 3
UNIT TEST

Choose a word from the box that best completes each sentence.

1. Jesus' birth in the town of Bethlehem in Judea fulfilled the words of

   the prophet _____ .

2. The great prophet _____ told King Hezekiah that God
   would not allow foreign nations to destroy Judah; he would always
   be with the people of Judah.

3. _____ , the son of Elizabeth and Zechariah, was sent
   by God like the prophets before him to prepare the way for the coming
   of the Messiah.

4. God called the prophet _____ from the southern
   kingdom of Judah to go to the northern kingdom of Israel and tell
   the people there to live justly or their kingdom would be destroyed.

5. King _____ began a reform of religious practices in
   Judah, banned pagan practices, and returned true worship to the
   Temple in Jerusalem.

6. The prophet-priest _____ told the people that God
   would purify those who remained true to him and would shepherd
   them back from exile to the promised land.

7. In the Book of _____ we are reminded that God alone
   can provide lasting happiness.

8. When Jews celebrate the festival of _____ , they recall
   that through God's help Esther saved God's people.

9. In the Book of _____ we read about God's rescue of his
   people through the brave actions of a remarkable woman.

Judith

Amos

Ecclesiastes

Ezekiel

Herod

Isaiah

John

Josiah

Malachi

Micah

Purim

continued on next page

Underline the correct answer.

10. God sent the prophet **(Jonah/Elijah)** to the northern kingdom of Israel to show the people that the gods worshiped by King Ahab were false gods.

11. The prophet **(Hezekiah/Jeremiah)** was accused of blasphemy, rejected, and imprisoned, but he never lost hope because he knew that God is always with his people.

12. The prophet Elijah anointed a man named **(Elisha/Isaiah)** to carry on his work among God's people.

13. When Judah was invaded a third time, the city of Jerusalem—including the Temple—was destroyed and even more people were deported to **(Babylon/Assyria)**.

14. The Book of **(Wisdom/Lamentations)** contains five poems describing the destruction of the kingdom of Judah and the sufferings of the people.

15. When Judas **(Maccabeus/Malachi)** rededicated the Temple, he asked the people to remember the event with a "feast of lights" that Jews celebrate today as the festival of Hanukkah.

16. During **(King Haman's/Herod's)** reign over Judea, an angel of God was sent to Mary to tell her she would be the Mother of the Son of God.

Write a paragraph to answer each question.

17–18. In the Book of Jonah we read of a prophet who is swallowed by a huge fish. What symbolic meaning does the story of Jonah have for us as Christians?

_____

_____

_____

_____

19–20. The prophet Isaiah, preaching to God's people in exile in Babylon, said that salvation would come only through the suffering of a servant of the Lord—a servant without sin. How are these words of Isaiah's important to Christians?

_____

_____

_____

_____

Witness

Part 1   I Open My Heart

As followers of Jesus, we are called to witness to him in the world. We are called to live as Jesus taught us and to choose good and avoid evil. Then we can spread the Good News of Jesus Christ and share God's love with others. We do this through witnessing to our Catholic faith in our words, our actions, and our decisions.

What are some ways you can share God's love through your words and actions? Draw your own image that depicts how you will witness and share the Good News.

Good News

Witness

Part 2 We Come Together for Prayer

Leader: In Baptism, we declare our beliefs and promise to live holy lives. Let us renew our baptismal commitment. Through the Paschal Mystery we have been buried with Christ in Baptism, so that we may walk with him in newness of life. And so, let us renew the promises of Holy Baptism, by which we once renounced Satan and his works and promised to serve God in the holy Catholic Church. And so I ask you:

Leader: Do you renounce sin, so as to live in the freedom of the children of God?

All: I do.

Leader: Do you renounce the lure of evil, so that sin may have no mastery over you?

All: I do.

Leader: Do you renounce Satan, the author and prince of sin?

All: I do.

Leader: Do you believe in God, the Father almighty, Creator of heaven and earth?

All: I do.

Leader: Do you believe in Jesus Christ, his only Son, our Lord, who was born of the Virgin Mary, suffered death and was buried, rose again from the dead and is seated at the right hand of the Father?

All: I do.

Leader: Do you believe in the Holy Spirit, the holy Catholic Church, the communion of saints, the forgiveness of sins, the resurrection of the body, and life everlasting?

All: I do.

Leader: And may almighty God, the Father of our Lord Jesus Christ, who has given us new birth by water and the Holy Spirit and bestowed on us forgiveness of our sins, keep us by his grace, in Christ Jesus our Lord, for eternal life.

All: Amen

(Adapted from the Renewal of Baptismal Promises, *Rite of Confirmation*)

Witness

Part 3 I Cherish God's Word

"You are the light of the world. A city set on a mountain cannot be hidden. Nor do they light a lamp and then put it under a bushel basket; it is set on a lampstand, where it gives light to all in the house. Just so, your light must shine before others, that they may see your good deeds and glorify your heavenly Father." (Matthew 5:14–16)

READ the quotation from Scripture. Read slowly. Pay close attention to what you are reading.

REFLECT on what you read. Think about:

- How can you be a light to others?
- Why do people hide their light?
- Whose witness has been a light for you?

SHARE your thoughts and feelings with God in prayer. Let your thoughts and feelings come naturally. Speak to God as a friend.

CONTEMPLATE, or sit quietly and allow your attention to remain focused on God's Word in the Scripture passage from the Gospel of Matthew above.

Saint-Paul de Vence, an historical hilltop village in France

Witness

Part 4 I Value My Catholic Faith

Write down your insights and observations from the group discussion activity you complete during this part of the retreat. Also write down any important points made during the discussion.

_____

_____

_____

_____

_____

_____

Following the discussion, complete these statements:

Two things I learned from my classmates' insights are

_____

_____

The discussion was helpful to me in the following ways:

_____

_____

I now understand that my call to be a witness and an evangelizer means

_____

_____

One way I will be more open to being a witness among my friends and family is

_____

_____

Witness

Part 5 I Celebrate Catholic Identity

After listening to the ideas your group has suggested, complete each sentence by writing ways you will be a witness to Jesus Christ at home, at school, or in your neighborhood.

I will witness in words by

_____

_____

_____

I will witness in actions by

_____

_____

_____

Now write a sentence stating your commitment to follow through on these actions.

My commitment:

_____

_____

_____

_____

_____

_____

Share your plan with your family members. Ask them to help you in carrying out your plan.

Witness

Part 6 I Honor My Catholic Identity

Leader: Lord God, guide us in proclaiming your Kingdom in this world. Give us the words to teach about you. Grant us courage to make you known through our actions. Open our hearts to learn about you from others.

Reader: "You are the light of the world." (Matthew 5:14)

Reflection (Leader): Because we are baptized into Christ, we are called to reflect his light in the world. Jesus taught us to reflect his light when he taught the Commandments, the Beatitudes, the Great Commandment, and the Law of Love. Living these and all that Jesus taught is the way we witness to him.

Leader: That we may teach about God through our words.

All: Lord, help us be your light.

Leader: That we may teach about God through our works.

All: Lord, help us be your light.

Leader: That we may learn about God from others, especially those whom we serve.

All: Lord, help us be your light.

Leader: Let us close by praying together in the words Jesus taught us.

(All join together in praying the Lord's Prayer.)

All: Our Father, who art in heaven,
hallowed be thy name;
thy kingdom come;
thy will be done on earth
   as it is in heaven.
Give us this day our daily bread;
and forgive us our trespasses
as we forgive those
   who trespass against us;
and lead us not into temptation,
but deliver us from evil. Amen.

Catholic Identity Retreat

Bringing the Retreat Home

Witness

Retreat Recap

Review the pages of your child's *Celebrating Catholic Identity: Morality* retreat. Ask your child to tell you about the retreat. Talk about the following:

- Through our Baptism, we are called to witness to our faith.
- We are called to evangelize: to spread the Good News of Jesus Christ and share God's love with others.
- We can witness through our words, our actions, and our decisions.

Light of the World

Complete Part 3 of your child's retreat together as a family. The Scripture passage is Jesus' declaration that we are light for the world. Think about and discuss the last question, *Whose witness has been a light for you?* Together pray for the strength and courage to follow Jesus and bring his light to others.

Take a Moment

Talk with your child about ways that you can evangelize others through your witness in your everyday life. Each of you should choose one specific situation in your life through which you will try to evangelize.

Family Prayer

Pray together the following prayer for evangelization.

*O*pen my heart to hear the Gospel and grant me the confidence to proclaim the Good News to others.

Pour out your Spirit, so that I might be strengthened to go forth and witness to the Gospel in my everyday life through my words and actions.
Amen.

(From the "Prayer for the New Evangelization," United States Conference of Catholic Bishops)

Christ Appearing to His Disciples at the Mount of Galilee, by Duccio di Buoninsegna (1260–1319)

For more resources, see the *Catholic Identity Home Companion* at the end of this book

Why We Believe
As a Catholic Family

What if someone asks us:

- What does the Catholic Church mean by the "New Evangelization"?

The following resources can help us to respond:

When we evangelize, we spread the Good News of Jesus Christ and share God's love with others. We can evangelize by speaking and acting in ways that reflect God's love, telling others about the wonderful things that Christ has done, and encouraging others who already believe in Christ to continue to grow in their faith.

What does Scripture say?

Jesus said to his disciples:

"Your light must shine before others, that they may see your good deeds and glorify your heavenly Father." (Matthew 5:16)

"Go, therefore, and make disciples of all nations, baptizing them in the name of the Father, and of the Son, and of the holy Spirit, teaching them to observe all that I have commanded you." (Matthew 28:19–20)

As Jesus' disciples today, we are called to proclaim his Good News. An important concern of the Church today is the New Evangelization, which is a call to each person to "deepen his or her own faith, have confidence in the Gospel, and posses a willingness to share the Gospel" (United States Conference of Catholic Bishops, *The New Evangelization: Disciples on Mission in the World*).

The focus of the New Evangelization is being evangelized and then going forth to evangelize. We not only evangelize people who have not heard the Good News of Jesus Christ, but also those who have heard it but need encouragement to live it.

What does the Church say?

There is a "situation, particularly in countries with ancient Christian roots, and occasionally in the younger Churches as well, where entire groups of the baptized have lost a living sense of the faith, or even no longer consider themselves members of the Church, and live a life far removed from Christ and his Gospel. In this case what is needed is a 'new evangelization' or a 're-evangelization'" (Saint John Paul II, *Redemptoris Missio*, 33).

"To evangelize, therefore, it is necessary to open ourselves once again to the horizon of God's Spirit, without being afraid of what he asks us or of where he leads us. Let us entrust ourselves to him! He will enable us to live out and bear witness to our faith, and will illuminate the heart of those we meet." (Pope Francis, General Audience, May 22, 2013)

Notes:

The Covenant Fulfilled in Jesus

Seasonal Chapter

DEAR FAMILY

In Unit 4 your child will grow as a disciple of Jesus by:

- understanding Jesus as teacher and healer who worked signs and wonders among the people
- thanking Jesus for giving his life for us and rising so that we would have new life
- appreciating the coming of the Holy Spirit on Pentecost and the witness of early Christians who were persecuted for their faith
- recognizing that the Church continues Jesus' ministry by sharing the Word of God, the Bible, celebrating the sacraments, and working for social justice
- living as Catholics who are united, holy, welcoming and faithful.

Fast Facts

The Church of the Beatitudes is built on the hill where many people believe Jesus first taught the Beatitudes. The Church overlooks the Sea of Galilee and is octagonal in shape, with each of eight sides representing one of the Beatitudes. The dome symbolizes the ninth saying, "for great is your reward in heaven."

What's the Word?

God continues to tell us who he is through his only Son, Jesus. What does Jesus teach us about God? Have each family member share one of the stories of Jesus' life and what it tells us about who God is. Give thanks to God for the Bible.

Reality Check

"Parents must regard their children as *children of God* and respect them as *human persons.*"

(*Catechism of the Catholic Church*, 2222)

Show That You Care

As disciples of Jesus Christ, we are called to work for the unity of Christians and to respect people of all faiths. As a family, learn more about one of the Christian churches or one of the other faiths. You may have friends who belong to another church or faith whom you could invite to share with you. Pray together for all God's people.

Picture This

The Unit 4 timeline is on pages 248–251. Look over the timeline together, and invite your 6th grader share an event which was most memorable to him or her. The timeline ends with today's disciples. What family events would you add to the timeline as significant moments of faith?

Take Home

Be ready for this unit's Take Home:

Chapter 22: Remembering favorite teachers

Chapter 23: Praying the Stations of the Cross

Chapter 24: Praying to the Holy Spirit

Chapter 25: Learning more about the Bible

Chapter 26: Redesigning *Project Disciple's* logo

Jesus, Teacher and Healer

✝ We Gather in Prayer

Reader: A reading from the holy Gospel according to Matthew

"As he was walking by the Sea of Galilee, he saw two brothers, Simon who is called Peter, and his brother Andrew, casting a net into the sea; they were fishermen. He said to them, 'Come after me, and I will make you fishers of men.' At once they left their nets and followed him. He walked along from there and saw two other brothers, James, the son of Zebedee, and his brother John. They were in a boat, with their father Zebedee, mending their nets. He called them, and immediately they left their boat and their father and followed him." (Matthew 4:18–22)

The Gospel of the Lord.

All: Praise to you, Lord Jesus Christ.

Leader: We want to follow Jesus—but what must we leave behind?

Reader 1: May we leave behind selfishness, and follow Jesus in the spirit of gratitude and generosity.

All: Jesus, we want to follow you.
(Response to all five petitions.)

Reader 2: May we leave behind injustice, and follow Jesus with hope and help for those who suffer.

Reader 3: May we leave behind fear and self-consciousness, and follow Jesus by using our talents and abilities to help others.

Reader 4: May we leave behind pride and arrogance, and follow Jesus by showing mercy and forgiveness.

Reader 5: May we leave behind anger and desires for revenge, and follow Jesus by seeking ways to live in peace with all.

♫ Pescador de Hombres/ Lord, You Have Come

Tú has venido a la orilla, no has buscado ni a sabios ni a ricos; tan sólo quieres que yo te siga.

Lord, you have come to the seashore, neither searching for the rich nor the wise, desiring only that I should follow.

Refrain:
Señor, me has mirado a los ojos, sonriendo has dicho mi nombre, en la arena he dejado mi barca, junto a ti buscaré otro mar.

O Lord, with your eyes set upon me, gently smiling, you have spoken my name; all I longed for I have found by the water, at your side, I will seek other shores.

The wedding at Cana — Jesus brings God's love to all people — Many become disciples — Sermon on the Mount, the Beatitudes — Jesus works many signs and miracles — At Last Supper, Jesus gives a new covenant — Jesus prays at Garden of Gethsemane — Judas betrays Jesus

Timeline for Chapters 22–26

God makes himself known in his Son.

WE GATHER

✝ *Jesus, open our hearts to your presence among us now and always.*

Why do you prepare for an important event? What are some ways that you get ready for it?

WE BELIEVE

After Jesus' baptism at the Jordan River, the Holy Spirit led him into the desert. Jesus stayed there for forty days and forty nights. He prayed to his Father and fasted as a sign of his obedience. Jesus was preparing for his public life among the people.

Jesus returned to Galilee after his time in the desert and began to preach this message: "This is the time of fulfillment. The kingdom of God is at hand. Repent, and believe in the gospel" (Mark 1:15). The Gospel is the Good News about God at work in Jesus Christ. Jesus showed that the **Kingdom of God** is the power of God's love coming into the world and into our lives. The Kingdom came into the world with the coming of God the Son.

The Jewish People had been waiting for this fulfillment of God's promises. They were waiting for God's Kingdom. They expected God's Kingdom to be one of justice and fair rule.

Many hoped for Israel to be restored to its place of power. They were familiar with the idea of God as king. In the Old Testament God was considered the King of the universe and King of Israel. For this very reason the prophet Samuel did not want to appoint a human king to rule over God's people.

However, the Kingdom Jesus announced was not political. It was the power of God's love coming into the world and changing it. It was the power of God's love active in the lives of the people.

Jesus said the Kingdom, or reign, of God is near. Jesus was saying that:

- because Jesus is God, God's presence and rule can be found in him and in the things he said and did

- freedom from sin and the gift of God's life of grace are offered to everyone

- by living in God's presence and for the Kingdom, people can begin to live in God's life, the very life that we believe is life with God forever.

Kingdom of God
the power of God's love coming into the world and into our lives

con't ➤

Jesus' Ministry Jesus' mission was to share the life of God his Father with all people and to reconcile all people to God. Jesus brought God's love to all people and began to change the world. "The people were astonished at his teaching, for he taught them as one having authority." (Mark 1:22) He taught about the love of God his Father and encouraged all people to turn to God.

Jesus accepted and welcomed all people into his life. He showed concern for the hungry, and he often sat at table and ate with people who were ignored or neglected by the rest of society.

Because he is God the Son, Jesus' life was also a sign of God the Father's love and care. And the Third Person of the Trinity, God the Holy Spirit, was truly active in Jesus' life.

During his ministry Jesus also forgave the sins of those who sought God's forgiveness and healed those who were suffering from many different kinds of illnesses. These actions of healing and forgiving were special signs that Jesus was not only human, but also divine.

The things that Jesus said and did are the greatest Revelation of who God is and of how God loves us. And the ways we speak and act and live our faith show our belief in God's own Son, Jesus Christ.

As Catholics...

God revealed his Kingdom to us in the words of Christ, in the works of Christ, and in the very presence of Christ among us. After Christ's Resurrection the Church was planted like a seed in the world. Our mission is to bring forth the fruits of the Kingdom of God. What are these fruits? They are many, "but the greatest of these is love" (1 Corinthians 13:13).

What are some of the other fruits, or signs, of the Kingdom of God?

WE RESPOND

Think about the Kingdom of God. Work together to list some signs that God's love is active in our lives. Using these signs as captions, make a poster entitled "The kingdom of God is at hand" (Mark 1:15).

"The kingdom of God is at hand." (Mark 1:15)

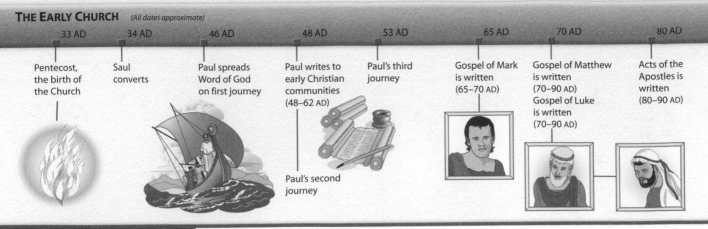

33 AD	34 AD	46 AD	48 AD	53 AD	65 AD	70 AD	80 AD
Pentecost, the birth of the Church	Saul converts	Paul spreads Word of God on first journey	Paul writes to early Christian communities (48–62 AD)	Paul's third journey	Gospel of Mark is written (65–70 AD)	Gospel of Matthew is written (70–90 AD) Gospel of Luke is written (70–90 AD)	Acts of the Apostles is written (80–90 AD)

Paul's second journey

Timeline for Chapters 22–26

Many people heard Jesus' message and became his disciples.

WE GATHER

✝ *Holy Spirit, give us the strength to live as disciples of Jesus Christ.*

Who do you spend time with? Share with? To whom do you listen? From whom do you learn?

WE BELIEVE

Jesus' message gave people hope. Many people wanted to get to know Jesus better. They wanted to learn more about God's love for them. They wanted to experience the peace and comfort that Jesus offered people. So they began to follow him.

Jesus invited all different kinds of people to follow him and live by his teachings. These women and men became his disciples. One day a large crowd followed Jesus to the mountains.

The message that Jesus gave to the people that day has become known as the *Sermon on the Mount*. Jesus told the people how to live as his disciples.

In the first part of the Sermon on the Mount, Jesus taught the people about the meaning of true happiness and the way to achieve that happiness. Jesus said that people would be happy only if they trusted in God and lived as he did.

We call these teachings that describe the way to live as Jesus' disciples the **Beatitudes**. In the Beatitudes *blessed* means "happy." As disciples of Jesus, we too are called to follow the Beatitudes. As Christians, we trust that the Holy Spirit helps us and the whole Church to do this.

Jesus' message of hope for all those who live the Beatitudes is: "Rejoice and be glad, for your reward will be great in heaven" (Matthew 5:12).

WE RESPOND

🏃 Read about the Beatitudes on page 251. As Jesus' disciples we, too, can find true happiness by living out each Beatitude. List practical ways that can show others that we are living out each of the eight Beatitudes.

Key Word

Beatitudes teachings of Jesus that describe the way to live as his disciples

Jesus' disciples can live the Beatitudes by:

1. _____
2. _____
3. _____
4. _____

5. _____
6. _____
7. _____
8. _____

Choose one of the actions from your list and try to live it this week.

TODAY

86 AD   90 AD   313 AD   325 AD   380 AD   381 AD

Book of Revelation is written (86–90 AD)

Gospel of John is completed (90–100 AD)

Christianity is accepted in the Roman Empire

Council of Nicea

Christianity becomes official religion of Roman Empire

Bishops meet in Constantinople

You are a disciple of Jesus Christ

The Beatitudes

📖 Matthew 5:3–10

"Blessed are the poor in spirit, for theirs is the kingdom of heaven." (Matthew 5:3)	This Beatitude tells us about our attitude toward the things we have; we should not be overly attached to possessions. Our confidence should be in God. We are called to share whatever we have with others.
"Blessed are they who mourn, for they will be comforted." (Matthew 5:4)	We are to be signs of hope despite the sadness, evil, and injustice we see in the world. As Jesus' disciples we are to comfort those who suffer injustice and loss.
"Blessed are the meek, for they will inherit the land." (Matthew 5:5)	The meek are the humble—that is, those who realize that their talents and abilities come from God. We are to use our God-given talents and abilities to do what is good, showing love for God and others.
"Blessed are they who hunger and thirst for righteousness, for they will be satisfied." (Matthew 5:6)	The greatest desire of those who hunger and thirst after righteousness is for God's power and presence to be at work in the world. As Jesus' disciples we try to do God's will. We put our trust in God and carry out Christ's work of justice.
"Blessed are the merciful for they will be shown mercy." (Matthew 5:7)	Those who show love and forgive others will themselves receive love and forgiveness in God's Kingdom. We are to show compassion to all people.
"Blessed are the clean of heart, for they will see God." (Matthew 5:8)	The clean of heart are those who are open to God and God's law. They are sincere in everything they do. We are to be faithful Christians and find Christ in others.
"Blessed are the peacemakers, for they will be called children of God." (Matthew 5:9)	God wants all people to love one another and to have the peace that comes from loving him and trusting in his will. We are called to be reconcilers in our homes, communities, and world. We are to bring people together.
"Blessed are they who are persecuted for the sake of righteousness, for theirs is the kingdom of heaven." (Matthew 5:10)	Prophets were often persecuted when they brought people God's message. We are to live out our Christian faith even when others do not understand our beliefs.

Jesus taught about living and growing closer to God.

WE GATHER

✝ *Jesus, you are the light of the world.*

What are some things that are essential, or necessary, in life? Did you ever have to try to live without them?

WE BELIEVE

In the Sermon on the Mount, Jesus went on to speak to his disciples about two items from everyday life: salt and light. He said, "You are the salt of the earth. But if salt loses its taste, with what can it be seasoned? . . . You are the light of the world. . . . your light must shine before others, that they may see your good deeds and glorify your heavenly Father" (Matthew 5:13, 14, 16).

When Jesus called his disciples to be like "salt" and "light" for each other and for all people, he was telling them that just as salt and light were important and necessary, so were they. Jesus wanted his disciples to show the way to him and to the Father. Jesus wanted his disciples to take an active part in their communities and to serve the Kingdom of God by sharing God's love and life with others.

🧍 List some benefits of salt and light in our lives.

_____

_____

_____

How can we be like salt and light in our communities? How can we help others to live and grow in God's love?

_____

_____

_____

_____

Jesus told his disciples, "Love your enemies, and pray for those who persecute you" (Matthew 5:44). Jesus wanted his followers to be identified by their love for one another and for all people. By acting out of love, they could bring others to believe in Christ and to give glory and praise to the Father.

As disciples of Jesus, we too can be salt and light for others. We can help people to live and grow in love for God.

About Prayer During his Sermon on the Mount, Jesus also taught his disciples about prayer. Through prayer, they could stay close to God. They could speak to God and listen to God speaking to them.

Jesus himself often prayed in silence and alone. He went into the mountains or desert to put himself in the presence of God, his Father. However, Jesus also prayed with others. He studied the Scriptures in the synagogue, and observed the Sabbath. With his friends and family he participated in the great Jewish feasts.

While preaching the Sermon on the Mount, Jesus gave his disciples advice on the ways to pray. He told them that God the Father knows what we need before we ask. Jesus instructed them to pray to God our Father. So he taught them a very special prayer—the Lord's Prayer.

The Lord's Prayer is one of the most important prayers in the Gospels and of the Church. This prayer is also called the Our Father. As followers of Jesus Christ, we pray the Lord's Prayer during Mass and at many other times in our lives.

The Lord's Prayer sums up Jesus' whole message of trust in and love for the Father. Each time we pray this prayer, we ask God to act in our lives and in the world. We ask the Holy Spirit to help us make the Kingdom come alive in people's hearts and lives. We hope for the Lord's return at the end of time.

Catholic cathedral carved in salt mines near Kracow, Poland.

We pray:	Our words mean:
Our Father, who art in heaven hallowed be thy name;	God is present to all who love him. We have become God's people and he is our God. We look forward to being with him forever.
thy kingdom come; thy will be done on earth as it is in heaven.	We ask God to unite us with the work of Christ and pray for God to bring about his Kingdom. We pray to God for the ability to do his will.
Give us this day our daily bread; and forgive us our trespasses as we forgive those who trespass against us;	We ask God for everything we need for ourselves and for the world. We use his gifts to work toward his plan of salvation. We ask God to heal us and we ask for forgiveness from others when needed. We follow the example of Christ and forgive those who have hurt us.
and lead us not into temptation, but deliver us from evil. Amen.	We pray that God will protect us from all that could draw us away from his love. We ask him to guide us to choose good in our lives, and we ask him for the strength to follow his law.

WE RESPOND

How can prayer help you to show that the Kingdom of God has begun?

Work in a group and list different ways that prayer can be part of our lives.

Pray the Lord's Prayer together.

Jesus worked signs and wonders among the people.

WE GATHER

✝ *Mary, Mother of God, help us to be close to your son.*

Sometimes people say it is a miracle when a team wins a game. Talk about the many things that people today think of as miracles. Do you think these events and happenings are miracles? How do you define a miracle?

WE BELIEVE

Jesus traveled through all of Galilee, "teaching in their synagogues, proclaiming the gospel of the kingdom, and curing every disease and illness among the people" (Matthew 4:23). Jesus worked many miracles. A miracle is an extraordinary event that is beyond human power and brought about by God. It is an action beyond the ordinary laws of nature. Jesus' miracles were all signs that he was the Son of God and that the Kingdom of God had arrived in him.

According to the Gospel of John, Jesus performed his first sign or miracle at a wedding feast in Cana of Galilee.

📖 John 2:1–12

One day Jesus and his mother, Mary, and some of Jesus' other disciples went to a wedding in the village of Cana. Cana was a few miles from Nazareth. At the wedding, however, the wine ran out in the middle of the banquet. Mary went to Jesus and told him that there was no more wine. Then Mary told the servants, "Do whatever he tells you" (John 2:5).

Jesus listened to his mother Mary. She knew the wedding party needed his help. Jesus pointed to some jars and told the servants, "Fill the jars with water." After they filled them to the top, Jesus said, "Draw some out now and take it to the headwaiter" (John 2:7, 8).

The servants did as he said. But Jesus had changed the water into wine. When the headwaiter tasted it, he was amazed that the wine was so good. He called the bridegroom and said to him, "Everyone serves good wine first, and then when people have drunk freely, an inferior one; but you have kept the good wine until now" (John 2:10).

Through this miracle, Jesus revealed not only that he was human, but also that he was divine. Through signs and his deep compassion and concern for others, the Kingdom of God continued to be made known. And his followers began to see who Jesus was and to believe in him and praise God.

Jesus' Miracles Everywhere Jesus went, to villages, towns, or farms, people brought those who were in need to him. Jesus did not work miracles as a show or to make himself popular. Jesus helped those who expressed faith in him.

We know from other accounts in the Gospels that Jesus worked many miracles during his public ministry. Some of these miracles involved nature or everyday needs, such as calming a storm or feeding a multitude of people. From the Gospel of Matthew we learn that as Jesus' disciples were crossing the river in a boat, a great storm frightened them. Jesus "rebuked the winds and the sea, and there was great calm" (Matthew 8:26).

Another time Jesus was worried about a crowd of thousands of people who had been listening to him preach and had had nothing to eat. Among all the people there were only seven loaves of bread and a few fish. Jesus gave thanks and broke the loaves and gave them to his disciples to give to the people. "They all ate and were satisfied. They picked up the fragments left over—seven baskets full." (Matthew 15:37)

Other miracles that Jesus worked involved people. For example, Jesus healed people who were lame and others who were sick. They were cured and could then walk and be well. Most often these healings were brought about by a simple word, and sometimes by a touch. Once two blind men followed Jesus asking him for help. When Jesus approached them, he asked if they believed he could help them. They said yes, and Jesus touched their eyes saying, "Let it be done for you according to your faith" (Matthew 9:29). Immediately their eyes were opened, and they could see.

Jesus worked miracles because he loved people, especially those suffering and in need. He wanted them to have his Father's comfort and peace in their lives. He also wanted to strengthen their belief in the power of God's love and forgiveness. And many that Jesus healed left their own towns and followed him.

WE RESPOND

How can you show that you are Jesus' disciple?

PROJECT

Show What you Know

Write the first part of each Beatitude in different squares. Then, write the remaining part of the Beatitudes in the other squares. Cover each square with paper. With a partner, play a Beatitude Memory Game by choosing squares to find each match.

"Blessed are the poor in spirit,		for theirs is the kingdom of heaven."	

Reality Check

All kinds of media (TV shows, commercials, Web sites, music, email campaigns) tell us how to find happiness. List a few examples:

_____

_____

As a disciple of Jesus Christ, what do you think of these messages?

_____

_____

Pray Today

In his gift of the Lord's Prayer, Jesus encouraged us to turn to God for all our needs. Pray the Lord's Prayer each day.

DISCIPLE

Pray
Learn
Celebrate
Share
Choose
Live

Saint Stories

Saint Angela de Merici was concerned with the lack of education that was available for girls. She founded the Company of Saint Ursula, known as the Ursulines. The Ursulines were the first group of women religious to work outside the cloister and the first teaching order of women. The Church celebrates the feast day of Saint Angela de Merici on January 27.

↪ DISCIPLE CHALLENGE

• What is another name for the Ursulines?

_____

• Underline the phrases that tell what the Ursulines were "first" to do.
• Visit *Lives of the Saints* on **www.webelieveweb.com** to learn more about Saint Angela de Merici.

Fast Facts

The Sisters of the Good Shepherd provide support to women and families through counseling. They help those in prison and those trying to start their lives again. They staff social service offices, and work to change unjust laws.

What's *the* Word?

Jesus used parables to teach about the Kingdom of God. Read the parables found in Mark 4:30–32 and Matthew 13:47–50. What is the Kingdom of God compared to in each of these parables?

_____

↪ **DISCIPLE CHALLENGE** What image could you use today to explain the Kingdom of God?

_____

Take Home

Read the *Saint Stories* feature about Saint Angela de Merici with your family. Point out that like Jesus, Saint Angela de Merici was a teacher. Invite family members to recall favorite teachers and talk about ways these teachers made a difference in their lives. Discuss ways your family can help educate children throughout the world.

CHAPTER TEST

Underline the correct answer.

1. An extraordinary event that is beyond human power and brought about by God is a (**Beatitude/miracle**).

2. The (**Torah/Gospel**) is the Good News about God at work in Jesus Christ.

3. The (**Beatitudes/Apostles**) are the teachings of Jesus that describe the way to live as his disciples.

4. The (**Kingdom of God/Lord's Prayer**) is the power of God's love coming into the world and our lives.

Short Answers

5. What message did Jesus give to the people at the Sermon on the Mount?

   _____

6. What are two things we ask God when we pray the words of the Lord's Prayer?

   _____

7. What did Jesus tell his followers about the Kingdom of God?

   _____

8. Why did Jesus work miracles?

   _____

Write a paragraph to answer this question.

9–10. What did Jesus do to show God's love to people?

   _____

   _____

   _____

   _____

Jesus, Redeemer and Savior

23

✠ We Gather in Prayer

Leader: Lord Jesus, you are the Savior and Redeemer of the world. Blessed be your name.

All: Blessed be your name for ever.

Leader: Our passage from death to new life can only be made in our dying and rising with Christ. Listen as Saint Paul reminds his friends of the Paschal Mystery.

Reader 1: "You were buried with him in baptism, in which you were also raised with him through faith in the power of God, who raised him from the dead."(Colossians 2:12)

All: Lord Jesus, you are the Savior and Redeemer of the world.

Reader 2: "And whatever you do, in word or in deed, do everything in the name of the Lord Jesus, giving thanks to God the Father through him." (Colossians 3:17)

All: Lord Jesus, you are the Savior and Redeemer of the world.

Leader: It is Christ's perfect sacrifice of love and obedience that saved us from sin and grants us salvation. All praise and honor be yours, now and for ever.

All: Amen.

Jesus gave us a new covenant.

WE GATHER

✝ *Jesus, thank you for your presence in the Eucharist.*

Think of some leaders in different countries or cities. Are they popular with everyone? Why or why not?

WE BELIEVE

During the time that Jesus was with his disciples and preaching among the people, many people said that he was the Messiah. This worried some of the authorities in Jerusalem. They feared that someone as popular as Jesus might lead a revolt against the Roman government.

Despite the political tension Jesus and the disciples went to Jerusalem as the feast of Passover approached. They were a family to one another. So like every other family, they prepared the Passover meal. At sundown they gathered for the meal, and as was the custom, they reclined on couches arranged around a low table.

Everything about the meal—the unleavened bread, the wine, the lamb, the bitter herbs— had a special meaning. The foods were symbols that reminded Jewish families of the great events of the Exodus from Egypt under the leadership of Moses. The Passover meal also reminded them of their covenant with God. It has the same meaning for Jews today.

Jesus, however, gave the Passover meal a new meaning. During the meal Jesus took some bread, prayed over it, broke it, and gave it to the disciples saying, "This is my body, which will be given for you" (Luke 22:19). Then he took a cup of wine, prayed over it, and gave it to them saying, "This cup is the new covenant in my blood, which will be shed for you" (Luke 22:20). Like God had done before, Jesus was giving his followers a new covenant and a new covenant meal. The Passover celebration now had a new meaning. As the priest of the new covenant, Jesus was offering himself as the Paschal lamb. Jesus told his disciples to "do this in memory of me" (Luke 22:19). We call the Passover meal that Jesus shared with his disciples on the night before he died the **Last Supper**.

Jesus' disciples continued to share this meal as a memorial to Jesus. Jesus was with them as they broke the bread and drank from the cup. Christ's own Body and Blood were present under the appearances of bread and wine. Jesus' love and his sacrifice would forever be remembered in the celebration of the Eucharist. For Christians the Eucharist is the new Passover of God's people.

The Final Hours Jesus knew that one of his Apostles would soon betray him. He knew that the next day would be one of suffering and of death. So he went to the Mount of Olives. His disciples went there, too. In these final hours before his suffering began, Jesus prayed to his Father in the olive grove called Gethsemane. And Jesus told his disciples that they should pray, too.

Key Word

Last Supper the Passover meal that Jesus shared with his disciples on the night before he died

Leonardo da Vinci (1452–1519), *The Last Supper*

As he prayed, Jesus asked to be relieved of the pain that he would suffer, and yet at the same time he wanted to do his Father's will. During his hours of prayer Jesus chose to be obedient and to trust his Father. Jesus freely chose to offer his life for us so that we might be freed from sin.

Jesus had given himself in the Eucharist and was now preparing to give his life for all of humanity.

WE RESPOND

Illustrate the Passover of the Jewish People and the new Passover that has been given to us by Jesus Christ. What can you do to remember Jesus' Last Supper this week?

Jesus gave his life for us.

WE GATHER

✝ *Jesus, help us never to turn from you.*

What are the reasons that there might be unrest or revolt in some countries, cities, neighborhoods? What are some of the ways that governments deal with these problems? Are the ways always peaceful? always just?

WE BELIEVE

While Jesus was praying in Gethsemane, Judas, one of his Apostles, entered the garden. He came with Temple guards and a group of people who had been angered by Jesus' teachings. Judas had promised to hand over Jesus to these men for thirty pieces of silver. Judas had told them that the one he would kiss was the one they were looking for. So Judas went to Jesus, greeted him, and kissed him. Jesus said, "Friend, do what you have come for" (Matthew 26:50). Then the guards took hold of Jesus, and though Peter offered a struggle, they arrested Jesus.

First they took Jesus before Caiaphas, the high priest. Caiaphas insisted that Jesus was guilty of blasphemy, of referring to God in a disrespectful or irreverent way.

Then this group took him before Pontius Pilate, the Roman governor. When Judas learned what had happened to Jesus because of his betrayal, he regretted what he had done. He tried to return the thirty pieces of silver and said, "I have sinned in betraying innocent blood" (Matthew 27:4). But it was too late to stop what had begun!

Pilate found nothing for which to condemn Jesus. Yet some leaders of the people had said that Jesus must die because he called God his Father. Pilate feared that there would be unrest or even a revolt unless he took action. Pilate ordered that Jesus be whipped and crucified.

Jesus was crucified between two criminals. The dying Jesus was insulted by those who passed him as well as by the soldiers, chief priests, and scribes. They said that if he were the king of Israel he would be able to save himself as he had saved others. When Jesus took his last breath, the veil of the sanctuary in the Temple was torn in two. The soldier who stood in front of Jesus and watched him die said, "Truly this man was the Son of God!" (Mark 15:39).

View of Jerusalem including the Church of the Holy Sepulchre

We further read in the Gospel of Mark that there were women watching from a distance. Mary Magdalene, Mary the mother of the younger James, and Salome had followed Jesus when he was in Galilee. Other women followers who had come with Jesus to Jerusalem were there, too.

After Jesus died, his body was placed in the tomb. When Jesus Christ died, his human soul united to his divine person, joined those who had died. Christ opened the gates of Heaven for those who had followed God's will. Christians call the day that marks Jesus' Death Good Friday because it was on this day that Jesus died to save us.

WE RESPOND

Jesus is our Redeemer. By his Death and Resurrection Jesus gained our salvation and brought us the hope of new life.

Let us imagine that we are walking with Jesus during the last days of his life.

Our first stop is the *Chapel of the Cenacle*. The word *cenacle* comes from a Latin word meaning "dining room." In the Upper Room on the second floor, Jesus celebrated the Last Supper with his Apostles. They ate the Passover meal together, a meal that celebrated the passing over of the Jews from slavery to freedom. At this meal, Jesus gave us the gift of his Body and Blood, the Eucharist. This building is also the site honored as David's tomb. So in this one building we remember David, the king of Israel, and Jesus, a descendant of David and Savior of the world.

The Garden of Gethsemane, Jerusalem

Our second stop is the *Garden of Gethsemane*. This garden was a special place for Jesus. This was where he went after the Last Supper to prepare for his eventual suffering on the Cross. It was here that he endured the agony in the garden.

The Church of the Holy Sepulchre, Jerusalem

Our last stop is the *Church of the Holy Sepulchre*. This is an impressive stone building with a shining dome. It combines two churches. The upper chapel of the church is said to be the site of Jesus' Crucifixion. The site of Jesus' tomb is said to lie beneath the dome, but the actual tomb was destroyed.

If you were in these sacred places, what would you pray for? What would you say to Jesus, who died and rose here, and is with us now, today?

The Chapel of the Cenacle, Jerusalem

Jesus Christ rose from the dead.

WE GATHER

✝ *Alleluia, we give praise to you, Jesus!*

Have you ever heard of or experienced an event that does not seem to have a natural explanation?

How did it make you feel? Why?

WE BELIEVE

As it had been foretold in the Scriptures, Jesus was raised from the dead on the third day after his Death. The mystery of Jesus' being raised from the dead is called the **Resurrection**.

📖 Mark 16:1–8

"When the sabbath was over, Mary Magdalene, Mary, the mother of James, and Salome bought spices so that they might go and anoint him. Very early when the sun had risen, on the first day of the week, they came to the tomb. They were saying to one another, 'Who will roll back the stone for us from the entrance to the tomb?' When they looked up, they saw that the stone had been rolled back; it was very large. On entering the tomb they saw a young man sitting on the right side, clothed in a white robe, and they were utterly amazed. He said to them, 'Do not be amazed! You seek Jesus of Nazareth, the crucified. He has been raised; he is not here. Behold, the place where they laid him. But go and tell his disciples and Peter, "He is going before you to Galilee; there you will see him, as he told you."' Then they went out and fled from the tomb, seized with trembling and bewilderment. They said nothing to anyone, for they were afraid."

The Holy Women at the Sepulchre by Laura James (Contemporary Artist)

264

Imagine that you are a news reporter in Jerusalem. You are interviewing Mary Magdalene and the other women on their return from Jesus' empty tomb. With a group role-play the interview.

Mark 16:9–11

The Risen Jesus Appears to Mary   "When he had risen, early on the first day of the week, he appeared first to Mary Magdalene. . . . She went and told his companions who were mourning and weeping. When they heard that he was alive and had been seen by her, they did not believe."

We can read in the Gospel of Mark that the risen Christ appeared to other disciples, too. They also told the group what they had seen, but the group of disciples still did not believe. They finally believed once Christ appeared to them.

Through the gift of faith we believe in Jesus Christ and his Resurrection. By faith we not only believe in Jesus risen among us, but also live as his disciples each day.

Resurrection the mystery of Jesus' being raised from the dead

WE RESPOND
♫ **Jesus Is Risen**

Refrain:
Alleluia! Alleluia! Alleluia!
Jesus is risen, alleluia!
That Easter morning at break of day,
friends of the Lord went to see where
   he lay.
The angel who sat at the tomb did say:
"He is not here, he is risen!" (Refrain)
All the apostles were filled with fear.
Then in the midst of them did he
   appear and say to them:
"Peace be upon you here.
See for yourselves, I am risen!" (Refrain)
Now it no longer could be denied,
seeing his feet and his hands and his side.
"Indeed you are Lord! You are God!"
   they cried.
"Conquering death, you have risen!"
(Refrain)

As Catholics...

In the Gospel of Luke, we read that Mary Magdalene was one of the many people Jesus healed. She became one of his closest followers. She often traveled with Jesus and the Apostles, and she was present at Jesus' Death and burial. In the Gospel of John we read that the risen Jesus first appeared to Mary and sent her out to tell the other disciples the Good News of his Resurrection. Mary Magdalene is a symbol of hope in the new life that comes from Christ. We honor Mary as a saint. Her feast day is July 22.

Think of a person that you consider a symbol of hope in new life. Why do you think this is so?

Christar appeared to his disciples.

WE GATHER

✝ *Jesus, help us to always believe in you.*

Think about the stories and events that you hear about or that people tell you about. Do you believe all of them? Why or why not?

WE BELIEVE

The risen Jesus appeared to his disciples to strengthen them and to increase their faith in his Resurrection. He wanted his disciples to believe in all that he had told them and in what he had done for humanity.

Later on the day of Jesus' Resurrection, the Apostles were gathered together behind locked doors. They feared that the people in authority might also arrest them. Jesus came and stood among them. He showed them his side and his hands and said, "Peace be with you. As the Father has sent me, so I send you." Then he breathed on them and said, "Receive the holy Spirit" (John 20:21, 22).

God breathed life into the first human beings. As God breathes life into every human being, Jesus breathed the Gift of the Holy Spirit upon his disciples. This began the new life in which humanity now can share because of Jesus' Resurrection.

The Holy Spirit that Jesus breathed on his Apostles is the same Holy Spirit who gives us life. The Holy Spirit guides us as we live each day. Jesus has not left us alone, but is with us always.

📖 John 20:24–29

Thomas, one of Jesus' Apostles, was not with the others when Jesus appeared to them. He did not believe that they had seen Jesus. He said to the other Apostles, "Unless I see the mark of the nails in his hands and put my finger into the nailmarks and put my hand into his side, I will not believe" (John 20:25).

Later in the week all of the disciples were together again, and Thomas was with them. They were inside and all the doors were locked. Jesus appeared right in the middle of them and told Thomas, "Put your finger here and see my hands, and bring your hand and put it into my side, and do not be unbelieving, but believe" (John 20:27). Thomas told Jesus he believed he was the Lord, his God. But Jesus reminded Thomas that he believed because he had now seen. Jesus said, "Blessed are those who have not seen and have believed" (John 20:29).

As disciples of Christ we are called to believe everything we have learned about Jesus from the Gospels and the other writings of the New Testament. We are called to believe that Jesus Christ died and rose to new life. We are called to believe what the Church teaches us about Christ.

We believe that Jesus is the Son of God, our Savior. We believe that through the risen Jesus we have new life and the hope of sharing this life with him forever.

WE RESPOND

Think about the appearances of Jesus after his Resurrection. Prepare a short advertisement using your favorite appearance to convince the public that Jesus is risen!

PROJECT

Pray
Learn
Celebrate
Share
Choose
Live

Show What *you* Know

You are a journalist living in the time of Jesus. Write a news article to explain the Key Words Last Supper and Resurrection.

Saint Stories

Saint Elizabeth of Portugal was born a Spanish princess in 1271. She was married to King Denis of Portugal at age twelve, and became the Queen of Portugal before she was a teenager! Saint Elizabeth of Portugal is remembered for her charity and kindness toward the poor and as a peacemaker. The Church celebrates her feast day on July 4.

➥ **DISCIPLE CHALLENGE** Saint Elizabeth showed charity and kindness to others. How can you do the same?

Fast Facts

 INRI

The letters *INRI* that appear on the crucifix are an acronym of the Latin *Iesus Nazarenus, Rex Iudaeorum*, which translates to English as Jesus of Nazareth, King of the Jews. Pontius Pilate ordered this inscription to be placed on Jesus' Cross. (See John 19: 19.)

What's *the* Word?

In the Gospel of Luke there is a story of the risen Jesus' appearance to two of his disciples on the road to Emmaus. Read Luke 24:13–35 with a friend. Take turns reading the verses. Would you have recognized Jesus?

DISCIPLE

More to Explore

The Congregation of the Most Holy Redeemer was founded by Saint Alphonsus Liguori, and serves all around the world to spread the Good News and deepen the faith of youth, young adults, and adults. Its members are priests, brothers, and lay missionaries who follow the example of Christ the Redeemer by preaching God's Word to the poor and abandoned. Known as the Redemptorists, they work in parishes, preach at parish programs, run retreats and conference centers, work with those suffering from AIDS and other terminal illnesses, serve as missionaries throughout the world, and manage Liguori Publications, a Catholic publishing company.

DISCIPLE CHALLENGE

- Underline the phrase that describes how the Redemptorists follow the example of Christ the Redeemer.
- Circle the name of the Redemptorists' founder.
- Name three ways the Redemptorists serve.

_____

_____

Visit www.cssr.com to learn more about the Redemptorists.

Question Corner

Who Am I?

I betrayed Jesus for thirty pieces of silver.

_____

I ordered Jesus to be whipped and crucified.

_____

I was first to see the risen Jesus.

_____

I needed to see "proof" before I could believe that Jesus had appeared after his Resurrection.

_____

Take Home

As a family, read about the Stations of the Cross on page 328. Visit **www.webelieveweb.com** to find appropriate stations and meditations to use at your parish church, or at a nearby shrine or retreat center that has outdoor stations. Then, pray the Stations of the Cross. At each station after silent reflection, pray:

We adore you, O Christ,
    and we bless you:
Because by your holy cross,
    you have redeemed the world.

Afterwards, gather together as a family and talk about the experience.

CHAPTER TEST

Complete the following.

1. At the Last Supper when Jesus was celebrating the _____ meal with his

   disciples, he gave them the _____.

2. The mystery that Jesus _____ on the third day after his Death is called the

   _____.

3. The risen Jesus appeared to his _____ to strengthen them and to increase

   their _____ in his Resurrection.

4. Christians call the day that marks Jesus' Death _____, because on this day

   Jesus died to _____.

Write True or False for the following sentences.
Then change the false sentences to make them true.

5. _____ On the evening of the Resurrection, the risen Jesus appeared to all
   his Apostles.

   _____

6. _____ On the night before he suffered and died, Jesus prayed to his Father.

   _____

7. _____ Christians celebrate the Eucharist as the new Passover given to us by Christ.

   _____

8. _____ By his Death, Jesus gains our salvation and brings us the hope of new life.

   _____

Write a paragraph to answer this question.

9–10. What happened at the Last Supper?

_____

_____

_____

_____

The Church Begins

24

✝ We Gather in Prayer

Leader: Come, Holy Spirit, fill the hearts of your faithful.

All: And kindle in them the fire of your love.

Reader: A reading from the Letter of Saint Paul to the Ephesians

"You are fellow citizens with the holy ones and members of the household of God, built upon the foundation of the apostles and prophets, with Christ Jesus himself as the capstone. Through him the whole structure is held together and grows into a temple sacred in the Lord; in him you also are being built together into a dwelling place of God in the Spirit . . . it has now been revealed to his holy apostles and prophets by the Spirit, that the Gentiles are coheirs, members of the same body, and copartners in the promise in Christ Jesus through the gospel." (Ephesians 2:19–22; 3:5–6)

The Word of the Lord.

All: Thanks be to God.

Leader: The Holy Spirit moves us to become one in Christ's body, his Church. From the apostles to the martyrs to all the holy ones in the faith, we have learned that the Spirit knows our needs even before we ask the Father. Jesus teaches us to pray. The Spirit leads us to pray in freedom as sons and daughters of God. And so we pray.

All: Amen! Amen! Amen!

271

With the coming of the Holy Spirit the Church began.

✝ *Holy Spirit, fill our hearts with your love.*

Have you ever been at a "Grand Opening" of a new store or business? What kinds of things were happening? How were people acting and reacting to all the activities? Give some examples.

_____

_____

_____

_____

❈ ❈ ❈ ❈

WE BELIEVE

Jesus was about to change the disciples' lives again. He had to leave them as they knew him and return in all his glory to his Father in Heaven. But he left them with the mission that he had begun. He had brought the Good News of the Kingdom of God. He showed the people his Father's love and forgiveness. He spoke to them about the power of the Holy Spirit. He lived in the spirit of justice and peace. And Jesus passed his mission on to his disciples. He wanted them to continue to bring more people into the community of believers.

Jesus knew that the Apostles and other disciples were fearful because of his arrest and Crucifixion. He saw their hope now that he had risen and was with them. Yet he would soon leave them and he knew that they needed strength and courage to carry on his mission. He knew that the Holy Spirit was the power and force that would guide the community of believers. The Holy Spirit would help them to live out their faith and love in the one God.

Jesus told his disciples that they were his witnesses, the ones who would now spread the Good News. Then he said, "And [behold]

I am sending the promise of my Father upon you; but stay in the city until you are clothed with power from on high" (Luke 24:49).

Jesus then went with his disciples "as far as Bethany, raised his hands, and blessed them. As he blessed them he parted from them and was taken up to heaven" (Luke 24:50–51). We call this the Ascension.

The disciples went back to Jerusalem as Jesus had instructed them. They were filled with joy and praised God, remembering all that had just taken place. Mary, the mother of Jesus, and other women and men who were disciples of Jesus prayed and stayed close to one another.

During this time after Jesus' Ascension, Peter told the others, "My brothers, the scripture had to be fulfilled which the holy Spirit spoke beforehand through the mouth of David, concerning Judas, who was the guide for those who arrested Jesus" (Acts of the Apostles 1:16).

Peter went on to say that Judas had died and that another person must be chosen to take Judas' place. This person must be a witness to everything the Apostles had seen and heard. So they chose two men and then prayed, "You, Lord, who know the hearts of all, show which one of these two you have chosen to take the place in this apostolic ministry from which Judas turned away to go to his own place" (Acts of the Apostles 1:24–25).

These two men then chose lots. Matthias drew the one that showed that he had been chosen to take Judas' place as one of the Apostles.

📖 Acts of the Apostles 2:1–4, 7, 17, 41

The Coming of the Holy Spirit   While the Jewish feast of Weeks, or Pentecost, was taking place the disciples were gathered together. "And suddenly there came from the sky a noise like a strong driving wind, and it filled the entire house in which they were. Then there appeared to them tongues as of fire, which parted and came to rest on each one of them. And they were all filled with the holy Spirit and began to speak in different tongues, as the Spirit enabled them to proclaim." (Acts of the Apostles 2:2–4) Everyone was astounded and Peter told them that the prophecy of Joel was now fulfilled.

"God says,
'that I will pour out a portion of my spirit
   upon all flesh.'" (Acts of the Apostles 2:17)

How wonderful it was that each person understood what was being said in his or her own language! The fact that this happened helps us to know that Christ's message of love and peace is for all people.

We call the day the Holy Spirit came upon the first disciples **Pentecost**. It was on this day that Peter and the other Apostles baptized about three thousand people. This was the beginning of the Church. After this day Peter and the other Apostles continued to preach and baptize. Many believers became members of the Church. And the Church was made strong through the power of the Holy Spirit.

WE RESPOND

What can you personally do to share Christ's message of love and peace? How can his message be shared throughout the entire world? Explain.

🎵 **Spirit of God, Come to Us**

Refrain:
   Spirit of God, fill our hearts,
   Spirit of God, fill our minds;
   Help us to give, help us to live as
      signs of your love.

We are your people, we are your own
faithful companions joined as one;
come to us now, Spirit of God,
enkindle within us the
   fire of your love.
(Refrain)

Spirit of God, come to us;
Spirit of Jesus, live in us;
help us to be signs of your peace,
signs of compassion,
   forgiveness and hope.
(Refrain)

Key Word

Pentecost the day on which the Holy Spirit came upon the first disciples

273

The Good News of Christ spread to many places.

WE GATHER

✝ *Lord, help us to be faithful members of your Church.*

🏃 Brainstorm a list of ways you spread important news so that everyone who needs to know about it gets the message.

WE BELIEVE

From the beginning the Apostles tried to help the members of the Church to live according to Jesus' teachings. In carrying out Jesus' command to love God, themselves, and others, the disciples shared everything. They contributed to a common fund to help needy members. We learn from Scripture that "they devoted themselves to the teaching of the apostles and to the communal life, to the breaking of the bread and to the prayers" (Acts of the Apostles 2:42).

Some disciples called themselves "followers of the Way," recalling that Jesus described himself as "the way, and the truth, and the life" (John 14:6). Others called themselves Nazarenes, indicating that they were followers of Jesus of Nazareth. It was not until about ten years after Jesus' Death, in a large city called Antioch, that the followers of Jesus Christ were first called "Christians."

As the numbers of disciples increased and they spread throughout Judea and beyond, the Temple authorities in Jerusalem became uneasy. Peter and the other Apostles were arrested. But they were released the next day because they had done nothing against the existing laws.

As Peter and the others continued to preach, fear about their influence and acceptance grew. It was not long before a persecution of Christ's disciples broke out.

📖 Acts of the Apostles 9:1–8, 17–18

One of the leaders of these persecutions was a young Pharisee and Roman citizen named Saul.

When Saul heard that Christians were active in Damascus, a busy commercial center in Syria, he asked the high priest for permission to arrest Christians there and bring them back to Jerusalem for trial. The high priest granted his request. As Saul approached Damascus, however, he had an experience that changed his whole life. A blinding light flashed around him. He fell to the ground and heard a voice saying to him "Saul, Saul, why are you persecuting me?" He said, "Who are you, sir?" The voice replied, "I am Jesus, whom you are persecuting" (Acts of the Apostles 9:4–5). With these words Jesus was telling Saul that in persecuting Christians, he was persecuting Jesus because Jesus and his followers were one body, the Church.

When Saul got up from the ground, he opened his eyes but could not see. The men he was traveling with brought him to Damascus. Three days later he recovered his sight in the presence of one of Jesus' disciples and Saul was baptized. This event is one of the most well-known examples of conversion in the Bible.

Within a short time Saul, better known by his Roman name, Paul, became one of the great leaders of the early Church. In three missionary journeys, Paul brought the Good News of Jesus Christ to the major cities of the eastern Roman Empire.

- His first journey took him to the island of Cyprus and to Antioch and other cities of Syria and Asia Minor (modern Turkey).

- His second journey, which is the most extensive, included an eighteen-month stay in Corinth, Greece.

- Most of his third journey was spent establishing the Church community in Ephesus, a large and important city in Asia Minor.

During his travels Paul wrote letters to the new Christians in these places. Some of these letters can be found in the New Testament.

In caring for these members of the Church, Paul took all kinds of risks. He suffered insults, the hatred of his enemies, shipwreck, and even imprisonment. Yet Paul never wavered from his faith. He led many to believe in Jesus and to become members of the Church.

From the moment of his conversion, Paul's life was guided by his devotion to Jesus, who was the center of his preaching and teaching.

WE RESPOND

Imagine that you, like Paul, have an experience that strengthens you to preach about Jesus Christ. What might that experience be?

Work in a group to make a map of the journeys that you would take to bring the Good News of Jesus to those who need to hear it in today's world.

Christians were persecuted for their faith.

WE GATHER

✝ *Lord, help us to be your witnesses.*

Have you ever seen or experienced persecution? Why do you think so many people throughout the world are persecuted?

WE BELIEVE

Paul's missionary trips were very important to the development of the Church. He preached the Good News of Jesus Christ to people of different cultures and customs. Because of his work, Christianity spread beyond Judea and to people other than only those of the Jewish faith. It grew to include Greeks and Romans. Thus from its beginning, the Church has included people of different cultures who speak different languages, have unique customs, and live throughout the world.

As the Church grew, the Roman government became more threatened. Christians refused to honor and worship the false gods of the Roman Empire. More importantly, the Roman laws required people to acknowledge the emperor as a god, yet the Christians would not do this.

Christianity was not an accepted religion during the first three centuries, and this put the Christians at risk. Many had to keep their faith secret. They gathered for worship in the homes of fellow Christians, and tried to spread the Good News without angering the Roman officials. The Romans believed that Christians put the authority and security of the empire at risk. These fears and misunderstandings led to the persecution of Christians. Some were imprisoned and forced to accept false gods. Others were ridiculed and treated as outcasts.

These conditions, however, did not stop Christians from believing in Christ. Many even became martyrs for their faith. A **martyr** is a person who dies rather than give up his or her belief in Jesus Christ. The word *martyr* actually comes from the Greek word for "witness." We do not have a record of all of the thousands of Christians who died for their faith. However, there are some martyrs whose stories have been passed down to us. Some of the information we have is folklore, but this adds to our desire to learn more about the great witness of the early days of the Church.

martyr person who dies rather than give up his or her belief in Jesus Christ

Saint Lawrence Lawrence lived in Rome during the third century. He was one of the deacons of the Roman Church. He had a great responsibility in caring for the goods of the Church and making sure those in need were helped. In the year 257 Pope Sixtus was arrested and put to death. The following year Lawrence also became a martyr.

There are many legends and devotions surrounding Saint Lawrence. One of these is that when the pope was led away by the Roman soldiers, he told Lawrence that he would also die in three days. So Lawrence sold all the sacred vessels. He then gave all the Church's money to the poor, the widows, and the orphans of Rome. When the chief Roman officer heard this, he ordered Lawrence to bring all the Church's valuables to him.

Lawrence gathered all the Christians he could find and all the people who were neglected and abused by society. He then presented them to the chief Roman officer as "the Church's treasure." We celebrate Saint Lawrence's feast day on August 10.

Saint Cecilia Cecilia is another well-loved martyr and saint of the Church. She is believed to have lived in Rome during the third century. Her family was of high standing in Rome, and she was brought up in the Christian faith. Cecilia wanted to dedicate her life to Christ. But her father wanted her to marry a man of high office who was not Christian. It is said that during the wedding ceremony Cecilia was silently singing to God and praying for his help. Cecilia convinced her husband that an angel of God protected her, and soon her husband and his brother became Christians. These two men were martyred, and Cecilia is said to have buried them. She, too, was then persecuted and martyred. We celebrate the feast day of Saint Cecilia, patroness of music, on November 22.

Saint Agnes Agnes lived during the third century in Rome. At age thirteen, she dedicated her life to Christ and vowed to remain pure of heart. It is said that she was a beautiful young woman whom many men wanted to marry. She refused to worship the false gods of many of the people of her time and was treated immodestly and ridiculed for her chaste ways. However, this abuse did not weaken her faith. She withstood the mistreatment and finally her life was taken because she refused to give up her Christian ways. Thus, she too died as a martyr. We celebrate Saint Agnes's feast day on January 21.

As Catholics...

In recent years the Catholic Church has honored the Christian martyrs of the twentieth and twenty-first centuries. In May 2000, the Vatican welcomed Christians of different faith communities to participate in a prayer service to honor these martyrs. Among those remembered were Father Christian de Chergé and the monks of Our Lady of Atlas in Algeria (Catholic), Margherita Chou (Catholic), Pastor Paul Schneider (Lutheran), W.G.R. Jotcham (Baptist), and His Holiness Tichon, Patriarch of the Russian Orthodox Church. These women and men gave their lives as a witness to their faith in Christ. It is important to remember their lives and to work to stop religious persecution and violence.

Do some research and find out more about martyrs of recent centuries.

WE RESPOND

List some ways people give witness to their faith today.

_____

_____

_____

_____

_____

_____

All Christians are called to be witnesses to Christ. How can you be a witness to Christ this week?

Christianity became an accepted religion.

✝ *Father, lead us to be holy in you.*

In the United States we all are free to practice our religion. What are some ways this right is protected?

WE BELIEVE

The fourth century was a dramatic one for the Church. In the year 313 the Roman emperors declared that Christianity was accepted in the Roman Empire. In the year 380 Christianity became the official religion of the Roman Empire. The years of persecution were finally ending. However, not all Romans accepted Christianity, and sometimes even members of the same family did not practice the same faith. The family of Saint Martin of Tours is one example of this.

Saint Martin of Tours   Martin is one of the first saints that we remember not as a martyr but as a witness who was able to live out his Christian faith. Martin was born in a Roman province in the early years of the fourth century. He felt a strong calling to serve God. His parents continued to worship false gods, so Martin had to study Christianity secretly. At age fifteen he joined the Roman army. He did not want to serve in the military, but he was required to do so because his father had served in the military.

As a young soldier he showed great compassion for those in need. Once he passed a beggar and tore half of his cloak to cover the man and keep him warm. That night Jesus appeared to Martin and soon after Martin was baptized. A few years later he left the army and went to Tours, France. There he spoke out against those who were misinterpreting the faith. The people of Tours respected Martin greatly.

Eventually Martin became the Bishop of Tours. He devoted his time to stopping false beliefs in France. He prayed, taught, and preached everywhere. Through his work many came to believe in Christ. Martin lived until he was at least eighty years old. At his request, he was buried in the Cemetery of the Poor. We celebrate the feast of this bishop and saint on November 11.

Professing the Faith   As we know, the Apostles shared their faith with the early Church. Eventually it became necessary to summarize the faith into professions of faith, or creeds, for those being baptized. One of the earliest creeds, the Apostles' Creed is still prayed today. It can be found on page 325.

The Apostles' Creed is divided into three parts. The first part is about the First Person of the Blessed Trinity and the great work of creation. The second part is about the Second Person of the Blessed Trinity and the redemption all of us have because of him. The final part is about the Third Person of the Blessed Trinity from whom the Church and our holiness come.

During the fourth century, and later throughout the Church's history, some Church members questioned these teachings. It became necessary for the Church to come together to ensure that the teaching of Jesus and the Apostles was passed on to future generations.

In the year 325 the bishops gathered together in Nicea for the first Ecumenical Council. An *Ecumenical Council* is a gathering of the pope and bishops to discuss and make decisions on issues of faith, Christian living, and the life of the Church. In Nicea they discussed Jesus, the Blessed Trinity, and the Church. They again gathered in Constantinople in 381 to make clear the Church's teachings on all these subjects. The result of these two councils is another creed which we still say today at Mass. It is the Nicene Creed. It can be found on page 327.

Both the Apostles' Creed and the Nicene Creed are part of Tradition. Tradition refers to the written and spoken beliefs and practices that have been passed down to us from the time of Christ and the Apostles. Papal writings and council documents are other examples of Tradition, as is the Church's liturgy. The Catholic Church teaches us that Tradition is one of the two means by which God's Revelation comes to us. The Bible is the other. Together they make up the one source of Revelation. As the Church relies on the Bible as a book of faith, the Church looks to Tradition as a living witness of faith.

WE RESPOND

Profess your faith by praying the Apostles' Creed or Nicene Creed together.

The Third Council of Constantinople (680–681) from a fresco in the Vatican circa 1868.

PROJECT

Show What you Know

Use the code to find each . Then, write a sentence using the word.

A	B	C	D	E	F	G	H	I	J	K	L	M	N	O	P	Q	R	S	T	U	V	W	X	Y	Z
1	2	3	4	5	6	7	8	9	10	11	12	13	14	15	16	17	18	19	20	21	22	23	24	25	26

1. ___ ___ ___ ___ ___ ___
    13   1   18   20   25   18

_____

2. ___ ___ ___ ___ ___ ___ ___ ___ ___
   16   5   14   20   5   3   15   19   20

_____

Fast Facts

Saint Paul was one of the great leaders of the early Church. June 2008–2009 was declared the "Year of Saint Paul" by Pope Benedict XVI. Special liturgies, publications, Web sites, events, videos, and symposiums were based on the 2,000th anniversary of the birth of Saint Paul.

Reality Check

Take this Evangelizer Survey.

I can be an evangelizer by:

❏ speaking and acting in ways that reflect God's love

❏ telling others about the wonderful things that Christ has done

❏ encouraging others who already believe in Christ to continue to grow in their faith.

❏ other _____

DISCIPLE

Pray
Learn
Celebrate
Share
Choose
Live

Saint Stories

As a religious in the Daughters of Charity, Saint Catherine Laboure experienced visions of the Virgin Mary. In one of the visions, Mary instructed Catherine to have a medal honoring the Immaculate Conception made. This medal is commonly known as the miraculous medal. The Church celebrates Saint Catherine Laboure's feast day on November 25.

Visit *Lives of the Saints* on **www.webelieveweb.com** to learn more about saints and holy people.

Make *it* Happen

We are called to give witness to our faith. We give witness when we speak and act based upon the Good News. We tell others about the wonderful things that Christ has done. We show them what it means to be a disciple. Giving witness to our faith is an important part of the Church's mission of evangelization. Evangelization takes part in our everyday lives. We evangelize those who have not yet heard the message of Jesus Christ. We also evangelize those who have heard the message but need encouragement to live out the gift of faith that is theirs.

↳ **DISCIPLE CHALLENGE** Be an evangelizer! Live out the Gospel, and the people around you will see your faith in action. How can you do this today?

_____

_____

_____

Now, pass it on!

Take Home

The Church was made strong through the power of the Holy Spirit. Call upon the Holy Spirit to strengthen your family. Pray together the following prayer:

Come Holy Spirit,
fill the hearts of your faithful.
And kindle in them the fire of your love.
Send forth your Spirit and they shall be created.
And you will renew the face of the earth.
Amen.

281

Underline the correct answer.

1. Christianity was (**accepted/not accepted**) as a religion during the first three centuries.

2. The Church began with the coming of (**the Holy Spirit/Matthias**).

3. (**Romans/Nazarenes**) were followers of Jesus Christ who were later called Christians.

4. The Apostles' Creed and the Nicene Creed are part of (**Tradition/Scripture**).

Short Answers

5. What are two ways the Holy Spirit helps Christ's disciples?

_____

6. What do we call the day on which the Holy Spirit came upon the first disciples?

_____

7. Why was the fourth century important for the Church?

_____

8. Why is Paul considered to be a great leader of the early Church?

_____

Write a paragraph to answer this question.

9–10. What are some ways Christians have given witness to Christ?

_____

_____

_____

_____

The Bible and the Church Today

25

✝ We Gather in Prayer

Leader: The prophets such as Amos, Micah, Jeremiah, Isaiah, and John the Baptist announced God's special love for those who are poor and in need. They called the people to live justly.

Reader: Jesus, the Messiah, began his ministry by proclaiming these words of the prophet Isaiah in the synagogue in Nazareth,

"The Spirit of the Lord is upon me,
   because he has anointed me
      to bring glad tidings to the poor.

He has sent me to proclaim liberty to captives
   and recovery of sight to the blind,
      to let the oppressed go free,
and to proclaim a year acceptable to the
      Lord" (Luke 4:18–19).

♫ God Has Chosen Me

God has chosen me,
God has chosen me to bring good
   news to the poor.
God has chosen me,
God has chosen me to bring new
   sight to those searching for light:
God has chosen me, chosen me:

Refrain:
And to tell the world that God's
   kingdom is near,
To remove oppression and break
   down fear,
Yes, God's time is near,
God's time is near,
God's time is near, God's time is near.

God is calling me,
God is calling me in all whose cry is
   unheard.
God is calling me,
God is calling me to raise up the
   voice with no power or choice:
God is calling me, calling me: (Refrain)

The New Testament is made up of different types of writings.

WE GATHER

✝ *Jesus, you are Lord.*

Some families keep a scrapbook or memory box that is passed from generation to generation. What might be in such a book or box? Why? How does your family record and share memories?

WE BELIEVE

The Bible is a book of faith. It is a record of the ways that God has remained faithful to his people. The Old Testament tells us who God is by telling us what God has done for the Jewish People and for us. It gives us a basic understanding of who God is and what our relationship to him should be.

Christians see the events and truths of faith in the Old Testament as leading us to Jesus and his teachings found in the New Testament. From the New Testament we learn about God's final Revelation in Jesus Christ and the salvation that comes from Christ. We learn about the first Christian communities and the beginning of the world-wide Church.

The New Testament is a collection of twenty-seven books. The writers of these books were inspired by the Holy Spirit to use their own abilities to record the truths of faith that are so important for living as Christians. Like the Old Testament, the New Testament includes different types of writings.

The Gospels   The Gospels of Matthew, Mark, Luke, and John are in many ways historical writings. The writers of the Gospels describe Jesus' mission and ministry, his call to discipleship, and his love. They help us to understand that Jesus Christ is Messiah and the Son of God. This is why Christians consider the Gospels the most sacred books of the Bible.

Scholars believe that the Gospel of Mark was the first to be written around the years 65 to 70. The Gospels of Matthew and Luke are thought to have been written between the years 70 and 90, and the Gospel of John was completed between the years 90 and 100.

Matthew   Mark   Luke   John

The Letters to the Christian Communities
The letters, or Epistles, include twenty-one writings from leaders such as Paul, James, Peter, John, and Jude to different Christian communities. These letters have a variety of purposes. Some are written to discuss specific problems in the community, to instruct the people on how to live and worship, and to explain the role of the leaders of the community.

The letters include words of encouragement to new Christians who sometimes struggled in following Jesus' example of love and service. Many of these letters appear to have been written between the years 48–62. These were the years when Paul was in prison. A few letters were written much later, possibly during the early years of the second century.

Other Writings   The Acts of the Apostles and the Book of Revelation are the other books of the New Testament. The Acts of the Apostles records the coming of the Holy Spirit and the ministry of the Apostles. It describes the beginning and growth of the Church and the various missionary trips of the Apostles and disciples. The Acts of the Apostles, which is actually a continuation of the Gospel of Luke, was probably written between the years 80 and 90.

The Book of Revelation is the final book in the New Testament. In many ways it is like parts of the Old Testament Books of Ezekiel, Zechariah, and Daniel. The Book of Revelation is based on visions and dreams and the interpretation of them. It is believed to have been written around the years 86 to 90.

As a Christian prophecy, the Book of Revelation deals with Christ's second coming at the end of time. The book uses symbols, poetry, and images. Sometimes its imagery is difficult to understand. However, the purpose of the Book of Revelation is not to foretell specific events, but to spread the message of God's Kingdom.

We treat both the Old and New Testaments as sacred, or holy. The Holy Spirit inspired the biblical writers, so God is the true author of Scripture. Our God is a living God, one who is present to us today and always. The Bible helps us to know that God loves us and is with us today. God is acting in our lives, calling us to learn from our ancestors in faith, calling us to respond to his love and to follow his Son.

WE RESPOND

 List some ways Scripture is a part of your life.

_____

_____

_____

_____

_____

_____

_____

The Bible is an important source for Christian living and worship.

WE GATHER

✝ *Help us to hear and live your word, Lord.*

Think about something new that you are learning to do, like rollerblade, play the piano, or use sign language. Who or what are your guides to learning these things?

WE BELIEVE

The Bible is an important guide for Christian living. From the Bible we learn the Ten Commandments, the Beatitudes, the Great Commandment, and Christ's new commandment. These laws and teachings are the foundation of our moral life as Catholics. They help us to relate to God, ourselves, and one another.

Jesus built upon the teachings of the Old Testament writers. He used their words to teach his own disciples about following God's law. The Shema, the prayer prayed daily by Jews of Jesus' time and by Jewish people today, reminded the people to love God with all their hearts, souls, and strength. And the people had been instructed since the beginning of their covenant with God, "You shall love your neighbor as yourself" (Leviticus 19:18).

When Jesus was asked which commandment of God's law was the greatest he combined the two teachings into one. "You shall love the Lord, your God, with all your heart, with all your soul, and with all your mind. This is the greatest and the first commandment. The second is like it: You shall love your neighbor as yourself." (Matthew 22:37–39)

Jesus Christ is our model for just and right living. He obeyed God his Father and accepted the law as his guide. In fact, he told his disciples, "Do not think that I have come to abolish the law or the prophets. I have come not to abolish but to fulfill" (Matthew 5:17).

Jesus fulfilled the law by living it completely and totally. He showed us the way to love God and one another. His love changed the way people lived. He called each of us to follow his example when he gave us the *new commandment*. "I give you a new commandment: love one another. As I have loved you, so you also should love one another. This is how all will know that you are my disciples, if you have love for one another." (John 13:34–35)

Prayer and Worship Sacred Scripture is an essential part of the liturgy, the Church's official public worship. God's word is proclaimed at every Mass. In fact, the first main part of the Mass is called the Liturgy of the Word.

On Sundays and certain feast days of the Church, the Liturgy of the Word includes three readings and a Responsorial Psalm. The first reading is usually from the Old Testament. We hear of God's saving action in the lives of his people. We then sing or recite a Responsorial Psalm. The second reading is from one of the New Testament books other than the four Gospels. This reading encourages us to follow Christ's teachings and to be faithful disciples. The third reading is always from one of the four Gospels.

We show our reverence for the Good News of Jesus Christ by standing for the proclamation of the Gospel. The deacon or priest kisses the Book of Gospels, which was also honored in procession at the beginning of the Mass. And while the deacon or priest proclaims the Gospel, altar servers often stand on either side of him holding candles. These are just some of the ways we show how important the Gospels are to our lives as Christians.

The deacon or priest then gives a homily to help us understand what God's word means to us today. The homily helps us to reflect on the ways we are called to live as faithful followers of Christ.

Hearing the Word of God is also a part of the other sacraments and liturgical celebrations of the Church. The Liturgy of the Hours is a beautiful combination of praying, singing, and listening to God's Word.

We can use the Bible in study and personal prayer, too. By reflecting on God's Word we can get to know God and ourselves better.

This reflection can help us to understand God's will for us.

WE RESPOND

Discuss some ways that you can learn more about Scripture. This week choose one of these ways and then share what you have learned with your class.

As Catholics...

Christ calls all of us to love one another as he has loved. When we read the Gospels we find many examples of the way Jesus lived. He cared for the needs of others, especially those who were neglected, poor, or oppressed. Jesus identified himself with those he served, and he once told his disciples, "whatever you did for one of these least brothers of mine, you did for me" (Matthew 25:40). The Corporal Works of Mercy come from this part of Matthew's Gospel. All the Works of Mercy are acts of love that help us to care for the needs of others. They can be found on page 329.

The Corporal Works of Mercy deal with the physical and material needs of others. The Spiritual Works of Mercy deal with the needs of people's hearts, minds, and souls.

Select one Work of Mercy and perform it this week.

287

The Church continues Jesus' ministry through the Seven Sacraments.

WE GATHER

✝ *Jesus, you are always near.*

Think of the people in your life who are special to you. Are there certain things that remind you of them even when they are not present? Discuss your answers.

WE BELIEVE

The Gospels record Jesus' ministry of welcoming, healing, forgiving, and feeding others. One special way the Church continues his ministry is through the sacraments. A sacrament is an effective sign given to us by Jesus through which we share in God's life. We call the life of God within us grace. Grace is God's gift to us. We can live each day knowing that God lives in us.

We believe that Christ instituted the sacraments so that his followers would always experience his presence. In the sacraments we find many parallels to the prayer and worship of the Jewish People. For example, all of the celebration of the sacraments include readings from Scripture. They also include blessings and gestures that are based on Jewish rituals. In the Jewish faith the ritual gesture of anointing with oil was and is a sign of consecration for a God-given mission. Anointing with oil is an important part of the Sacraments of Baptism, Confirmation, the Anointing of the Sick, and Holy Orders. The laying on of hands, which is also an essential part of the sacraments and is a sign of God's blessing and presence, comes from Jewish customs, too.

The sacraments are part of the liturgy of the Church, and they are our most important celebrations. The whole Body of Christ celebrates each sacrament. The priest and other members of the Church who participate in the sacraments represent the whole Church. The sacraments join Catholics all over the world with Jesus and with one another. They unite us as the Body of Christ.

Sacraments of Christian Initiation Our initiation into the Church takes place through three sacraments: Baptism, Confirmation, and the Eucharist. Baptism begins our new life in Christ. Confirmation seals us with the Gift of the Holy Spirit and strengthens Christ's life in us. The Eucharist nourishes us with the Body and Blood of Christ so that we, too, can become more Christ-like.

Baptism is the sacrament in which we are freed from sin, become children of God, and are welcomed into the Church.

Confirmation is the sacrament in which we receive the Gift of the Holy Spirit in a special way.

The Eucharist is the Sacrament of the Body and Blood of Christ in which Jesus is truly present under the appearances of bread and wine.

Sacraments of Healing The Sacraments of Penance and Reconciliation and the Anointing of the Sick are known as Sacraments of Healing. Through these sacraments we experience God's forgiveness, peace, and healing touch.

Penance and Reconciliation is the sacrament by which our relationship with God and the Church is restored and our sins are forgiven.

The Anointing of the Sick is the sacrament by which God's grace and comfort are given to those who are suffering because of their old age or because they are seriously ill.

Sacraments at the Service of Communion Church members who receive these sacraments are strengthened to serve God and the Church through one of two particular vocations. This sacrament helps them to be faithful and true to their vows.

Holy Orders is the sacrament in which baptized men are ordained to serve the Church as deacons, priests, and bishops.

Matrimony is the sacrament in which a man and a woman become husband and wife and promise to be faithful to each other for the rest of their lives.

WE RESPOND

Write your answer to each of these questions.

What sacraments have you received?

_____

_____

How have you participated in the celebration of these sacraments?

_____

_____

How did your family and parish take part?

_____

_____

What are some signs of these sacraments?

_____

_____

Why are these sacraments important to your parish? to you?

_____

_____

Share your experiences with the class. Brainstorm ways you can encourage people your age to participate in the sacraments.

The Church continues Jesus' ministry through her work for social justice.

WE GATHER

✝ *Holy Spirit, fill me with love for God and others.*

🏃 Make a list of words and actions that would describe people who try to do the things God asks them to do.

WE BELIEVE

Through the prophets of the Old Testament, God spoke to his people. He told them to be faithful to the covenant and true to him, the one true God. The prophets encouraged the people to have hope and to trust in God. They called the people to work for social justice, and told them that love of God could not be separated from love of neighbor.

John the Baptist proclaimed the same message of the prophets who had gone before him. He prepared people for the Messiah who would bring a reign of true justice.

This is exactly what Jesus Christ, the Son of God and Messiah, did. Jesus worked for justice. He tried to make sure that people had what they needed. He healed the sick and fed the hungry. He listened to people when they told him about their needs. Jesus stood up for those who were neglected or ignored by society. And he spoke out against leaders who did not take care of people.

Catholic social teaching calls us to work for justice and peace as Jesus did. Jesus' life and teaching are the foundation of Catholic social teaching. There are seven themes of Catholic social teaching.

🏃 Read the chart and discuss the questions listed at the end of each theme.

Themes of Catholic Social Teaching

Life and Dignity of the Human Person
Human life is sacred because it is a gift from God. Because we are all God's children, we all share the same human dignity. Our dignity—our worth and value—does not come from the way we look or the things we accomplish. Our dignity comes from being made in the image and likeness of God. This dignity makes us equal. As Christians we respect all people, even those we do not know.

Call to Family, Community, and Participation
We are all social. We need to be with others to grow. The family is the basic community in society. In the family we grow and learn values. We learn what it means to be part of a group. Families are groups of people that contribute to society in many ways. As Christians we are involved in our family life and community.

Rights and Responsibilities of the Human Person
Every person has a fundamental right to life. This includes the things we need to have a decent life: faith and family, work and education, health care and housing. We also have a responsibility to others and to society. We work to make sure the rights of all people are being protected.

Option for the Poor and Vulnerable
We have a special obligation to help those who are poor and in need. This includes those who cannot protect themselves because of their age or their health. At different times in our lives we are all poor in some way and in need of assistance.

Dignity of Work and the Rights of Workers
People have the right to decent work, just wages, safe working conditions, and to participate in decisions about their work. There is value in all work. Our work in school and at home is a way to participate in God's work of creation. It is a way to use our talents. When we unite our work to Christ, it can be redemptive.

Solidarity of the Human Family
Solidarity is a feeling of unity. It binds members of a group together. Each of us is a member of the one human family, equal by our common human dignity. The human family includes people of all racial, cultural, and religious backgrounds. We all suffer when one part of the human family suffers whether they live near us or far away from us.

Care for God's Creation
God created us to be stewards, or caretakers, of his creation. We must care for and respect the environment. We have to protect it for future generations. When we care for creation, we show respect for God the Creator.

Questions

What are some ways the dignity of students or teachers is not respected during class? Why do you think this happens?

What are some conflicts in your school that have been resolved in a way that recognizes the dignity of those involved?

What are some virtues that individuals practice? that families practice? that neighbors practice?

How does the practice of these virtues influence society as a whole?

What is the difference between needing and wanting something?

What are some ways people might be poor?

What are some ways people are vulnerable?

How might different kinds of work make people feel?

How can we make people feel respected and valued for whatever work they do?

What are some problems or challenges that we face in our country?

How are they similar to those of other countries? How are they different?

What are some examples of society not protecting the environment?

How can these situations be changed?

Key Word

Catholic social teaching
the teaching of the Church that calls all members to work for justice and peace as Jesus did

The whole Church is called to live by this social teaching. Together we can work to change the things in society that allow injustice. Society should promote virtue, not obstruct it. Together we can work to promote virtue in society by keeping spiritual values primary. Those in authority must serve the common good using morally acceptable means. This means providing social conditions that allow people to reach their fulfillment.

WE RESPOND

In groups select one theme of Catholic social teaching. Dramatize some examples of people following the teaching and of people not following it. What are the effects of each of these examples on our society?

PROJECT

Show What *you* Know

How can you teach others about Catholic social teaching?
Be creative. Write your ideas here:

Celebrate!

The Seven Sacraments are part of the liturgy of the Church, and they are our
most important celebrations.

 DISCIPLE CHALLENGE Invite your friends and family to take a "sacrament survey."
Ask them which sacraments they have received. Record your results here:

Name	Sacraments Received

DISCIPLE

Pray
Learn
Celebrate
Share
Choose
Live

Saint Stories

Saint Thomas Aquinas is known as one of the greatest theologians in the history of the Church. He was a Dominican priest and a brilliant student. He is the patron saint of all universities and of students. The Church celebrates his feast day on January 28.

Visit *Lives of the Saints* on **www.webelieveweb.com** to learn more about saints and holy people.

What's *the* Word?

"They [the early Christians] devoted themselves to the teaching of the apostles and to the communal life, to the breaking of the bread and to the prayers... Every day they devoted themselves to meeting together in the temple area and to breaking bread in their homes. They ate their meals with exultation and sincerity of heart, praising God and enjoying favor with all the people. And every day the Lord added to their number." (Acts of the Apostles 2:42, 46–47)

• Which sacrament is described in the first verse?

_____

• Circle the sentence above that implies that more and more people were being baptized and following Jesus.

Question Corner

As you near the end of the Grade 6 *We Believe* program, what questions do you still have about the Bible?

_____

_____

_____

_____

_____

Take Home

Read the *Question Corner* with your family. Talk about your response(s). Work together to find the answers. Invite family members to share favorite Bible stories or passages that were introduced to them through the Grade 6 *We Believe* program.

CHAPTER TEST

Write True or False for the following sentences.
Then change the false sentences to make them true.

1. _____ Catholic social teaching calls us to work for justice and peace as Jesus did.

_____

2. _____ The writers of the New Testament were inspired and guided by Paul to record the truths of faith God wanted revealed to us.

_____

3. _____ The sacraments join Catholics all over the world with Jesus and one another, and unite the Church as the Body of Christ.

_____

4. _____ The dignity of work is an important source for Christian living and worship.

_____

Short Answers

5. What kinds of books are in the New Testament?

_____

6. Name two ways we live out Jesus' new commandment.

_____

7. What is a sacrament?

_____

8. There are seven themes of Catholic social teaching. List three.

_____

Write a paragraph to answer this question.

9–10. How does the Church use Scripture?

_____

_____

_____

_____

The Church in the World

26

✝ We Gather in Prayer

Leader: Blessed be God who made us to be his Church.

Blessed be the name of the Lord.

All: Now and for ever.

Reader: A reading from the holy Gospel according to Matthew

All: Glory to you, O Lord.

Reader: Jesus "said to them, 'But who do you say that I am?' Simon Peter said in reply, 'You are the Messiah, the Son of the living God.' Jesus said to him . . . 'you are Peter, and upon this rock I will build my church.'"
(Matthew 16:15–18)

The Gospel of the Lord.

All: Praise to you, Lord Jesus Christ.

🎵 Who Am I?

Who do people say I am?
Tell me who I am!
Are you Elijah? No, I'm not.
John the Baptist? No, I'm not.
Jeremiah? No, I'm not.

Who do you say I am?
Tell me who I am!
You are Jesus! Yes, I am.
Christ the Lord! Yes, I am.
Son of God! Yes, I am.

On your faith I'll build my Church.
We will build your Church!
Will you follow? Yes, we will!
Love each other? Yes, we will!
Share the Good News? Yes, we will!

Tell the people who I am.
Tell them who I am.
We will tell the people,
you are Christ the Lord, Son of God!

We live as one people.

✝ *Holy Spirit, increase our faith.*

Sometimes we may say to others that we believe in peace, justice, and family. What do you believe in? How do you show others what you believe in?

WE BELIEVE

Each time we gather for Mass, we profess our faith as a community. We do this by praying the Apostles' Creed or the Nicene Creed. We declare our belief in the Blessed Trinity, Christ, and the Church. In the Nicene Creed we state, "We believe in one holy catholic and apostolic church." One, holy, catholic, and apostolic are the four essential features, or identifying marks, of the Church. They are also called the **marks of the Church**.

The members of the Church believe in and follow the one Lord, Jesus Christ. The Church is one because its members are joined to Christ, who "is the head of the body, the church" (Colossians 1:18). Saint Paul wrote, "As a body is one though it has many parts, and all the parts of the body, though many, are one body, so also Christ. For in one Spirit we were all baptized into one body, whether Jews or Greeks, slaves or free persons" (1 Corinthians 12:12–13).

The Church is one because:

• Jesus Christ unites us by his Death and Resurrection

• the one Holy Spirit draws us together and guides us as a community

• the pope and bishops are called to lead us and continue the work of the Apostles

• the Seven Sacraments unite us and enable us to share in God's grace.

Members of the Church share the same Baptism in the name of the Father, and the Son, and the Holy Spirit. Because of our common Baptism, we participate in the Eucharist, another very important sign of our unity. In the Eucharist, we are nourished by the Word of God and receive the Body and Blood of Christ. We are joined more closely to Christ and one another to form the Body of Christ, the Church. And we show that we are filled with the life of Christ by the way that we live.

The Church and Other Christian Communities
The Catholic Church teaches that it is the Church founded by Christ himself. It is the one, holy, catholic, and apostolic Church. However, the Catholic Church respects all other Christians, recognizes the good in other Christian traditions, and has an especially close connection to the members of the Orthodox Churches. Other followers of Christ include: Episcopalians, Lutherans, Methodists, Presbyterians, Baptists, and Pentecostals.

Catholics have many things in common with other Christians. Most Christians are baptized and believe that Jesus is both divine and human. They believe that he died and rose to save us from sin. Christians also share the belief that the Bible was inspired by the Holy Spirit. For Christians throughout the world the Bible is the most important book.

But Jesus wanted his followers to be united. At the Last Supper Jesus prayed, "I pray not only for them, but also for those who will believe in me through their word, so that they may all be one" (John 17:20–21). So the Catholic Church works with other Christian communities to bring about the unity of the Church. This work to promote the unity among all Christians is called **ecumenism**.

The task of ecumenism involves all of us. We are called to know and understand our faith and the teachings of the Church. We are called to participate in our parish and grow as disciples of Christ. We are called to pray that all Christians may be one. A special time to pray for this is during the Week of Prayer for Christian Unity that takes place each January.

Key Words

marks of the Church the four essential features of the Church: one, holy, catholic, and apostolic

ecumenism the work to promote unity among all Christians

WE RESPOND

Make a poster illustrating some possible ways to bring about ecumenism.

How can you show that you believe in ecumenism?

Ecumenical Prayer Service, Toronto, Canada

We live as a holy people.

WE GATHER

✝ *Father, holy is your name.*

The word *holy* is an adjective. What are some of the nouns you would use it to describe? What in your life do you consider holy?

WE BELIEVE

We learn from the Old Testament stories of creation that the one true God is good and holy. We know that he shared his goodness with all of his creation, most especially with humans. When God's people struggled to remain good and faithful, God continued to be with them. His prophets called the people to be holy through worship and just living. God so loved his people and wanted to share his life with them that he sent his only Son to be their Messiah.

Christ offered his goodness and holiness to all of us through his life, Death, Resurrection, and Ascension. Christ shares his holiness with us today through the Church. **Holiness** is sharing in God's goodness and responding to his love by the way we live. This holiness comes from the gift of God's life that he shares with us through the sacraments and from living as faithful Christians every day. The gifts of the Holy Spirit help us to respond to the love God offers us, and to follow Christ's example of loving service.

The Apostles taught the early Christians that by Baptism they shared in the very life of Christ. They knew that this union with Christ meant that they shared in his holiness, too. All the baptized were considered "holy ones." Saint Paul wrote to the new community at Corinth, "Do you not know that you are the temple of God, and that the Spirit of God dwells in you? . . . the temple of God, which you are, is holy" (1 Corinthians 3:16, 17).

To Paul, *holy* was another way of saying "belonging to God." He told the Corinthians, "you have been sanctified in Christ Jesus, called to be holy, with all those everywhere who call upon the name of the Lord Jesus Christ" (1 Corinthians 1:2).

Paul, Peter, and the other Apostles encouraged Christ's disciples to live lives of holiness. We, too, share this call to holiness. We look to Jesus as our model for holy living. We live this life of grace as Jesus' disciples. He lived his life in perfect love of God the Father and in service to others, and he wants us to lead holy lives, too. Our holiness grows as we respond to God's love in our lives and live as Christ asks us to live.

List some signs of holiness in the world today. Who are some people who you think live holy lives?

Models of Holiness From the beginning of the Church, some of God's holy ones have been remembered in a special way. The martyrs were the first to be honored for heroic virtue and faithfulness to God. "Heroic virtue" is a term used to describe people who are brave, committed to the faith, and Christ-like in distinctive ways. Heroic virtue motivates people to do things that are very difficult.

holiness sharing in God's goodness and responding to his love by the way we live; our holiness comes through grace

298

Saints have stood up for their faith in many ways. Some saints preached the Good News of Christ in times when the Church was misunderstood by society. Others put Jesus' words into action in the midst of discrimination or injustice. Many others dedicated their lives to prayer and penance. These women and men are friends and servants of God. Their lives are models for us.

The Church officially declares a disciple of Christ a saint by a process called *canonization*. We remember and celebrate each canonized saint on a special day during the Church year. For many saints, this day is the day of their death, which we see as the beginning of their new life with God in Heaven.

The lives of the saints teach us about true discipleship. Because the saints are closely united to Christ, they pray for us constantly. They help the Church to grow in holiness. Their love for the Church is great.

It is important to remember that we are all God's holy ones and that his Church is holy. But we are human, and the Church is a human community. We are tempted and at times we do not live as God calls us to live. However, through the grace of the Sacrament of Penance, we are again freed from sin and made holy. The Sacrament of the Eucharist also strengthens us to follow Christ's example of holiness. Praying, respecting all people, living fairly, and working for justice and peace help us to respond to God's grace in our lives and to help the Church to grow in holiness.

WE RESPOND

How can you grow in holiness this week?

In groups identify some ways you and your families can show others that you "belong to God."

_____

_____

_____

As a class plan to present some of these ways to a class of younger students. Design the presentation to include role-plays that involve the younger students.

Venerable Pierre Toussaint

Saint Elizabeth of Portugal

Saint Cecilia

Saint Martin of Tours

Saint Paul

Saint Mary Magdalene

As Catholics...

On All Saints' Day, November 1, we remember and honor all of Christ's faithful followers who lived holy lives on earth and now live in happiness with God forever. We not only celebrate the lives of canonized saints but also all people who are saints with God. This is a good time to celebrate the lives of our patron saints—the saints whose names we share, the saints for whom our schools and parishes are named, and the saints that our families honor.

On All Souls' Day, November 2, we remember all people who have died, particularly those in our own families and parishes. We pray that they may know God's love and mercy and share in eternal life.

Who are some of the people you remember on these special days?

We live as a welcoming people.

WE GATHER

✝ *God our Father, help us to love all your children.*

There are specific conditions to being a member of certain clubs or groups. Discuss what conditions you think are necessary to being in the choir, on a sports team, in the chess club, or in the art club.

WE BELIEVE

The word *catholic* means "universal." The Church is open to all people everywhere. We welcome all who seek God's love and mercy. This has been true since the beginning of the Church.

Jesus commissioned the Apostles and sent them to make disciples of all nations. Some of them traveled to Rome, Antioch, and other parts of the world to preach the Gospel message. They baptized believers and established local Church communities. This was the beginning of the universal Church.

Catholics belong to a great variety of cultures, and they live their faith in different ways. Their different customs and traditions are a true gift to the Church. We are blessed that all are part of the life of the Church. All of us together are still one in Christ.

No matter what the racial or cultural heritage of our parish communities, we are a community of faith. We may be from different countries. We may speak different languages and have different customs. But we are united by our love for Christ and our common call to holiness. Together we make the Church catholic, and we participate in the sacraments, learn about our faith, and grow as members of the Church. We are united and strengthened to love as Jesus loved and to continue his work for justice and peace.

🧍 Illustrate ways your parish is one community made up of many different people.

The Mission of the Church The Church is missionary because she is catholic. All people are invited to believe in Jesus and to be baptized in the faith of the Church. Extending this invitation to faith is an important part of the Church's mission. The mission of the Church is to share the Good News of Christ and to spread the Kingdom of God.

We are the Church, and each of us is called to take part in the mission of the Church. We are called to share the Good News of Christ and to live lives of holiness. We can do this by our prayers, good works, and everyday living.

Some members of the Church share in her mission as missionaries. Single and married people, priests, and religious sisters and brothers can be missionaries. Students of many ages, adults, and entire families can serve as missionaries.

Missionaries share their faith with those they serve. They also may build homes, schools, and hospitals with the people that they serve. They may teach people to farm and to provide for their needs in other ways, too. These works of service put the Good News of Christ into action.

Respect for All Faiths   There are many other religions beside Christianity. As Catholics we respect the rights of others to practice and live their faith. As you have learned, Christianity has its roots in Judaism. The Jewish People are our ancestors in faith, and many of our beliefs, prayer practices, and traditions are based in Judaism. For example, we share the belief in the one true God and follow the Ten Commandments.

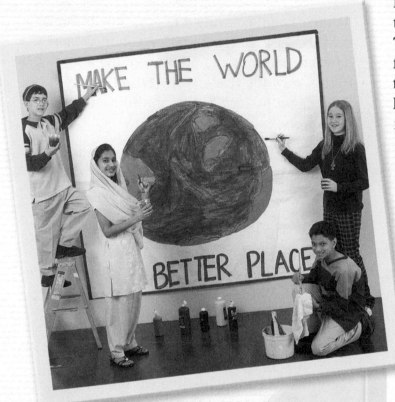

Today Jewish People everywhere continue to live their faith in the one true God. God's covenant with the Jewish People is a wonderful sign of God's great love for the people he first made his own. Jewish People continue to live by that covenant today.

Islam is another religion with which Christians and Jews share belief in the one true God. People who practice the religion of Islam are called Muslims. Muslims, Jews, and Christians have the important connection of worshiping God and consider Abraham a common ancestor. Muslims follow the teachings of the prophet Muhammad, who lived in the sixth and seventh centuries.

People of other religions and faiths include Buddhists, Hindus, and members of many native tribes. There are many other people of faith. They, too, follow a set of beliefs and show their faith in different ways. In communities around the world, there are people of different religions living and working together. The Church respects the rights of all people to practice their faith, and we join with them in trying to make the world a better place. People who die for the faith, catechumens, and those who through no fault of their own do not know Christ or his Church, but who seek God and do their best to follow his will, may achieve salvation even if they have not been baptized.

WE RESPOND

 What might your class do to show respect for people whose beliefs are not the same as yours? List three ideas here and then decide on ways to make them a part of your daily life.

_____

_____

_____

_____

_____

We live as a faithful people.

WE GATHER

✝ *Holy Spirit, guide all those who spread the Good News of Christ.*

🏃 Write some sentences in which the word *foundation* is used in different ways. Share your sentences with the class.

WE BELIEVE

The Church is apostolic because she is built on the faith of the Apostles. ". . . you are fellow citizens with the holy ones and members of the household of God, built upon the foundation of the apostles and prophets, with Christ Jesus himself as the capstone" (Ephesians 2:19–20).

Jesus chose the Apostles to care for and lead the community of believers. The faith we profess and practice is based on the faith that the Apostles shared and spread. For instance, the Apostles' Creed tells us about Jesus, his teachings, and the teachings of the Apostles. The Apostles' Creed has an important place in the Church. From the early years of the Church in Rome, this was the creed that those being baptized professed.

The life and leadership of the Church is based on that of the Apostles. When the Apostles established local communities of believers, the Apostles appointed local leaders to represent them in the community. The Apostles passed on to these leaders what Christ had given them: the Gift of the Holy Spirit and the authority to carry out the mission of Jesus Christ. These leaders preached the Good News and shared the teachings of the Apostles. They continued the Apostles' ministry and acted under their leadership. They were the successors of the Apostles and eventually became known as bishops.

As the Church continued to grow, the bishops, the successors of the Apostles, commissioned others to continue the ministry of the Apostles. In this way, the leadership of the Church throughout history can be traced back to the Apostles.

The bishops of today are called to continue the ministry of the Apostles. As the Bishop of Rome, the pope is the successor of the Apostle Peter, who was the first leader of the Church of Rome. The pope continues Peter's ministry and has a special responsibility to care for the Church. The bishops, with the pope as their head, are called to lead and guide the whole Church.

The whole Church shares in the mission that Christ first gave to his Apostles. But as a body has different parts with different functions, so the members of the Church have different roles in sharing in this mission.

The Laity The laity are the baptized members of the Church who share in the Church's mission to bring the Good News of Christ to the world. The laity are also known as laypeople or the Christian faithful. Right now you are a layperson. All Catholics begin their lives as members of the Christian faithful. Most remain laypeople their entire lives, and serve God and share in the mission of the Church as single people or married people.

You are a layperson, and every day you are growing as Jesus' disciple. You do not have to wait to be an adult to be an active member of the Church. You can live and share your faith right now. As a layperson you are called to share the Good News at home, in school, and in your neighborhood. You can take part in your parish celebrations and activities. Every day you can live as Jesus taught. You can be an example of Christian living for others.

Laypeople are called to bring the Good News of Christ to their work places and local communities. Women and men in the laity are called to be involved in city, state, and national governments. In these situations they often take on leadership positions and make many decisions. They have a responsibility to act and make decisions based on the teachings of Jesus and on their faith.

Laypeople are called to participate in the celebration of the sacraments and to support their parishes. They may serve on the parish pastoral council or in the various parish ministries. In their dioceses they may lead or work in areas such as catechesis, education, worship, youth ministry, and peace and justice ministries.

It is truly a blessing that all in the Church can work to bring about God's reign. We are one people who can show by our love of others that we are living as Christ's disciples in the world.

WE RESPOND

What are the different ways that the Church serves the world?

What are the different ways that people your age participate in the mission of the Church?

PROJECT

Show What *you* Know

Across

3. the successor of the Apostle Peter and leader of the Church

4. the work to promote unity among all Christians

Down

1. a word that means "universal"

2. sharing in God's goodness and responding to his love by the way we live

6. The _____ of the Church are the four essential features of the Church: one, holy, catholic, and apostolic.

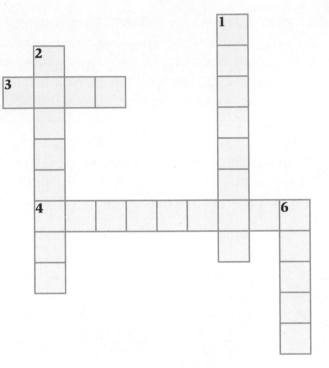

Question Corner

How do you share in the Church's mission as a sixth-grader? Check all that apply.

❏ I share the Good News at home, at school, and in my neighborhood.

❏ I take part in parish activities.

❏ I live as Jesus taught.

❏ I am an example of Christian living.

❏ I participate in the celebration of the sacraments.

❏ other _____

Now, pass it on!

D1SC1PLE

Pray
Learn
Celebrate
Share
Choose
Live

Saint Stories

Saint Maximilian Kolbe was a Franciscan priest. During World War II, he was imprisoned in a Nazi concentration camp. There he offered his life in place of another man, a husband and father, who had been chosen to die. Saint Maximilian is an example of unselfish love for all people. The Church celebrates his feast day on August 14. How can you show that you are unselfish at home? in your community?

_____

Visit *Lives of the Saints* on www.webelieveweb.com to learn about more saints and holy people.

Pray Today

We are called to pray that all Christians may be one. A special time to pray for this is during the Week of Prayer for Christian Unity. The Week of Prayer for Christian Unity is traditionally celebrated every year from January 18 to 25.

↳ DISCIPLE CHALLENGE Write a prayer for Christian unity.

_____

_____

_____

_____

Take Home

Redesign the logo for *Project Disciple* with your family. You might want to use the outline on the left for your ideas.

Be sure to live it out!

Complete the following.

1. The Church is one because _____

_____

2. The Church is holy because _____

_____

3. The Church is catholic because _____

_____

4. The Church is apostolic because _____

_____

Circle the letter of the correct answer.

5. _____ is sharing in God's goodness and responding to his love by the way we live.

   a. Ecumenism   **b.** Catholic   **c.** Holiness

6. The _____ are all the baptized members of the Church who share in the Church's mission to bring the Good News of Christ to the world.

   a. bishops   **b.** laity   **c.** Apostles

7. The Catholic Church is the Church founded by _____.

   a. Jesus Christ   **b.** Peter   **c.** Paul

8. The work to promote unity among all Christians is called _____.

   a. ecumenism   **b.** holiness   **c.** marks of the Church

Write a paragraph to answer this question.

9–10. What can young people do to help the Church to grow?

_____

_____

_____

_____

"The love of God has been poured into our hearts by his Spirit living in us, alleluia."

Introductory Rites, Pentecost Vigil Mass

SEASONAL CHAPTER 27

This liturgical chapter celebrates the entire Easter season.

During the Easter season, we celebrate our new life in Christ and the coming of the Holy Spirit.

WE GATHER

✝ *Lord Jesus, may we rise with you to new life in the Holy Spirit!*

Think of a time when a person was welcomed into your family. How did you celebrate?

WE BELIEVE

The Easter season is a special time to rejoice in the new life we have in Christ. It is a time for bringing new members into the Church—for celebrating the Sacraments of Baptism and Confirmation, both of which lead to the table of the Eucharist. And during the Easter season the whole Church grows in their experience of the risen Christ, and through liturgical celebrations, reflects with joy on Christ's Paschal Mystery. We welcome the new members of the Church and pray with them each week.

The Easter season lasts for fifty days. During this time we celebrate the Resurrection and Ascension of Jesus Christ and the coming of the Holy Spirit on Pentecost. We hear stories of the risen Jesus' appearances to his disciples. We learn about the beginning of the Church from the Acts of the Apostles.

Easter Monday in Nigeria The day after Easter Sunday is an important day of worship in Nigeria. In many towns and villages Catholics and other Christians gather in a common place which they name "Galilee" for the day. They believe that, like the Apostles and first disciples, they are to be in "Galilee" to meet the risen Lord. Christians of all faiths gather together to celebrate Christ's Resurrection with preaching, singing and dancing, sharing a meal, and participating in all types of sports and games. This "Galilee" gathering is possible because Easter Monday is traditionally a public holiday in Nigeria.

Ascension   During the season of Easter we recall the last event of Jesus' public life, his Ascension. Jesus ascended, or returned to his Father in heaven forty days after he rose from the dead. Thus the Church celebrates the feast of the Ascension around forty days after Easter. In many dioceses of the United States this feast is a holy day of obligation. We read about Jesus' Ascension in the Acts of the Apostles.

Christ the Redeemer,
Rio de Janiero

Acts of the Apostles 1:3–12

Forty days after his Resurrection, the risen Jesus had gathered with his Apostles outside of Jerusalem. He told them, "'You will receive power when the holy Spirit comes upon you, and you will be my witnesses in Jerusalem, throughout Judea and Samaria, and to the ends of the earth.' When he had said this, as they were looking on, he was lifted up, and a cloud took him from their sight." (Acts of the Apostles 1:8–9).

The Apostles went back to the upper room and waited in prayer.

Pentecost Fifty days after Easter we celebrate the Feast of Pentecost. The word *Pentecost* comes from a Greek word meaning "fiftieth." Pentecost is celebrated on the last Sunday and final day of the Easter season. On Pentecost Sunday we celebrate the coming of the Holy Spirit to the first disciples. We also celebrate the beginning of the Church, and we rejoice because the Holy Spirit fills our hearts today.

The Jewish feast of Pentecost was celebrated fifty days after Passover, as a thanksgiving for the harvest. The "first fruits" of field and orchard were blessed and shared. So it is fitting that on this feast God the Father and God the Son, chose to share the "first fruits" of Jesus' Resurrection—the Holy Spirit, the power sent from on high. This Gift of the Holy Spirit was a great gift of God's love. The Apostles now shared in the fellowship of the Holy Spirit.

What a difference the Holy Spirit made in the lives of the Apostles! During Jesus' trial and Death, the Apostles were afraid. After his Resurrection, they remained hidden. When the Holy Spirit came, the Apostles began to remember the words of Jesus and to act on them. They began preaching and teaching. They were no longer alone. Neither are we alone because the Holy Spirit will be with us always.

The Apostles and Mary spent the time between the Ascension and Pentecost in prayer. The Church keeps the days between Ascension and Pentecost as days of waiting and prayer for the Holy Spirit. During this time the liturgy is full of prayerful longing for the coming of the Holy Spirit.

WE RESPOND

Pray this prayer together.

"Father,
let your Spirit come upon us with power
  to fill us with his gifts.
May he make our hearts pleasing to you,
  and ready to do your will."

Prepare for the feast of the coming of the Holy Spirit. Write a prayer, a poem, a favorite quotation from Scripture, or a "Spirit-filled" action you can do.

✝ We Respond in Prayer

Leader: Lord, send out your Spirit.

All: And renew the face of the earth.

Reader: A reading from the first Letter of Saint Paul to the Corinthians

"There are different kinds of spiritual gifts but the same Spirit; there are different forms of service but the same Lord. . . As a body is one though it has many parts, and all the parts of the body, though many, are one body, so also Christ. For in one Spirit we were all baptized into one body, whether Jews or Greeks, slaves or free persons, and we were all given to drink of one Spirit." (1 Corinthians 12:4–5, 12–13)

The Word of the Lord.

All: Thanks be to God.

🎵 Envía Tu Espíritu

Refrain

Envía tu Espíritu, envía tu Espíritu,
envía tu Espíritu,
sea renovada la faz de la tierra.
Sea renovada la faz de la tierra.

Spirit of the living God,
burn in our hearts,
and make us a people of hope
and compassion. (Refrain)

Wind of promise, wind of change,
friend of the poor,
empower your people to make
peace and justice. (Refrain)

PROJECT DISCIPLE

Pray Learn Celebrate Share Choose Live

Celebrate!

Answer the following questions about the season.

1. How long is the season of Easter? _____

2. During the season of Easter, what do we recall as the last event of

   Jesus' public life? _____

3. What are we celebrating on Pentecost Sunday? _____

4. When do we celebrate Pentecost? _____

5. Which feast during the Easter season is also a holy day of obligation

   in many dioceses in the United States? _____

What's the Word?

"God raised this Jesus; of this we are all witnesses. Exalted at the right hand of God, he received the promise of the holy Spirit from the Father and poured it forth, as you see and hear." (Acts 2:32–33)

- What two liturgical events does Peter describe in this passage?

  _____

- Underline the phrase that describes how the Apostles are part of the Easter story.

Picture This

Design an e-card to send during the Easter season. If possible, include symbols of Easter in your design, such as the Paschal Candle, a flowering plant, a white dove, etc.

Take Home

The Irish phrase *Cead Mile Failte* (kayd me-lay fall-chuh) means "a hundred thousand welcomes." The season of Easter is a time of welcoming new members into the Church.

How can your family welcome these new members? Make a list here:

_____

_____

UNIT TEST

Fill in the circle beside the correct answer.

1. The Church teaches us that _____ is one of the two means by which God's Revelation comes to us. The Bible is the other.
   ○ Tradition ○ liturgy ○ the Council of Nicea

2. In the first part of the Sermon on the Mount, Jesus gave guidelines that describe the way to live as his disciples. These are the _____.
   ○ Gospels ○ Beatitudes ○ Lord's Prayer

3. _____ did not believe that the other Apostles had seen Jesus.
   ○ The Apostle Thomas ○ Mary Magdalene ○ Joseph of Arimethea

4. On his way to _____ to persecute Christians, Saul had an experience that changed his life.
   ○ Antioch ○ Damascus ○ Ephesus

5. One, holy, catholic, and apostolic are the four _____.
   ○ themes of Catholic social teaching ○ marks of the Church ○ models of holiness

6. The Apostle _____ was chosen to take Judas's place.
   ○ Matthias ○ Paul ○ Jerome

7. As a Christian prophecy, the Book of Revelation deals with _____.
   ○ the ministry of the Apostles ○ the life and work of Jesus ○ Christ's Second Coming

8. The work to promote the unity of all Christians is called _____.
   ○ ecumenism ○ social justice ○ holiness

9. We call the power of God's love coming into the world and into our lives the _____.
   ○ Gospels ○ Kingdom of God ○ marks of the Church

10. For Christians the _____ is the new Passover of God's People.
    ○ Eucharist ○ Gospels ○ Beatitudes

11. Christians call the day Christ died _____.
    ○ Sabbath ○ Good Friday ○ Pentecost

continued on next page 313

Write True or False for the following sentences. Then change the false sentences to make them true.

12. _____ The Gospels are effective signs given to us by Jesus through which we share in God's life, which we call grace.

_____

13. _____ It was at Antioch, about ten years after Jesus' Death, that his followers were first called Nazarenes.

_____

14. _____ The Lord's Prayer is one of the most important prayers in the Gospels and of the Church.

_____

15. _____ Catholic social teaching calls us to work for justice and peace as Jesus did.

_____

16. _____ The Apostles are all the baptized members of the Church who share in the Church's mission to bring the Good News of Christ to the world.

_____

Write a paragraph to answer each question.

17–18. If you were an early Christian and were arrested for your faith, what would you tell the Roman authorities?

_____

_____

_____

19–20. As members of the Church, each of us is called to take part in her mission. How can you, as a sixth grader, do this?

_____

_____

_____

Devotions and Pilgrimages

Part 1   I Open My Heart

As Catholics, we worship God in the liturgy and sacraments. But we can express our love for God in many other ways. One of these ways is by making a pilgrimage. A pilgrimage is a prayer journey taken to a shrine or sacred place.

Look at this image. A scallop shell is a symbol of pilgrimage, used by those on a pilgrimage to the tomb of Saint James in Santiago de Compostela in Spain.

Trace, decorate, and cut out the shell. Keep the shell with you on your "Devotions and Pilgrimages" retreat.

Obradoiro Square and Santiago de Compostela Cathedral, Galicia, Spain

Devotions and Pilgrimages

Part 2 We Come Together for Prayer

Leader: Union with God is the beginning and the end of life's pilgrimage. Let us call on him with confidence, saying:

All: (*Response for each petition*) Lord, be the companion of our journey.

Reader 1: Father all-holy, of old you made yourself the guide and the way for your people as they wandered in the desert; be our protection as we begin this journey, so that we may return home again in safety. For this we pray: (*Response*)

Reader 2: You have given us your only Son to be our way to you; make us follow faithfully and unswervingly. For this we pray: (*Response*)

Reader 3: You guide your pilgrim Church on earth through the Holy Spirit; may we seek you in all things and walk always in the way of your commandments. For this we pray: (*Response*)

Reader 4: You lead us along right and peaceful paths; grant that we may one day see you face to face in heaven. For this we pray: (*Response*)

(*Now write your own intercession in the space below. Take turns praying and responding to these intercessions aloud.*)

Leader: All-powerful God, you always show mercy toward those who love you, and you are never far away from those who seek you. Remain with your servants on this holy pilgrimage and guide their way in accord to your will. Shelter them with your protection by day, give them the light of your grace by night, and, as their companion on the journey, bring them to their destination in safety. We ask this through Christ our Lord.

All: Amen.

(Adapted from Blessing of Pilgrims)

Catholic Identity Retreat

Devotions and Pilgrimages

Part 3   I Cherish God's Word

"Then [two disciples] said to each other, 'Were not our hearts burning [within us] while [Jesus] spoke to us on the way and opened the scriptures to us?' So they set out at once and returned to Jerusalem where they found gathered together the eleven and those with them who were saying, 'The Lord has truly been raised and has appeared to Simon!' Then the two recounted what had taken place on the way and how [Jesus] was made known to them in the breaking of the bread.

While they were still speaking about this, he stood in their midst and said to them, 'Peace be with you.'" (Luke 24:32–36)

READ the quotation from Scripture. Read slowly. Pay close attention to what you are reading.

REFLECT on what you read. Think about:

- When have you recognized Jesus on your journey of faith?

- The gift of peace Jesus gives to his followers.

- How can you offer peace to others?

SHARE your thoughts and feelings with God in prayer. Let your thoughts and feelings come naturally. Speak to God as a friend.

CONTEMPLATE, or sit quietly and allow your attention to remain focused on God's Word in the Scripture from the Gospel of Luke above.

People on a pilgrimage to Croagh Patrick, a mountain in Ireland related to the life of Saint Patrick

Devotions and Pilgrimages

Part 4 **I Value My Catholic Faith**

The Stations of the Resurrection is a devotion begun in 1988 by Father Sabino Palumbieri in Rome. Praying these stations is like taking a pilgrimage to the many places mentioned.

Look at the one of the Stations of the Resurrection that your team has received. Read the corresponding Scripture passage, and in the space below jot down notes about what should be the illustration for this station.

Then work with your team to illustrate your station on the poster board or drawing paper. Now pray the Stations of the Resurrection holding up your illustrations and reading the Scripture passages aloud.

Devotions and Pilgrimages

Part 5 I Celebrate Catholic Identity

Mary, the Mother of Jesus, is honored by many devotions and in shrines and sites of pilgrimage throughout the world. Below are images of two pilgrimage sites you can visit to honor Mary.

Find out about the stories of these Marian devotions and see if any signs or miracles at this site were attributed to Mary's intercession. Which of these two shrines would be your first choice to visit? Why?

_____

_____

Share your choice with the group.

Shrine of Our Lady of Knock, a pilgrimage site in Ireland

Image of Our Lady of Guadalupe in the Basilica of Our Lady of Guadalupe, Mexico City, a pilgrimage site in Mexico

Catholic Identity Retreat

Devotions and Pilgrimages

Part 6 I Honor My Catholic Identity

Forty Hours is a devotion to Jesus in the Blessed Sacrament. During Forty Hours, the Blessed Sacrament is placed in a vessel called a *monstrance* and displayed for forty consecutive hours. People sign up to take turns being present with the Blessed Sacrament during the entire forty hours. They pray, sing, and meditate. Imagine you are participating in Forty Hours at your parish. Pray silently to Jesus in the Blessed Sacrament.

Pray the Glory Be to the Father together:

Glory be to the Father
and to the Son
and the Holy Spirit,
as it was in the beginning
is now, and ever shall be
world without end. Amen.

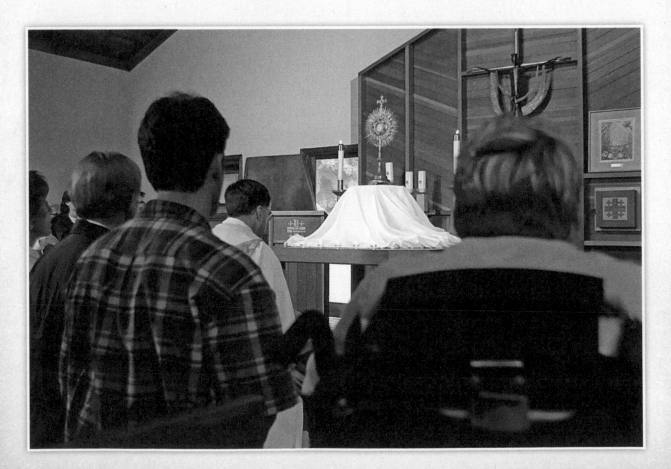

Catholic Identity Retreat

Bringing the Retreat Home

Devotions and Pilgrimages

Retreat Recap

Review the pages of your child's *Celebrating Catholic Identity: Prayer* retreat. Ask your child to tell you about the retreat. Talk about the following:

- Devotions and pilgrimages are among the ways we express our love for God.

- The Church's rich heritage of devotions and pilgrimages honor Jesus, Mary, and many of the saints.

- A pilgrimage is a prayer journey taken to a shrine or sacred place.

A Virtual Pilgrimage

Through the centuries, Christians have made pilgrimages to the Holy Land. Make a pilgrimage to the Holy Land "virtually" with your child. Explore a Web site for Holy Land tours or another online guide featuring the various holy sites that Christians might visit. Discuss any images of holy sites that capture your interest, and talk about the events in Jesus' life to which these locations relate.

Basilica of the National Shrine of the Immaculate Conception, Washington, D.C.

Take a Moment

Make a pilgrimage close to home with your family. Learn about any local Catholic shrines by searching for Catholic shrines in your area online or contacting your parish or diocese. If possible, plan a family pilgrimage to one of these holy sites. You might also want to make a family pilgrimage to your local cathedral, which is a sign of unity of your diocese or archdiocese.

Family Prayer

Choose a devotion that your family can make your own. For example, perhaps you can make a habit of praying a daily prayer to Mary or a favorite saint.

Detail, Church of the Nativity, Bethlehem, holy site believed to be Jesus' birthplace

For more resources, see the *Catholic Identity Home Companion* at the end of this book.

Why We Believe
As a Catholic Family

What if someone asks us:

- Why do Catholics believe in miracles?
- Why do Catholics make pilgrimages to holy sites?

The following resources can help us to respond:

A miracle is an extraordinary event that is beyond human power and brought about by God. Throughout history God has shown his power and love through many signs and miracles. Miracles remind us of the continued presence of God in our lives. The signs and miracles that Jesus worked attest that he was sent by God the Father. They manifest that God's Kingdom is present in Jesus Christ, God the Son.

🌿 What does Scripture say?

"[Elijah] called out to the Lord: 'O Lord, my God, let the life breath return to the body of this child.' The Lord heard the prayer of Elijah; the life breath returned to the child's body and he revived."
(1 Kings 17:21–22)

Jesus said, "Unless you people see signs and wonders, you will not believe" (John 4:48).

Jesus said, "But I have testimony greater than John's. The works that the Father gave me to accomplish, these works that I perform testify on my behalf that the Father has sent me" (John 5:36).

God has continued to send signs and miracles to help us to believe in him and in his presence among us. Some signs and miracles are very personal, but others have happened at specific places throughout the world. Often the Virgin Mary, one of the saints, or even an image of Jesus has been seen by people at these sites, and churches or shrines have been established there to remember these events. Catholics go to these sites to express their love for God and to stand at the very sites where visions and miracles have been recorded. The Church determines whether these signs or miracles are authentic from God. The Church recognizes signs and miracles as being works of God either directly or through the prayers and intercessions of a specific saint or saints.

🌿 What does the Church say?

"Besides sacramental liturgy and sacramentals, catechesis must take into account the forms of piety and popular devotions among the faithful. The religious sense of the Christian people has always found expression in various forms of piety surrounding the Church's sacramental life, such as the veneration of relics, visits to sanctuaries, pilgrimages, processions, the stations of the cross, religious dances, the rosary, medals, etc." (CCC, 1674; see Denzinger Schonmetzer, 601, 603, 1822)

"[Miracles'] essential purpose is to indicate that the human person is destined and called to the kingdom of God. These signs therefore confirm in different ages and in the most varied circumstances the truth of the Gospel, and demonstrate the saving power of Christ who does not cease to call people (through the Church) on the path of faith."
(Saint John Paul II, General Audience, January 13, 1988)

Notes:

Explain the importance to Christians of each of these passages from Scripture. Then illustrate each passage.

1. "Now this is eternal life, that they should know you, the only true God, and the one whom you sent, Jesus Christ." (John 17:3)

2. "God created man in his image;
   in the divine image
      he created him;
   male and female
      he created them."
   (Genesis 1:27)

3. "Have dominion over the fish of the sea, the birds of the air, and all the living things that move on the earth." (Genesis 1:28)

4. "This is the sign of the covenant I have established between me and all mortal creatures that are on earth." (Genesis 9:17)

5. "Do not do the least thing to him. I know now how devoted you are to God, since you did not withhold from me your own beloved son." (Genesis 22:12)

Across

1. Moses' brother, who helped him explain God's message to the Israelites.

3. The sweet, bread-like food God provided to the Israelites in the wilderness.

5. Poetic prayers intended to be chanted or sung in public worship.

8. David's son, who succeeded him as king of Israel.

11. The first king of Israel, chosen by God and anointed by Samuel.

12. David's father, who summoned his son from the fields at Samuel's command.

13. The center of worship of the one true God that Solomon built in Jerusalem.

14. A Moabite woman whose story shows us that sadness can be turned into joy when we follow God's plan for us.

Down

1. The _____ of the covenant, the box in which the tablets of the Ten Commandments were kept.

2. The land God promised to the Israelites.

4. The night on which God spared the Israelites as he struck down the firstborn of the Egyptians.

5. Delilah, who betrayed Samson, was a _____ woman.

6. The man to whom God spoke from a burning bush, calling him to lead his people from slavery.

7. The son of Hannah whom God called to be a prophet.

9. Through God's actions and her firm faith in him, _____ helped free Israel from its enemies.

10. A poem or song expressing sorrow, mourning, or regret.

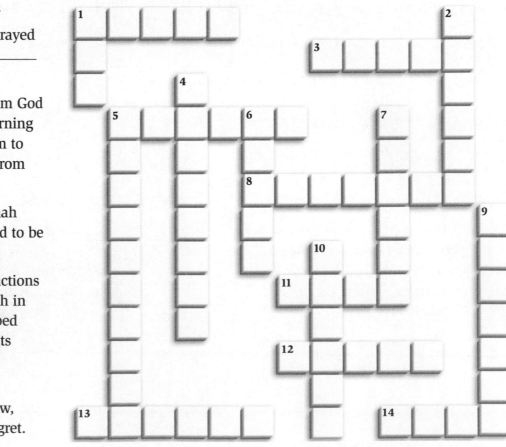

ALTERNATIVE ASSESSMENT

Amos	Elijah	Elisha	Ezekiel	John
Habakkuk	Isaiah	Jeremiah	Malachi	Micah

Write the name of the prophet that fits the description below.

1. This man was the first prophet sent by God to the northern kingdom of Israel to preach that the one true God is the only God; his name means "Yahweh is my God."

_____

2. God summoned this shepherd from the southern kingdom of Judah to call the people of the northern kingdom back to God.

_____

3. When God's people were in exile in Babylon, God told them that Babylon was an instrument for purifying Judea of its sins.

_____

4. The prophet Elijah anointed this man and threw his cloak over him as a sign that he was called to the mission of a prophet.

_____

5. This prophet was accused of blasphemy, attacked, and imprisoned by God's people, but he continued to speak out against the sins he saw around him.

_____

6. This prophet mentioned a messenger who would prepare the way for repentance and true worship.

_____

7. This prophet and priest warned God's people against all forms of social injustice, idolatry, and superstition.

_____

8. This great prophet foretold that salvation would come only through the suffering of a servant of the Lord. This servant would be without sin.

_____

9. This prophet foretold that a new David would restore the Chosen People.

_____

10. This son of Elizabeth and Zechariah preached and prophesied throughout Judea to prepare the way for the coming of the Messiah.

_____

As a member of the Church, you are called to continue Jesus' ministry. Choose four from the following and write a summary:

- the Lord's Prayer

- the Beatitudes

- Spiritual Works of Mercy

- Corporal Works of Mercy

- the Seven Sacraments

- the seven themes of Catholic social teaching

- the Bible.

_____

_____

_____

_____

_____

_____

_____

_____

_____

_____

_____

_____

_____

_____

Then describe ways that each of the four you have summarized above can be used to spread the Good News of Jesus Christ. Present your ideas in the form of a demonstration, a poster, or a song.

This year I learned about God's actions in the lives of his people throughout history.

I learned about

- the patriarchs _____
  _____

- Moses and the Exodus _____
  _____

- the prophets _____
  _____

- Jesus _____
  _____

2

✂ Cut on this line.

As a disciple of Jesus, I share my faith with others.

I can share stories from the Bible with

- ○ a younger child or children

- ○ a close friend

- ○ my family

- ○ _____

Three of my favorite stories I would like to

share are _____

_____

_____

6

As a disciple of Jesus, I live out my faith by following ancestors of faith.

An ancestor of faith who is an example

- of asking God for forgiveness _____
  _____

- of being just and fair _____
  _____

- of caring for the needs of others _____
  _____

- of being Jesus' disciple _____
  _____

I will continue to live out my faith by

_____

_____

7

As Jesus' disciple I celebrate the sacraments with the Church.

I have received the Sacraments of

_____

_____

I celebrated these sacraments with

_____

_____

I am preparing to receive the Sacrament of

_____

_____

I am preparing by _____

_____

_____

3

CONGRATULATIONS ON COMPLETING YOUR YEAR AS A GRADE 6 DISCIPLE!

Fold on this line.

A RECORD OF MY JOURNEY AS A GRADE 6 DISCIPLE

_____
Name

✂ Cut on this line.

As a disciple of Jesus, I am called to make loving choices.

This year I made a loving choice in interacting

- with my family _____
  _____

- with my friend(s) _____
  _____

- in school _____

When I heard about the needs of others, I chose to

_____

_____

_____

As a disciple of Jesus, I pray every day.

A prayer I like to pray from the

- Old Testament is _____
  _____

- New Testament is _____
  _____

I like to pray

○ by myself

○ with friends and family

○ with my parish

A prayer for guidance I will pray this summer

is _____

_____

✝ We Gather in Prayer

🎵 Though the Mountains May Fall

Though the mountains may fall
and the hills turn to dust,
yet the love of the Lord will stand
as a shelter for all who will call on his name.
Sing the praise and the glory of God.

Leader: Let us gather together to give thanks to our God.

All: God, we thank you for faithfulness and love. We thank you for our ancestors in faith, who have shown us your ways of love.

Leader: God, we thank you for revealing yourself to us through the words and actions of your Son, Jesus Christ.

All: God, help us continue Jesus' mission and share the Good News of your love with everyone we meet.

Leader: God, we ask for the Holy Spirit's guidance in being loving and faithful disciples. As we look forward to a safe and happy summer, help us to remember that Jesus is with us.

All: Amen!

The Lives of the Saints

Saint Joan of Arc

➤ **Born:** January 6, 1412 ➤ **Died:** May 30, 1431 ➤ **Feast Day:** May 30

What she said

"About Jesus Christ and the Church, I simply know they're just one thing, and we shouldn't complicate the matter."

What the world was like

Joan of Arc lived at the time of the beginning of the Renaissance, which was a revival of classical art, architecture, literature, and learning. This was a time of transition from medieval times to modern times.

When Joan of Arc was born, France was involved in the Hundred Years War with England. Because of this war, much of the farmland in France was ruined and people were starving because of lack of food. During Joan's life, many people in France died from the Black Death, a deadly plague that was spreading throughout Europe. People lived in fear of not only the English and the plague, but also of local French people who raided towns and villages.

Who she was

Joan of Arc grew up in France. Her father was a farmer. Although she did not have much formal education, her mother taught her prayers. Joan always listened to her parents and tried to do what they asked of her. She attended Mass every day and she tried to help the poor. She was quiet and preferred to play alone rather than with others. She enjoyed playing in the woods and she was good at spinning and weaving cloth.

While Joan was growing up, there was a war going on between France and England. This war had lasted almost one hundred years. France was divided and had no king. Joan began hearing the voices of Saint Michael, Saint Catherine, and Saint Margaret. They told Joan that she was chosen by God to unite France and to help Charles be crowned king. Joan was very surprised because she knew nothing about politics or about the military. She wanted to serve God, but she did not know how to help her country. Finally, she realized that this was God's will and he would lead her.

At first she was laughed at, but soon Joan was leading the French army with a banner that said "Jesus and Mary." She began winning battles. Soon the English were gone from many towns in France. The French soldiers loved Joan. Eventually, she saw Charles crowned the king of France.

Later Joan was captured and became a prisoner of the English. She was sentenced to death. Although she was afraid, Joan remained faithful to God and calmly went to her death holding a crucifix.

What this saint means to us today

Joan of Arc was faithful to God's will in her life. Even when she was laughed at, she kept her focus on God and what he asked her to do. It seemed to be impossible for a teenage girl to become a soldier, lead an army, and unite the country of France, but Joan did just that because of her faith.

When things seem to be impossible in our lives, we can be like Joan and let our faith guide us.

The Lives of the Saints

Name _____

Saint Joan of Arc

Joan of Arc grew up in France when her country was at war with England. She was the daughter of a farmer and lived a very simple and quiet life. She attended Mass every day and loved God very much. As a teenager, she heard the voices of Saint Michael, Saint Catherine, and Saint Margaret telling her that God had a special mission for her. God wanted Joan to unite France and to help Charles be crowned the king. Though this seemed impossible, Joan became the leader of the French army and won many battles. She was brave and helped to defend and unite her country. Because of her victories, Charles was crowned king of France with Joan by his side.

In the space below, write about a time that you found the courage to do something that you thought was right.

_____

_____

_____

_____

_____

_____

_____

_____

_____

_____

For saints, games, study guides and more,
visit **www.webelieveweb.com**.

Congratulations! Throughout your **We Believe** program you have learned, celebrated, prayed, chosen, shared, and served as a disciple of Jesus Christ.

Now, you are moving toward a more mature faith and a deeper relationship with Jesus Christ and the Catholic Church. As a junior high student, you will be experiencing a continuation of the **We Believe** program that is especially designed for you: **We Live Our Faith**.

There are two texts, one for each junior high year: **We Live Our Faith** *as Disciples of Jesus* and **We Live Our Faith** *as Members of the Church*.

Both texts are based on questions that real junior high students—like you—asked. You will have the opportunity to learn about what your faith can mean to your life as an older student.

The most important things I have learned about my faith this year are:

_____

_____

As a junior high student, I want to learn more about Jesus and the Church. Here is a question I hope to get answered.

_____

_____

_____

We are blessed to be disciples of Jesus Christ and members of the Church!

Prayers and Practices

Glory Be to the Father

Glory be to the Father
and to the Son
and the Holy Spirit,
as it was in the beginning
is now, and ever shall be
world without end. Amen.

Our Father

Our Father, who art in heaven,
hallowed be thy name;
thy kingdom come;
thy will be done on earth
    as it is in heaven.
Give us this day our daily bread;
and forgive us our trespasses
as we forgive those
    who trespass against us;
and lead us not into temptation,
but deliver us from evil. Amen.

Hail Mary

Hail Mary, full of grace,
the Lord is with you!
Blessed are you among women,
and blessed is the fruit
    of your womb, Jesus.
Holy Mary, Mother of God,
pray for us sinners,
now and at the hour of our death.
Amen.

Morning Offering

O Jesus, I offer you all my prayers,
works, and sufferings of this day
for all the intentions of your most
Sacred Heart. Amen.

Evening Prayer

Dear God, before I sleep
I want to thank you for this day,
so full of your kindness and your joy.
I close my eyes to rest
safe in your loving care.

Apostles' Creed

I believe in God, the Father almighty,
    Creator of heaven and earth,

and in Jesus Christ, his only Son,
    our Lord,
who was conceived by the Holy Spirit,
born of the Virgin Mary,
suffered under Pontius Pilate,
was crucified, died, and was buried;
he descended into hell;
on the third day he rose again
from the dead;
he ascended into heaven,
and is seated at the right hand
    of God the Father almighty;
from there he will come to judge
    the living and the dead.

I believe in the Holy Spirit,
    the holy catholic Church,
    the communion of saints,
    the forgiveness of sins,
    the resurrection of the body,
    and life everlasting. Amen.

Find other versions of some of these
prayers at www.webelieveweb.com

The Angelus

The angel spoke God's message to Mary,
and she conceived of the Holy Spirit.
Hail Mary. . . .

"I am the lowly servant of the Lord:
let it be done to me according to your word."
Hail Mary. . . .

And the Word became flesh
and lived among us.
Hail Mary. . . .

Pray for us, holy Mother of God,
that we may become worthy of the promises
of Christ.

Let us pray.
Lord,
fill our hearts with your grace:
once, through the message of an angel
you revealed to us the Incarnation of your Son;
now, through his suffering and death
lead us to the glory of his resurrection.
We ask this through Christ our Lord.
Amen.

Hail, Holy Queen

Hail, holy Queen, mother of mercy,
hail, our life, our sweetness, and our hope.
To you we cry, the children of Eve;
to you we send up our sighs,
mourning and weeping in this land of exile.
Turn, then, most gracious advocate,
your eyes of mercy toward us;
lead us home at last
and show us the blessed fruit of your womb, Jesus:
O clement, O loving, O sweet Virgin Mary.

The Canticle of Mary, the Magnificat

"My soul proclaims the greatness of the Lord;
    my spirit rejoices in God my savior.
For he has looked upon his handmaid's lowliness;
    behold, from now on will all ages call me
        blessed.
The Mighty One has done great things for me,
    and holy is his name.
His mercy is from age to age
    to those who fear him.
He has shown might with his arm,
    dispersed the arrogant of mind and heart.
He has thrown down the rulers from their thrones
    but lifted up the lowly.
The hungry he has filled with good things;
    the rich he has sent away empty.
He has helped Israel his servant,
    remembering his mercy,
according to his promise to our fathers,
    to Abraham and to his descendants forever."
                                    (Luke 1:46–55)

Memorare

Remember, most loving Virgin Mary,
never was it heard
that anyone who turned to you for help
was left unaided.

Inspired by this confidence,
though burdened by my sins,
I run to your protection
for you are my mother.
Mother of the Word of God,
do not despise my words of pleading
but be merciful and hear my prayer.
Amen.

Note:
The Ten Commandments are found on page 110.
The gifts of the Holy Spirit are found on page 147.
The Beatitudes are found on page 251.
The Seven Sacraments are found on pages 288–289.
The seven themes of Catholic social teaching are found on pages 290–291.
The Prayer to the Holy Spirit is found on page 281.

Nicene Creed

I believe in one God,
   the Father almighty,
   maker of heaven and earth,
   of all things visible and invisible.

I believe in one Lord Jesus Christ,
   the Only Begotten Son of God,
   born of the Father before all ages.
   God from God, Light from Light,
   true God from true God,
   begotten, not made, consubstantial
      with the Father;
   through him all things were made.
   For us men and for our salvation
      he came down from heaven,
   and by the Holy Spirit
      was incarnate of the Virgin Mary,
         and became man.

For our sake he was crucified
      under Pontius Pilate,
   he suffered death and was buried,
   and rose again on the third day
      in accordance with the Scriptures.
   He ascended into heaven
      and is seated at the right hand
         of the Father.
   He will come again in glory to judge
         the living and the dead
         and his kingdom will have no end.

I believe in the Holy Spirit, the Lord,
   the giver of life,
who proceeds from the Father and the Son,
who with the Father and the Son is
   adored and glorified,
who has spoken through the prophets.

I believe in one, holy, catholic
   and apostolic Church.
I confess one Baptism for the
   forgiveness of sins
and I look forward to the resurrection of the
   dead and the life of the world to come.
Amen.

The Rosary

A rosary is made up of groups of beads arranged in a circle. It begins with a cross followed by one large bead and three small ones. The next large bead (just before the medal) begins the first "decade." Each decade consists of one large bead followed by ten smaller beads.

Begin the Rosary with the Sign of the Cross. Recite the Apostles' Creed. Then pray one Our Father, three Hail Marys, and one Glory Be to the Father.

To pray each decade, say an Our Father on the large bead and a Hail Mary on each of the ten smaller beads. Close each decade by praying the Glory Be to the Father. Pray the Hail, Holy Queen as the last prayer of the Rosary.

The mysteries of the Rosary are special events in the lives of Jesus and Mary. As you pray each decade, think of the appropriate Joyful Mystery, Sorrowful Mystery, Glorious Mystery, or Mystery of Light.

The Five Joyful Mysteries
1. The Annunciation
2. The Visitation
3. The Birth of Jesus
4. The Presentation of Jesus in the Temple
5. The Finding of the Child Jesus in the Temple

The Five Sorrowful Mysteries
1. The Agony in the Garden
2. The Scourging at the Pillar
3. The Crowning with Thorns
4. The Carrying of the Cross
5. The Crucifixion and Death of Jesus

The Five Glorious Mysteries
1. The Resurrection
2. The Ascension
3. The Descent of the Holy Spirit upon the Apostles
4. The Assumption of Mary into Heaven
5. The Coronation of Mary as Queen of Heaven

The Five Mysteries of Light
1. Jesus' Baptism in the Jordan
2. The Miracle at the Wedding at Cana
3. Jesus Announces the Kingdom of God
4. The Transfiguration
5. The Institution of the Eucharist

Stations of the Cross

From the earliest days of the Church, Christians remembered Jesus' life and Death by visiting and praying at the places where Jesus lived, suffered, died, and rose from the dead.

As the Church spread to other countries, not everyone could travel to the Holy Land. So local churches began inviting people to "follow in the footsteps of Jesus" without leaving home. "Stations," or places to stop and pray, were made so that stay-at-home pilgrims could "walk the way of the cross" in their own parish churches. We do the same today, especially during Lent.

There are fourteen "stations," or stops. At each one, we pause and think about what is happening at the station.

1. Jesus is condemned to die.
2. Jesus takes up his cross.
3. Jesus falls the first time.
4. Jesus meets his mother.
5. Simon helps Jesus carry his cross.
6. Veronica wipes the face of Jesus.
7. Jesus falls the second time.
8. Jesus meets the women of Jerusalem.
9. Jesus falls the third time.
10. Jesus is stripped of his garments.
11. Jesus is nailed to the cross.
12. Jesus dies on the cross.
13. Jesus is taken down from the cross.
14. Jesus is laid in the tomb.

The Canticle of Zechariah

"Blessed be the Lord, the God of Israel,
for he has visited and brought redemption
   to his people.
He has raised up a horn for our salvation
within the house of David his servant,
even as he promised through the mouth of his
   holy prophets from of old:
   salvation from our enemies and from the
   hand of all who hate us,
     to show mercy to our fathers
and to be mindful of his holy covenant
and of the oath he swore to Abraham our father,
and to grant us that, rescued from the hand
   of enemies,
without fear we might worship him in holiness
   and righteousness
   before him all our days.
And you, child, will be called prophet of the Most High,
for you will go before the Lord to prepare his ways,
to give his people knowledge of salvation
   through the forgiveness of their sins,
because of the tender mercy of our God
   by which the daybreak from on high will visit us
to shine on those who sit in darkness and
   death's shadow,
   to guide our feet into the path of peace."

(Luke 1:68–79)

Act of Contrition

My God,
I am sorry for my sins with all my heart.
In choosing to do wrong
and failing to do good,
I have sinned against you
whom I should love above all things.
I firmly intend, with your help,
to do penance,
to sin no more,
and to avoid whatever leads me to sin.
Our Savior Jesus Christ
suffered and died for us.
In his name, my God, have mercy.

Prayer for Vocation

Dear God,
You have a great and loving plan
for our world and for me.
I wish to share in that plan fully,
faithfully, and joyfully.

Help me to understand what it is
you wish me to do with my life.
Help me to be attentive to the signs
that you give me about preparing for the future.

Help me to learn to be a sign
of the kingdom, or reign, of
God whether I'm called to the
priesthood or religious life,
the single or married life.

And once I have heard and understood
your call, give me the strength
and the grace to follow it
with generosity and love. Amen

The Precepts of the Church

1. You shall attend Mass on Sundays and holy days of obligation and rest from servile labor.

2. You shall confess your sins at least once a year.

3. You shall receive the sacrament of the Eucharist at least during the Easter season.

4. You shall observe the days of fasting and abstinence by the Church.

5. You shall help to provide for the needs of the Church.

Corporal Works of Mercy

Feed the hungry.
Give drink to the thirsty.
Clothe the naked.
Visit the imprisoned.
Shelter the homeless.
Visit the sick.
Bury the dead.

Spiritual Works of Mercy

Admonish the sinner.
   (Give correction to those who need it.)

Instruct the ignorant.
   (Share our knowledge with others.)

Counsel the doubtful.
   (Give advice to those who need it.)

Comfort the sorrowful.
   (Comfort those who suffer.)

Bear wrongs patiently.
   (Be patient with others.)

Forgive all injuries.
   (Forgive those who hurt us.)

Pray for the living and the dead.

The Holy Days of Obligation

(as celebrated by the Church in the United States.)

Solemnity of Mary, Mother of God (January 1)

Ascension (when celebrated on Thursday during the Easter Season)*

Assumption of Mary (August 15)

All Saints Day (November 1)

Immaculate Conception (December 8)

Christmas (December 25)

*(Some dioceses celebrate the Ascension on the following Sunday.)

Glossary

ark of the covenant (p. 113)
a wooden box in which the tablets of the Ten Commandments were kept

Beatitudes (p. 250)
teachings of Jesus that describe the way to live as his disciples

Bible (p. 25)
the written record of God's Revelation and his relationship with his people

blasphemy (p. 191)
a thought, word, or act that refers to God without respect or reverence

Blessed Trinity (p. 23)
the Three Persons in One God: God the Father, God the Son, and God the Holy Spirit

Book of Genesis (p. 33)
the first book in the Bible

Canaan (p. 69)
an area in western Palestine that included most of present-day Israel

Catholic social teaching (p. 291)
the teaching of the Church that calls all members to work for justice and peace as Jesus did

conscience (p. 39)
the ability to know the difference between good and evil, right and wrong

covenant (p. 33)
an agreement between God and his people

Divine Inspiration (p. 25)
the special guidance that the Holy Spirit gave to the human writers of the Bible

Divine Revelation (p. 23)
God's making himself known to us

ecumenism (p. 297)
the work to promote unity among all Christians

exodus (p. 98)
the biblical word describing the Israelites' departure from slavery to freedom

faith (p. 69)
a gift from God that enables us to believe in him and accept all that he has revealed

free will (p. 39)
the freedom and ability to choose

Gospel (p. 57)
the Good News about God at work in Jesus Christ

holiness (p. 298)
sharing in God's goodness and responding to his love by the way we live; our holiness comes through grace

hope (p. 199)
a gift from God that enables us to trust in God's promise to be with us always; it enables us to be confident in God's love and care for us

human dignity (p. 39)
the value and worth that comes from being made in God's image and likeness

idolatry (p. 173)
giving worship to a creature or thing instead of to God

Incarnation (p. 225)
the truth that the Son of God, the Second Person of the Blessed Trinity, became man

Kingdom of God (p. 248)
the power of God's love coming into the world and into our lives

lamentation (p. 196)
a sorrow that is expressed in the form of a poem

Last Supper (p. 260)
the Passover meal that Jesus shared with his disciples on the night before he died

manna (p. 109)
a sweet bread-like food that God provided for the Israelites in the desert

marks of the Church (p. 297)
the four essential features of the Church: one, holy, catholic, and apostolic

martyr (p. 277)
person who dies rather than give up his or her belief in Jesus Christ

miracle (p. 109)
an extraordinary event that is beyond human power and brought about by God

monarchy (p. 134)
kingdom or empire ruled by one person, either a king or queen

Mount Sinai (p. 109)
a mountain peak in the rocky southern part of the Sinai peninsula

Nazirite (p. 125)
a person consecrated to God who promised not to drink wine or strong drink, touch anyone or anything that had died, or cut or shave his or her hair

Original Sin (p. 50)
the first sin that weakened human nature and brought ignorance, suffering, and death into the world; we all suffer from its effects

parable (p. 211)
short story that has a message

Passover (p. 103)
the event in which God passed over the whole of Egypt, taking the lives of every firstborn Egyptian and sparing the Israelites

patriarch (p. 69)
a father, or founder, of a clan, a group of related families

Pentecost (p. 273)
the day on which the Holy Spirit came upon the first disciples

pharaoh (p. 75)
the king of Egypt

prophet (p. 132)
someone who speaks on behalf of God, defends the truth, and works for justice

proverb (p. 200)
a brief saying that gives wise advice

providence (p. 75)
God's plan for and protection of all creation

psalm (p. 150)
a poetic prayer designed to be sung or chanted to some kind of musical accompaniment

Resurrection (p. 265)
the mystery of Jesus' being raised from the dead

sin (p. 50)
a thought, word, deed, or omission against God's law

soul (p. 45)
the invisible spiritual reality that makes each of us human and that will never die

steward (p. 47)
a person who is given both the authority over what he or she cares for and the responsibility for seeing that it lives and grows

superstition (p. 196)
the false belief that living creatures or things possess powers that in fact they do not have

Ten Commandments (p. 111)
the laws of God's covenant given to Moses on Mount Sinai

Torah (p. 203)
the Hebrew name for the first five books of the Old Testament

Tradition (p. 25)
the Revelation of the Good News of Jesus Christ as lived out in the Church, past and present

vocation (p. 191)
God's call to serve him in a special way

wisdom (p. 147)
the knowledge and ability to recognize and follow God's will in our lives

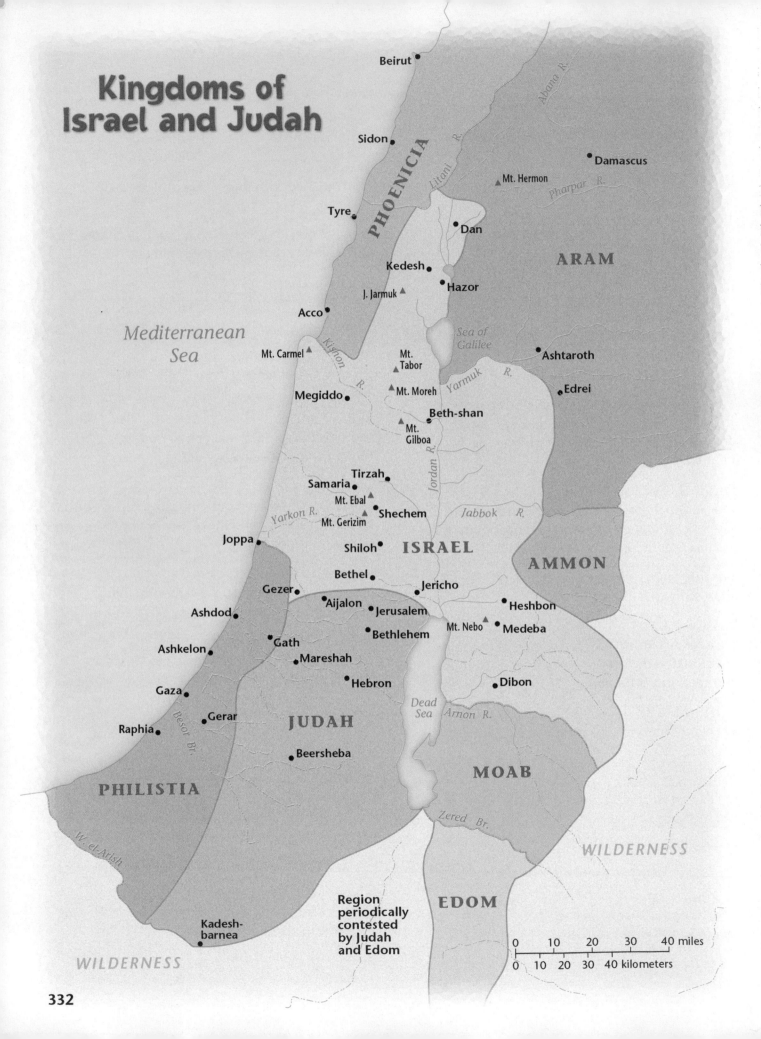

Kingdoms of Israel and Judah

Beirut

Sidon

PHOENICIA

Damascus

Mt. Hermon

Tyre

Dan

Kedesh

Hazor

J. Jarmuk

ARAM

Acco

Mediterranean
Sea

Mt. Carmel

Mt.
Tabor

Sea of
Galilee

Ashtaroth

Mt. Moreh

Edrei

Megiddo

Beth-shan

Mt.
Gilboa

Tirzah

Samaria

Mt. Ebal

Shechem

Jabbok R.

Mt. Gerizim

Shiloh

ISRAEL

AMMON

Bethel

Jericho

Gezer

Heshbon

Aijalon

Jerusalem

Joppa

Ashdod

Gath

Bethlehem

Mt. Nebo

Medeba

Ashkelon

Mareshah

Gaza

Hebron

Dibon

Gerar

Dead
Sea

Raphia

JUDAH

Arnon R.

Beersheba

MOAB

PHILISTIA

W. el-Arish

Besor Br.

Zered Br.

WILDERNESS

Region
periodically
contested
by Judah
and Edom

EDOM

Kadesh-
barnea

WILDERNESS

| 0 | 10 | 20 | 30 | 40 miles |

| 0 | 10 | 20 | 30 | 40 kilometers |

Litani R.

Pharpar R.

Abana R.

Kishon R.

Yarmuk R.

Jordan R.

Yarkon R.

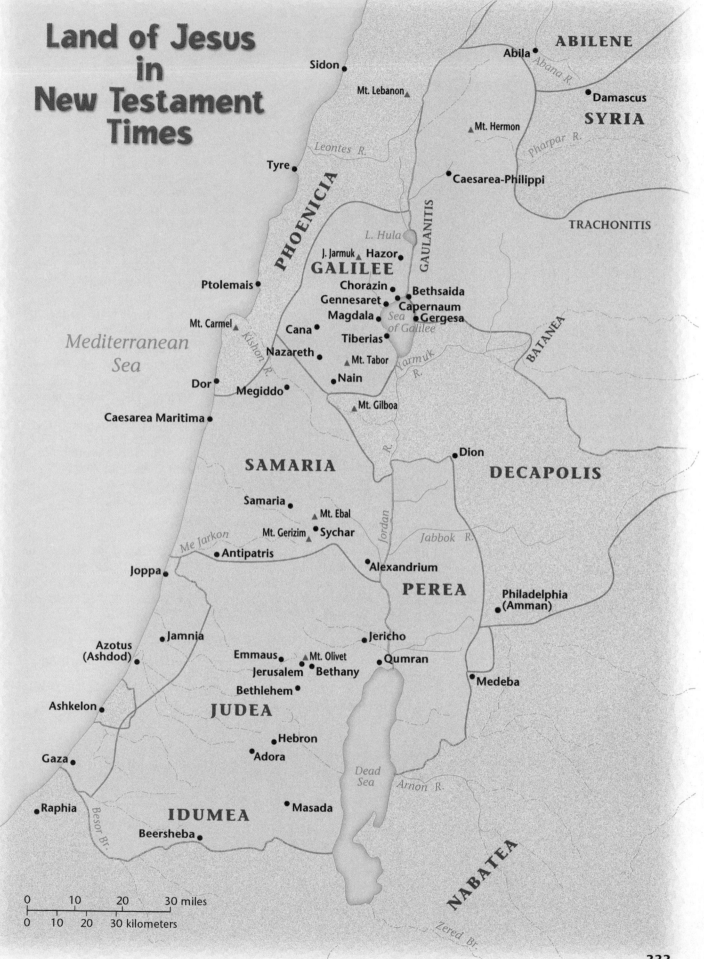

Land of Jesus in New Testament Times

ABILENE

Abila

Abana R.

Damascus

SYRIA

Mt. Hermon

Sidon

Mt. Lebanon ▲

Leontes R.

Pharpar R.

Caesarea-Philippi

TRACHONITIS

PHOENICIA

Tyre

L. Hula

J. Jarmuk ▲ Hazor

GALILEE

GAULANITIS

Chorazin

Ptolemais

Bethsaida

Gennesaret

Capernaum

Magdala

Gergesa

Sea of Galilee

BATANEA

Mt. Carmel ▲

Cana

Tiberias

Kishon R.

Nazareth

Mediterranean Sea

Mt. Tabor ▲

Yarmuk R.

Nain

Dor

Megiddo

Mt. Gilboa ▲

Caesarea Maritima

Dion

SAMARIA

DECAPOLIS

Samaria

Mt. Ebal ▲

Mt. Gerizim ▲ Sychar

Jordan R.

Jabbok R.

Me Jarkon

Antipatris

Alexandrium

PEREA

Joppa

Philadelphia (Amman)

Jamnia

Jericho

Azotus (Ashdod)

Emmaus

Mt. Olivet ▲

Qumran

Jerusalem

Bethany

Medeba

Bethlehem

Ashkelon

JUDEA

Hebron

Gaza

Adora

Dead Sea

Arnon R.

Raphia

IDUMEA

Masada

Beersheba

Besor Br.

NABATEA

Zered Br.

| 0 | 10 | 20 | 30 miles |
| 0 | 10 | 20 | 30 kilometers |

Index

The following is a list of topics that appear in the pupil's text.
Boldface indicates an entire chapter or section.

Catholic Identity Q&A

I n this section, you will find questions and answers that review the content in your *We Believe: Catholic Identity Edition* book this year. Each question in this section covers the key Catholic teachings in your book, in chapter order. Answer each question to review what you have learned—whether you use this section at home, in school, or in the parish. The answers provided will strengthen your understanding of your Catholic faith and help to reinforce your Catholic Identity.

The *CCC* references after each answer indicate where to find further information about that answer in the *Catechism of the Catholic Church*.

Q: What is Divine Revelation?

A: Divine Revelation is God making himself known to us. *CCC, 50, 53*

Q: How is God's Revelation handed down to us?

A: God's Revelation is handed down to us through Sacred Scripture and through Tradition. *CCC, 81–82*

Q: What is the Blessed Trinity?

A: The Blessed Trinity is the Three Persons in one God: God the Father, God the Son, and God the Holy Spirit. *CCC, 234, 261, 266*

CCC = Catechism of the Catholic Church

Q: What is the Bible?

A: The Bible is the written record of God's Revelation and his relationship with his people. It is a collection of books organized into parts called the Old and New Testaments. *CCC, 120*

Q: What is Divine Inspiration?

A: Divine Inspiration is the special guidance that the Holy Spirit gave to the human writers of the Bible. *CCC, 105, 106*

Q: What is Tradition?

A: Tradition is the Revelation of the Good News of Jesus Christ as lived out in the Church, past and present. *CCC, 78*

Q: What is the Old Testament?

A: The Old Testament is the part of the Bible, made up of forty-six books, in which we learn about God's relationship with the people of Israel. *CCC, 120*

Q: What is the New Testament?

A: The New Testament is the part of the Bible, made up of twenty-seven books, in which we learn about God's final Revelation in Jesus Christ and the salvation that comes from Christ. We learn about his mission, the first Christian communities, and the beginning of the Church. *CCC, 124, 140*

Q: What is a covenant?

A: A covenant is an agreement between God and his people. *CCC, 62, 64*

Q: What book of the Bible teaches us about creation?

A: We learn about creation in the Book of Genesis, the first book of the Bible. We learn that God is the source of all life and that he created the universe and all living things. *CCC, 289*

Q: How are human beings different from the other creatures God created?

A: Human beings are different because they are made in the image and likeness of God and have free will, conscience, and a soul. *CCC, 357, 362, 363*

Q: **What laws and teachings from the Bible give us a foundation for Christian living?**

A: From the Bible we learn the Ten Commandments, the Beatitudes, the Great Commandment, and Christ's New Commandment. These laws and teachings help us to relate to God, ourselves, and one another. *CCC, 131*

Q: **How is the Bible an important source for Christian worship?**

A: Sacred Scripture is an essential part of the liturgy, the Church's official public worship. *CCC, 132, 1177*

Q: **What is our soul?**

A: Our soul, our breath of life from God, is the invisible spiritual reality that makes each of us human and will never die. *CCC, 362–366*

Q: **What are the effects of Original Sin?**

A: Original Sin weakened human nature and brought ignorance, suffering, and death into the world. *CCC, 405, 418*

Q: **What is faith?**

A: Faith is a gift from God that enables us to believe in him and accept all that he has revealed. *CCC, 153–155*

Q: **What does the Church's liturgical year celebrate?**

A: Throughout the seasons of the liturgical year we celebrate the whole life of Christ, most especially his Paschal Mystery. *CCC, 1168, 1171–1173*

Q: **What is Ordinary Time?**

A: Ordinary Time is the season of the liturgical year in which we learn about the life of Christ and grow as his followers. It is celebrated twice during the liturgical year. It includes special days honoring Mary and the saints. *CCC, 1163, 1168, 1173*

Q: **What is a miracle?**

A: A miracle is an extraordinary event that is beyond human power and is brought about by God. *CCC, 547, 548*

Q: What are the Ten Commandments?

A: The Ten Commandments are the law of God's covenant given to Moses on Mount Sinai. *CCC, 2056–2058*

Q: What is a prophet?

A: A prophet is someone who is called by God to speak on behalf of God, defend the truth, and work for justice. *CCC, 64, 702, 2581*

Q: What is a psalm?

A: A psalm is a poetic prayer designed to be sung or chanted with musical accompaniment. The psalms are an important part of the liturgical life of all Christians. *CCC, 2586–2588*

Q: What is Advent?

A: Advent is a liturgical season of joyful expectation and preparation for the birth of God's Son, Jesus Christ, at Christmas. *CCC, 524*

Q: What do we celebrate during the season of Christmas?

A: During the season of Christmas we rejoice in the Incarnation, the truth that the Son of God became man. *CCC, 1171*

Q: What is idolatry?

A: Idolatry is giving worship to a creature or thing instead of to God. Idolatry is forbidden by the First Commandment. *CCC, 2113*

Q: What is a vocation?

A: A vocation is God's call to serve him. *CCC, 897, 898, 1877*

Q: What is hope?

A: Hope is a gift from God that enables us to trust in God's promise to be with us always. Hope enables us to be confident in God's love and care for us. *CCC, 1817–1818*

Q: What is a parable?

A: A parable is a short story that has a message. *CCC, 546*

Q: What special role did Mary have in God's plan?

A: Mary was chosen to be the Mother of God's own Son, Jesus Christ, who is our Savior. *CCC, 494*

Q: What is Lent?

A: Lent is the season of the liturgical year in which we prepare for the great celebration of Easter through prayer, penance, and good works. *CCC, 1438*

Q: What is the Easter Triduum?

A: The Easter Triduum, a time during the liturgical year, is our greatest celebration of the Paschal Mystery. It is the three days from Holy Thursday evening to Easter Sunday Evening. *CCC, 1168*

Q: What is the Paschal Mystery?

A: The Paschal Mystery is Christ's suffering, Death, Resurrection from the dead, and Ascension into Heaven. By his Paschal Mystery, Jesus saves us from sin and gives us life. *CCC, 1067*

Q: What do we celebrate during the Easter season?

A: During the Easter season, we celebrate our new life in Christ and the coming of the Holy Spirit. The Easter season lasts for fifty days. During this time we celebrate the Resurrection and Ascension of Jesus Christ and the coming of the Holy Spirit on Pentecost. *CCC, 1169*

Q: What is the Kingdom of God?

A: The Kingdom of God is the power of God's love coming into the world and into our lives. *CCC, 2046*

Q: What are the Beatitudes?

A: The Beatitudes are teachings of Jesus that describe the way to live as his disciples. *CCC, 1716, 1717*

Q: What is Jesus' mission?

A: Jesus' mission is to share the life and love of God his Father with all people and to save them from sin. *CCC, 422, 714*

Q: When did Jesus rise from the dead?

A: Jesus rose from the dead on the third day after his Death—the first Easter Sunday. The mystery of Jesus' being raised from the dead is called the Resurrection. *CCC, 1169*

Q: When did the Church begin?

A: The Church began on Pentecost with the coming of the Holy Spirit upon the first disciples. *CCC, 767*

Q: What are the marks of the Church?

A: The Church is one, holy, catholic, and apostolic. *CCC, 811*

Resources
for the Family

I n this section, you will find a treasury of resources to help build up your Catholic Identity at home, in your parish, and in the community. Learn more about key Catholic teachings from the themes of your child's *Celebrating Catholic Identity* retreats: **CREED**, **LITURGY & SACRAMENTS**, **MORALITY**, and **PRAYER**. For each theme, you will find Catholic prayers, practices, and devotions to share with those you love—and make a part of your daily lives as a Catholic family!

Family: "the place where parents pass on the faith to their children."

—Pope Francis
Apostolic Exhortation *Evangelii Gaudium*, 66

Spirituality and Your Sixth-Grade Child

Your sixth grader is in a stage of preadolescence—no longer a child but not yet a teenager emotionally or intellectually. Children at this age look for both the acceptance of peers and the approval and direction of adults. In trying to understand God and aspects of faith and practice, sixth graders are also more likely to be directed by reason than by imagination. Make an effort to discuss and share experiences and questions related to faith. Resist the urge to provide quick and easy answers to your child's questions. Rather, encourage your child's desire to explore the relationship between facts and ideas and to think things through.

Your sixth grader is also learning—from your example and interactions

with friends—that doing right is not simply the passive avoidance of what is wrong, but the active, responsible choice of what is good and just. Reinforce choices that demonstrate respect, dignity, and compassion for others.*

Your sixth grader is also capable of understanding the chronology of biblical stories and recognizing the various genres in which these sacred texts were written. Help foster this ability by taking time to read the Bible together.

*See *Catechetical Formation in Chaste Living,* United States Conference of Catholic Bishops, #17

119   Luke, |10|

— **Book**

— **Chapter**

— **Verse**

Passage Title —

Titles are sometimes added to show themes of the chapters, but these titles are not part of the actual words of the Bible.

Praise of the Father |21| *t u**At that very moment he rejoiced [in] the holy Spirit and said, "I give you praise, Father, Lord of heaven and earth, for although you have hidden these things from the wise and the learned you have revealed them to the childlike. Yes, Father, such has been your gracious will. 22 *v*All things have been handed over to me by my Father. No one knows who the Son is except the Father, and who the Father is except the Son and anyone to whom the Son wishes to reveal him."

— **Passage**

A passage is a section of a chapter made up of a number of verses.

This passage shows Luke 10:21–22, which means: the Gospel of Luke, chapter ten, verses twenty-one to twenty-two.

Reading the Bible . . . in Five Easy Steps

The Bible is a collection of seventy-three books written under the inspiration of the Holy Spirit. The Bible is divided into two parts: the Old Testament and the New Testament. In the forty-six books of the Old Testament, we learn about the story of God's relationship with the people of Israel. In the twenty-seven books of the New Testament, we learn about the story of Jesus Christ, the Son of God, and of his followers. The Bible is divided into books, which are divided into chapters, which are divided into verses. When you are given a Scripture passage to read, here are five easy steps that will help you to find it! With your child, follow these steps to look up **Lk 10:21–22**.

1. **Find the book.** When the name of the book is abbreviated, locate the meaning of the abbreviation on the contents pages found at the beginning of your Bible. *Lk* stands for Luke, one of the four Gospels.

2. **Find the page.** Your Bible's contents pages will also show the page on which the book begins. Turn to that page within your Bible.

3. **Find the chapter.** Once you arrive at the page where the book begins, keep turning the pages forward until you find the right chapter. The image above shows you how a chapter number is usually displayed on a typical Bible page. You are looking for chapter **10** in Luke.

4. **Find the verses.** Once you find the right chapter, locate the verse or verses you need within the chapter. The image above also shows you how verse numbers will look on a typical Bible page. You are looking for verses **21** and **22**.

5. **Start reading!**

The Gift of Faith

Does your family realize that faith is a *gift*? God gives us the gift of faith, which enables us to believe all that God has revealed to us and to respond positively to God, with all our heart and strength. Faith is one of the *theological* virtues. The other theological virtues are hope and love (also called charity). Explain to your child that a virtue is a good habit that helps us to act according to God's plan for us. Virtues help guide our conduct with the help of God's grace. Pray together to grow in these good habits! Start by praying the following Acts of Faith, Hope, and Love together today.

An Act of Faith

O God, we believe in all that Jesus has
   taught us about you.
We place all our trust in you
   because of your great love for us.

An Act of Hope

O God, we never give up on your love.
We have hope and will work for your
kingdom to come and for a life that lasts
forever with you in heaven.

An Act of Love

O God, we love you above all things.
Help us to love ourselves and one another
as Jesus taught us to do.

All About Angels

Angels are creatures created by God as pure spirits. They do not have physical bodies. Angels serve God as his messengers. They serve God in his saving plan for us and constantly give him praise. Everyone has a guardian angel. Encourage your child to pray to his or her guardian angel.

Prayer to My Guardian Angel

Angel of God,
my guardian dear,
to whom God's love commits me here,
ever this day be at my side,
to light and guard,
to rule and guide.
Amen.

A Fruitful Life

Your child's *Celebrating Catholic Identity: Liturgy & Sacraments* retreat explored the Sacrament of Confirmation. The Sacrament of Confirmation completes our Baptism as we are sealed with the Gift of God the Holy Spirit. Like the Apostles on Pentecost, we are given the strength to spread and defend the faith by our words and actions. Confirmation not only unites us more closely to Christ and the Church, it also strengthens the Gifts of the Holy Spirit within us. Share with your child that when we respond to the Holy Spirit and use the gifts we have received, the results are the fruits of Holy Spirit in our lives. These are listed below.

Fruits of the Holy Spirit

Love	Patience	Faithfulness
Joy	Kindness	Gentleness
Peace	Generosity	Self-control

All Things Liturgical

Talk with your child about the meaning of *liturgy*. The liturgy is the official public prayer of the Church. This includes the Mass and all the celebrations of the sacraments, as well as a collection of daily prayers called Liturgy of the Hours. In the liturgy we gather as a community joined to Christ to celebrate what we believe. Does your family know that the Church has its own liturgical year? In one liturgical year we recall and celebrate the whole life of Jesus Christ. The liturgical year begins in late November or early December with the season of Advent. It includes such seasons and feasts as Christmas, Lent, Easter, and Pentecost Sunday.

The Liturgy of the Hours

The Liturgy of the Hours is an official public prayer of the Church made up of psalms, other readings from Scripture and Church teachings, prayers, and hymns. It is celebrated at various times during the day and helps us to praise God throughout the entire day, thereby reminding us that God is always active and present in our lives. We can grow in the habit of daily prayer by praying the Liturgy of the Hours.

The Sacrament of Penance and Reconciliation

Review with your child the steps to receive the Sacrament of Penance and Reconciliation, which are given below. When we receive the Sacrament of Penance, we not only confess our sins, but we have to show that we are sorry. Another name for showing we are sorry is *repentance*. Find out when your parish celebrates the Sacrament of Penance and make a commitment as a family to receive this sacrament.

- The priest welcomes me, and we both make the Sign of the Cross.

- Sometimes the priest reads a story from the Bible about God's forgiveness.

- I confess my sins to the priest.

- The priest may talk to me about what I can do to make the right choices. He will give me a penance to do. A penance is a prayer or action that shows I am sorry for my sins. I will carry out my penance after the celebration of the sacrament.

- I pray the Act of Contrition, expressing my sorrow for my sins and my firm purpose to rely on God and not sin again.

- I receive absolution, or forgiveness, from my sins.

- With the priest, I thank God for his forgiveness.

Let the Moral Law Be Your Guide

How many moral decisions does your family face in a typical day? You probably make more moral choices each day than you are aware of. You may make some choices instinctively, as "second nature." Other times, you may need to carefully consider your decision. Either way, God has given you the guidance you need to choose what is good and right. God's guidance comes in different forms. Together, they make up what we know as the *moral law*. Review these four expressions of the moral law with your child. Ask your child to tell you what he or she has learned about the revealed law this year.

Four Expressions of the Moral Law

- The source of all moral law is the Divine Law, or Eternal Law. This law is called "eternal" because it is always true and never changes. It is reflected in everything God has created, from the beginning of time. The Eternal Law is "the source, in God, of all law" (*CCC*, 1952).

- Human beings have an awareness of good and evil, right and wrong, with which we are born. It is God-given, part of our human nature. This is the *natural law*. The natural law is the law of God within us, known by human reason. The natural law is understood through our consciences. The natural law helps us to be in right relationships with God, others, the world, and ourselves. It also helps us understand and follow other expressions of the moral law.

- God also revealed his law to us in Scripture. This is called *revealed law*. God's law was first revealed in the Old Testament, in the Ten Commandments that he gave to Moses on Mount Sinai. The Ten Commandments express what God has already placed in the human heart in the natural law. God's law is more fully revealed in the New Testament, in the law of love that Jesus taught. This is called the New Law. It is contained in the New Commandment of Jesus (see below).

- Finally, God gives us *civil law* and the *laws of the Church* to guide us. Civil law establishes rules for how we are to live as members of a community. The natural law provides the foundation for the creation of moral and just civil laws. The Church is also a source of moral guidance for us. Through her Tradition, or teaching, the Church helps us understand revealed law and how to live it. The Church also has her own laws to guide us. This is called *ecclesiastical law*. It includes the Precepts of the Church. Review the Precepts of the Church with your child, found in the *Prayers and Practices* section of this book.

New Commandment

Jesus gave us the following commandment. Let it guide all your relationships—at home, at school, in the parish, and in the community.

"I give you a new commandment: love one another. As I have loved you, so you also should love one another. This is how all will know that you are my disciples, if you have love for one another." (John 13:34–35)

How to Become a Saint

Yes, it is true, everyone in your family could become a saint! Having been made holy by your Baptism and united to Christ, you are actually called to be a saint. Saints were ordinary human beings, just like you, who were faithful disciples of Jesus. They are followers of Christ who lived lives of holiness on earth and now share in eternal life with God in Heaven. From the example of the saints' lives, we can learn ways to love God, ourselves, and others. We can learn how to be disciples of Jesus, as the saints were.

Have you or your child ever wondered how the Church decides who is named a saint? Here is a brief summary of this process.

The Canonization Process

If someone who has died was known for living an especially holy life, or was martyred for his or her Catholic faith, the bishop of this person's diocese may begin the process to consider the person for sainthood.

- The first step is an investigation into the person's life. People who knew him or her will be interviewed. The bishop will collect information on things the person said, wrote, and did. The information will be sent to the Vatican. When a person becomes a candidate for sainthood, he or she is known as "Servant of God."

- A group of cardinals at the Vatican, the Congregation for the Causes of Saints, will study the information about the candidate's life. They will consider whether the person is a role model for living Catholic virtues. If so, the person will be declared "Venerable."

- The next step is declaring the candidate "Blessed." This is called *beatification*. Beatification occurs if it can be shown that a miracle occurred in connection with the candidate, or if the person died a martyr for the faith. An example of a miracle might be a sudden cure or healing, with no reasonable medical explanation, when someone prayed for the candidate's help. The Vatican carefully reviews the evidence on any miracles.

- If a second miracle can be credited to the candidate, he or she can be named a saint, or canonized.

Crowds gathered for the canonization ceremony of Saints John XXIII and John Paul II, Popes, in St. Peter's Square, Vatican City, Rome

What Is a Novena?

Have you ever prayed a novena? A novena is a devotion of praying for nine consecutive days. The word *novena* comes from a Latin word meaning "nine." Novenas have been prayed since the earliest days of the Church. In fact, Mary and the Apostles prayed together for a period of nine days between Jesus' Ascension and his sending of the Holy Spirit on Pentecost (see Acts of the Apostles 1).

Often people pray a novena for a special need or intention. Many novena prayers are in honor of specific saints. Here is one prayer to Mary, the Church's greatest saint, that you might wish to pray with your family for nine days. Ask Mary for her help with your family's needs or intentions.

The Virgin Mary, Ghent Altarpiece, Saint Bavo Cathedral, Ghent, Belgium, by Jan van Eyck (1429)

Regina Caeli (Queen of Heaven)

Queen of Heaven, rejoice, alleluia:
for the Son you were privileged to bear, alleluia,
is risen as he said, alleluia.
Pray for us to God, alleluia.

Rejoice and be glad, O Virgin Mary, Alleluia!
For the Lord is truly risen, Alleluia.

Let us pray. O God, who gave joy to the world through the Resurrection of your Son, our Lord Jesus Christ, grant, we beseech you, that through the intercession of the Virgin Mary, his Mother, we may obtain the joys of everlasting life. Through the same Christ our Lord. Amen.

The Chaplet of the Divine Mercy

The Chaplet of the Divine Mercy is a devotion that is prayed using rosary beads. Saint Faustina Kowalska, who lived from 1905 to 1938 in Poland, gave this practice of praying for the mercy of Jesus Christ to the Church. The Church celebrates the Second Sunday of Easter as Divine Mercy Sunday.

4 After five decades, pray three times:

Holy God, Holy Mighty One, Holy Immortal One, have mercy on us and on the whole world.

3 On the ten small beads of each decade, pray:

For the sake of His sorrowful Passion, have mercy on us and on the whole world.

2 Then, on the large bead before each decade, pray:

Eternal Father, I offer You the Body and Blood, Soul and Divinity of Your dearly beloved Son, Our Lord Jesus Christ, in atonement for our sins and those of the whole world.

1 To pray the chaplet, begin with the Sign of the Cross, the Apostles' Creed, an Our Father, and three Hail Marys, just as you would when beginning the Rosary.